# PACIFIC ORDEAL

# Pacific Ordeal

## KENNETH AINSLIE

RUPERT HART-DAVIS
SOHO SQUARE LONDON
1956

*First impression 1956*
*Second impression 1956*

PRINTED IN GREAT BRITAIN BY EBENEZER BAYLIS
AND SON, LTD., THE TRINITY PRESS, WORCESTER
AND LONDON

In the interests of discretion many proper names have been changed, otherwise the events in this story took place as described.

# List of Illustrations

A map of the voyage appears on pages 8 and 9

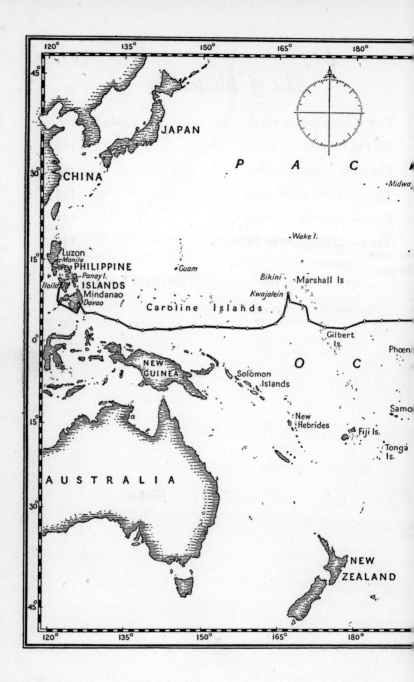

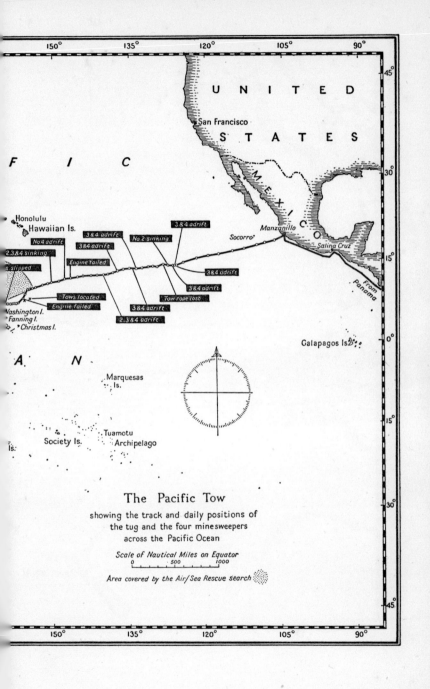

The Pacific Tow

showing the track and daily positions of
the tug and the four minesweepers
across the Pacific Ocean

Scale of Nautical Miles on Equator
0        500        1000

Area covered by the Air/Sea Rescue search

# *Chapter One*

It was a typical steaming hot Philippines day in May soon after the end of World War II. The temperature was ninety in the shade at the beginning of the biggest adventure and my toughest voyage in thirty-four years at sea.

I was manager and superintendent of UNRRA's Philippines China marine operations at the time. UNRRA's local agents were the Philippine Cargo Handlers Inc. who had a big office in Manila's 13th Street down near the docks. We were tidying up after the Japanese war which had ended just twenty-one months before, and my job had been to survey and have made seaworthy for despatch to China many small U.S. Navy and Army ships which, now the war was over, had been declared surplus. They were urgently required for river service to run food to millions of starving Chinese.

Adventures have odd beginnings. As I strolled into the Company's cool office that morning somebody startled me by calling out:

"Hello, Ainslie. I hear you're going to the States."

"It's news to me," I said, thinking my leg was being pulled. I learned later it wasn't. That afternoon Daley, one of the company's American executives, called me into his office.

"How would you like to go to the States?" he asked. "How soon could you leave?"

I asked him why.

He said: "We have bought an ex-U.S. Navy rescue tug. It's in Norfolk, Virginia, and we want a man to sail it across for us. We feel you are our best skipper. Besides you have worked hard for us in the last twelve months and now the UNRRA job is nearly finished, a pleasant voyage like this would be some small reward for your efforts and a holiday into the bargain. Will you take it?"

I pondered. He was right. I *had* worked hard for them, damned hard. Day and night for months life had had but one object for me—to search out every sort of ship that could be repaired and rush it north to China. I had scoured the Philippine ports and poked into every harbour and bay where suitable surplus craft might have been lying idle. When urgent appeals came for more and still more ships so that relief workers could get their rice up the Yangtse and the Hangchow and the Pearl Rivers that Chinese lives might be saved I had begun to look below the surface of the water. With the aid of diving gear we peered into the blue water of the many bays round the Luzon coast and found many more sunken vessels rusting on the sand, tropical growth slowly camouflaging them. Some were beyond repair but their engines and lockers often contained spares which we also desperately needed. Sometimes I had climbed into a diving suit and gone down to examine a hopeful looking wreck myself. It had been a hectic twelve months. Yes Daley *was* right. I did deserve a holiday. I could see the tug in my mind already. A restful cruise across the wide Pacific I knew so well. Plenty of sunbathing and in easy warm trade wind latitudes. "I'll go," I said. Daley looked pleased.

"How much time to get ready?" he asked. "Your crew will be picked in America but you will have to take a Filipino mate and second mate from here."

"I know just the men," I told him. "Give me two days."

I wandered out into the Manila sunshine. Already I was planning the voyage. Norfolk, Virginia, across the Caribbean, through the Panama Canal, probably a Pacific port in Mexico then Honolulu and Manila. Must be all of thirteen thousand miles, I thought, probably take about two months.

I called a taxi and set out to recruit my lieutenants. My first call was to a little house on the city outskirts. Ricardo Miranda was at home. He had worked under me for UNRRA and I knew him to be thoroughly reliable and trustworthy. He was thirty-nine, black haired and of dark complexion, always impeccably dressed and had had a particularly good education. He was a product of the Philippines Sea Frontier, a Filipino Dartmouth, and had spent most of his life in ships on the Philippines coast. When the Japs swarmed into Luzon in 1942 he went into the jungle and joined a guerrilla band.

Although he only held a Philippines second Mate's ticket I had found him dependable enough to give commands of small ships I had sent to China. Above all, he was a first-class navigator, and this was important, for I didn't fancy a "holiday" voyage in the chartroom.

Miranda had a particular affection for me. Once, during our UNRRA operations I had appointed him chief mate of a ship we had laid up for repairs in the Pasig River out of the typhoon danger area. There was friction between him and two Norwegian officers, one of whom I had suspended for pilfering deck stores. Both ganged up on him, and Miranda whipped out a foot-long knife and stabbed one of the Norwegians in the shoulder. I was in my office lower down the river when a member of the crew came running down to tell me about it. I hurried up to the ship and held an inquiry on the spot. It was soon obvious where the trouble lay; I sacked the Norwegians there and then. Miranda was specially faithful to me after that and I never heard of him using his knife again.

At first he was disappointed when I told him I wanted him only to be second Mate. Despite his second Mate's ticket he was proud of the fact that he had frequently sailed both as Mate and in command. But he came round in the end.

My second port of call was to the man I wanted to be

Mate. He held a Philippines Master's ticket and had commanded small coastal vessels. His name was Ramon Alonso, a fifty-four-year-old, five foot two, typically olive-complexioned little Filipino, but far less excitable than Miranda. I looked on him as a seaman of some experience upon whom I could place much of the responsibility. He knew how to handle and gain the respect of Filipino seamen, but I wasn't to discover until too late that over crews of mixed nationality his control was far from sure. Alonso was overjoyed at the prospect of the voyage.

"Yes, Captain Ainslie I will come," he said excitedly.

Five days later, on June 1, the three of us flew to San Francisco. I had an anxious moment at Manila Airport when up to a few minutes before our Skymaster was due to take off Alonso hadn't shown up. I had almost given him up when he tumbled harassed out of a taxi, apologizing profusely. It appeared he had been tying up some important private business at the last minute.

Looking down at the blue foam-flecked Pacific twelve thousand feet below us from my flying armchair, I little realized that the big ocean we were now flashing across in thirty-six hours was going to be our home for nearly six months. From the air even the stormiest of sea always seems to look comparatively smooth, and it gave me quite a feeling of detachment from it to watch the 7,000-mile blue carpet sliding monotonously by. A month later my feelings for that same ocean were to be far from detached.

We landed in San Francisco at 3.30 p.m. on June 2. The company's agents sent a car to meet us and we were whisked off to the California Hotel. Anxious to get some more details of my forthcoming voyage I lost no time in getting round to meet the agent himself. His name was Wyfield, an impressive man with an iron-grey moustache.

"I have sent your crew down to join the ship," he said in his soft drawl.

"You mean you have already picked them?" I asked astonished. "My Mate wanted to select them himself."

"That's right, Captain Ainslie. Take it from me you've got the best crew for the job we could find anywhere. Damn' fine sailors all of them; and experienced."

I did not know what Alonso would think of this. He was going to be annoyed. But it was too late now; I could only hope Wyfield was right. I asked him when we were leaving for Norfolk. He seemed a little vague and said there was no immediate hurry.

"Go and enjoy yourselves," he said, "and we will get in touch with you when the ship is ready."

As an afterthought I asked him the name of the tug.

"The *Wallace R. Gray*," he said. "Her U.S. Navy number was ATR 6, but we decided to call her after Colonel Gray."

Colonel Gray was the chief executive of the Islands Towage and Lighterage Company, owners of the tug. Just as I was leaving Wyfield gave me a letter he had received from the company. It wished me *bon voyage* and ended: "We sincerely hope that you will have a very pleasant voyage back to the Philippines and that it will prove uneventful." In the months that followed I was several times to remember that letter with irony.

I spent three days sightseeing in San Francisco. One day I was walking along the street when I heard a crowd of young 'Frisco men jeering at something. When I looked round I realized that I was the object of their attention. The words, "Take it off, buddy, the war's over now," drifted across to me. Then I suddenly remembered the rig I was wearing must have looked very like the uniform of an American Army officer. During the war I had been South-west Pacific Navigation Superintendent for the U.S. Armed Forces and, as was the custom in the Philippines where civilian tropical dress was at that time similar to Army dress anyway, was wearing out my uniform. But it obviously wasn't a San Francisco custom and I made a mental note to buy myself some less embarrassing clothes at the first opportunity.

The next day I got a message to report to the agents again. I jumped in a taxi and hurried round. Colonel Gray himself was waiting to see me. I had known him in Australia during the war when he was a Colonel in the U.S. Army Transport Command. He knew the Philippines shipping business better than any man I knew. He was handsome and rather distinguished looking and always could be relied upon to call a spade a spade.

He delivered my second shock in three days. "How much towing experience have you had?" he greeted me briskly. I didn't like the sound of this at all.

"Not very much," I told him guardedly. "Why?"

And then they told me.

Colonel Gray said, "We want you to tow four ex-U.S. minesweepers back to Manila for us." My heart sank. Four minesweepers thirteen thousand miles across the Pacific with a strange crew. At first it didn't appeal to me at all. The prospect of a sunshine cruise in a trim little tug was fast vanishing.

Gray must have sensed my disappointment. "Don't worry," he said. "You couldn't find a finer tug than this for the job. She's a slick looking 900-ton ex-U.S. Navy fast rescue craft, do better than $18\frac{1}{2}$ knots."

I wondered how much of that speed the four minesweepers would absorb. A month later I was to discover that they could, at times, comfortably devour $17\frac{3}{4}$ of those precious knots.

I asked him about refuelling arrangements. You need a lot of fuel to tow four vessels across more than thirteen thousand miles of ocean. I had assumed our route would be down the Florida coast, through the Windward Passage between Cuba and Haiti, across the Caribbean, through the Panama Canal, Manzanillo on the west coast of

Mexico, 3,090 miles across to Honolulu, another 3,240 to Guam and 1,800 on to Manila. But Gray told me I was to go from Manzanillo to Palmyra, not Honolulu. At Palmyra, around one thousand miles south of Hawaii, it appeared that special arrangements had been made for us to refuel at a U.S. Navy oiling depot. The fuel was cheaper too. Extra tanks aboard were to extend our normal range of one thousand miles to an additional distance then not known in San Francisco.

I asked Colonel Gray how long I was to be given to get my flotilla seaworthy and to get my towing gear rigged. I visualized quite a lot of work.

He smiled. "You have nothing to worry about on that score. The tows were rigged long ago. The minesweepers were in Charleston. The tug called in on its way down from Norfolk and picked them up. They left Charleston six days ago. We thought it best if you took over at Panama. Meanwhile there is another Captain and a Towmaster aboard."

It all sounded thoroughly unworkable to me. "It's a long tow," I said, "and it's my responsibility to get those five ships safely to Manila. Supposing I don't like the Towmaster's rig?"

Gray looked annoyed. "Look here, Ainslie, we've spent three months and a great deal of money rigging these tows and we can't afford any more delay. The Towmaster will go all the way; the tow-rig will be his responsibility."

For the second time that day I nearly quit, but I had agreed to go and go I would.

The authority of an American towmaster may have been well defined somewhere in an authoritative United States' shipping manual, but I was never to discover an accurate description of his duties. It is a purely American role. On a British tow the Master of the tug would be in supreme command of the whole operation, answerable to no one aboard. But an American Captain might, if his

17 PO—B

tow were lengthy, the voyage long and he without towing experience, employ a Towmaster to direct and advise on the technicalities of rigging towlines. But the Towmaster like the Pilot, is only an adviser. Final responsibility for the safety of all the ships under his command is always the captain's.

I imagined, therefore, that my Towmaster was to accompany us as a sort of technical adviser. How wrong I was.

The tug and four minesweepers which had left Charleston on May 30 were due in Cristobal on the Atlantic side of the Panama Canal about June 15.

On June 5 we boarded an airliner for Panama. Miranda and Alonso could have flown direct across Mexico. With their Philippine passports a Mexican visa was only a trifling formality. Not so for me. I held a British passport. Those enjoying Commonwealth citizenship it appeared were not so quickly admitted south of the border. It is roughly three thousand three hundred miles from San Francisco to Panama by the direct route. The route I had to take to avoid landing on Mexican soil was nearly five thousand miles. For convenience Miranda and Alonso came with me. We flew across the Southern States to Miami, Florida, down to Havana, Kingston, Baranquilla in Colombia and from there to Panama. It took four days. We booked in at the Internacional Hotel in Panama City and waited.

# Chapter Two

Six days later, on June 15, the *Wallace R. Gray* and her four minesweepers were reported off Cristobal. Panama City is on the Pacific side of the Isthmus, so I quickly took a train the sixty miles across, anxious to get a glimpse of my charges.

They must have arrived some hours before because they were already at anchor and the four minesweepers had been shorthauled, that is, hauled in close to the tug.

I shall never forget my first sight of the *Wallace R. Gray* lying there in Cristobal Bay. My heart warmed to her immediately. No harbour tug this, I thought. She looked far bigger and more powerful than I had imagined, and looked all of her gross 900 tons and 250 feet length. I liked her lines. Her wheelhouse and big funnel were streamlined and her Naval grey paint gave her the appearance of a fast sloop, particularly as she still carried her gun emplacements and was fitted with huge fire nozzles which look deceptively like heavy armament. On her foremast was the spidery outline of a radar installation. In her wartime role of fast rescue tug she had been based on the American coast ready to dash to the assistance of torpedoed ships. Her job then was either to tow the cripples back to port or help beach them before they sank. How many vessels she had saved in this way I never discovered. A shroud of mystery seemed to cover her career.

The minesweepers were smaller than I had been expecting. They were wooden 110-footers rather like the Royal Navy's Y.M.S.s, and I learnt were being taken to Manila merely for their valuable 200-h.p. diesel engines and big twin generators which had been carefully sealed and greased for the voyage. Their propellers and shafts had been drawn and the stern glands made watertight.

From the docks I couldn't see what sort of tow-rig was being used so I hired a launch and went out. As we approached the tug I saw that my first impression had been a little rose-tinted. She was quite the dirtiest vessel I had seen for a very long time. Although some work seemed to be going on aft nobody noticed me nor came to help me aboard. As I scrambled up the side I planted my hand squarely into the remains of the morning's breakfast which had been flung out of the galley. "There are going to be a few changes here before long," I told myself as I cleared the mess off my hand and sleeve. For a tug that had just completed a 1,860-mile tow there was an extraordinary absence of activity. It took me several minutes to find anyone at all. When I did he was a sloppy-looking seaman. "Where's the Skipper?" I asked him. He pointed disinterestedly towards the wheelhouse.

I found the Skipper and the first and second Mates there chatting. An atmosphere of casualness seemed to pervade the whole ship. They said the Towmaster was busy aft, supervising the stowing of the towing lines. The Towmaster seemed to be the only centre of work on the whole ship. I went aft to have a look at the towing gear, but most of it had been hauled in. He seemed to be having trouble making the crew do as he directed. They were trying to haul in the greasy 11-inch tow-rope and I got the impression none of them had had very much experience. And what a mixture they were—everything from jet black through olive to white.

The Towmaster, was a thick-set man, greying and muscular and in his early sixties. The most remarkable feature about him was his voice. It boomed with a kind of inescapable resonance. And in his job he had to use it frequently.

He did not appear to be very pleased to see me and

asked why I had not waited ashore until I heard from him. I told him we had run out of money while waiting for the tug to arrive and that the Company had cabled he would advance some cash. Leaving him I went in search of the Skipper whom I found in the saloon. He was a thirty-six-year-old American who had been a U.S. Navy convoy Commodore during the war. He hardly believed me when I showed him my orders.

"It doesn't make sense," he said. "The Mates and I signed on for the voyage to Manila. Not that we shall be sorry to leave her here."

I could get no more out of him except that the Towmaster was also Chief Engineer, and the information that the tow-lines had given trouble on the voyage down from Charleston and two of the minesweepers had been making water. The Towmaster wanted to modify and strengthen the lines and as there were better facilities for doing this at Balboa on the Pacific side of the Isthmus it was decided to push on through. For convenience in negotiating the canal locks which raise ships up on either side of the Isthmus to a connecting lake, eighty-five feet above sea level, we slipped the minesweepers. They were brought through later escorted by a canal tug after they had been pulled up on Cristobal slipway, and two of them recaulked.

Negotiating the canal I had a foretaste of the voyage ahead. It was in Miraflores Lock. I was on the bridge with the Captain from whom I was taking over. The canal Pilot ordered "touch astern". The telegraph clanged. To my amazement we began to surge forward. The engine-room had answered with "half ahead". The Pilot swore and shouted an order to the canal-side electric mules to whom we were made fast. Only their swift action saved us from crashing the preventer chains and lock gates and toppling into the next lock. We arrived safely in Balboa, but I began to look at my prospective crew a little closer after that.

Three days later on June 18 I assumed command. The little convoy was now mine. Alonso became Mate and Miranda my number two. I was disappointed not to have been stepping aboard at Charleston, but there was still plenty of sea between me and Manila—maybe nine thousand miles of it, I estimated. The log told me that the tow had taken sixteen days to reach Panama, averaging 4.37 knots on the 1,860-mile voyage. At that rate we should make the Philippines by October.

The sense of uneasiness I had felt on coming aboard had grown stronger as each day passed. From every quarter there seemed to be an undercurrent of dissatisfaction. I determined to get to the bottom of it all without further delay and ordered the whole ship's company—thirty-two including officers—to be mustered on the forecastle-head. Never in all my days at sea had I seen such a crew. Sixteen of them were Filipinos, the others included Americans, a Hawaiian, a Portuguese, a German and a Mexican.

"I seem to have inherited a legacy of dissatisfaction," I told them, from the bridge. "Something is wrong. We have a long voyage ahead of us and I don't intend making it with an unhappy crew. If any of you want to leave I'm giving you this opportunity to pay off."

I had expected that the most discontented of the crew would jump at this chance to go but I was quite unprepared for the result of my offer. It seemed that nearly all of them wanted to pay off. This was more than I had bargained for and I asked them what the trouble was.

A tall, powerfully built young American whose name I later discovered was Mark Todd, stepped forward and began a recital of complaints that painted a far from rosy picture of conditions aboard. The major trouble, however, seemed to be the question of authority. "We just don't know who to take orders from," he said. "As soon as the Captain's or Mate's orders are relayed to us they are countermanded. We never know what to do from one minute to the next, and it just won't work any longer. We're all fed up and want to leave the ship."

There was a lot more but the first thing to be done was to clear up this question of Command. I made it plain that after we had cleared Balboa I would be in sole charge. I took the opportunity of getting rid of those who looked like giving trouble. The first Assistant Engineer also left and they were all flown back to the States.

The Towmaster, who was still directing repairs to the minesweepers in Cristobal, had decided to relinquish his job as Chief Engineer and devote his full energies to his towmaster job. This meant securing a new Chief, which I found impossible in either Balboa, Panama or Colon. However, unknown to me at the time, the Towmaster had already cabled Manila to have two engineers flown from there. They arrived on June 28 and I found the new Chief was Solomon Cuesta, an elderly Filipino. He was 5 feet 1 inch tall and quite the smallest and most genial man aboard. A full row of gold teeth sparkled every time he smiled and in the beginning that was quite often. I knew him from my UNRRA days when he had helped me locate a lot of very hard-to-get equipment. And he handled Filipinos well. Unfortunately the *Wallace R. Gray* was to prove too much for him. He had been used to smaller craft and the burden of many of our subsequent breakdowns was to fall on the other engineers.

His first Assistant, forty-seven-year-old Filipino Romulo Gonzalez, who was flown from Manila at the same time was little better equipped. He too had been accustomed to smaller vessels. But his biggest handicap was a physical one. He was asthmatical and, I suspected, a bit tubercular. I knew him in Manila and had I known he was being considered would out of fairness to himself and the rest of the crew have tried to prevent his appointment. I had to insist that he use his own eating utensils aboard.

But we all admired the spirit he showed working as hard as the best in the face of his slowly losing battle with life.

It was the second and third Assistant Engineers who were to shoulder the major problems of the *Gray's* engine-room, and there were to be many. Without them we should never have reached Palmyra, let alone the Philippines. Our second Assistant was Hermann Schmidt, a German, short, blond, powerfully built and thirty-nine. Of his background I knew nothing. He never spoke of it and I never pumped him. He was an excitable fellow, quickly upset but always ready to pull far more than his own weight and proved one of the best engineers I have ever sailed with. Ashore, he was fond of the bright lights and had a reputation as a champion roller-skater. He had spent much of his time in American ships.

Johnnie Stephens, the third Assistant Engineer, had signed on in Charleston as a wiper. He was an American, came from South Carolina, and had been a wiper in the U.S. Navy. But he was too good to be wasted in this job and I later promoted him. He was about thirty-five, very tall, and the only time I was ever to hear him grumble was when he crashed his head into the maze of pipes with which the engine-room was fitted. "Many more months among these goddamned pipes, sir, and I'll have a permanent stoop," he used to say.

The "goddamned pipes" were an ingenious invention of the Towmaster's. Realizing that the long voyage was going to tax every ounce of power and gallon of fuel we had, he had made certain modifications to increase the efficiency of his engines. Before the ship had sailed from Charleston he had installed a great deal of extra piping to trap waste steam and divert it back to the cylinders. He had worked on it for weeks, tracking down every corner of the engine-room where steam, which could be short-circuited back to boost the engines, was normally being allowed to escape. The outcome of his ingenuity was, I am sure, one of the most efficient oil-burning, steam tugs that ever entered the Pacific.

Although I know something about engines and engine-rooms the *Gray's* with her confusing complexity of additional pipes, looking like a surrealist's nightmare, was more complicated than most. The way the engine-room team moved about down there, and in tropical heat—their thermometer sometimes showed one hundred and twenty degrees—remained, to me, one of the miracles of the voyage.

In addition to the Towmaster, my two Mates and the four engineers, there was one other officer who shared our little wardroom—we called it a wardroom because the *Gray* still retained much of her Naval character. He was Arthur Harris, our American radio officer and electrician. "Sparks" was to become the best friend I had aboard and the only one I ever really got to know. He was twenty-five, had a pretty wife back in Washington, and was a first-class radio operator. During the war he had been an operator in the U.S. Navy's big carrier *Yorktown*. He was aboard when the Japs sank her at Midway. He was trapped in the control room as she began to heel over but somehow had managed to struggle clear into the sea where he was later picked up. Always cool-headed and un-hurried, he was to prove to be quite the most valuable man aboard and was to play one of the bravest roles in our troubles to come. Two months before he had had not the least intention of going to sea again. But one day he happened to be a passenger on the same train in Virginia as the previous Skipper. The two got talking. "I need a radio operator," my predecessor had told him. "Why not join me?" Sparks liked the sound of the voyage back to the Western Pacific he had known during the war. He said he would have to discuss it first with his wife. She must have agreed for a few days later he was on a train for Charlestown and the *Gray*.

One of his jobs aboard was to edit the ship's newspaper—such as it was, which appeared regularly thrice weekly. Sparks picked up titbits of news by radio, typed them out and pinned copies in the officers' and crew's quarters. It was always read most avidly for its baseball scores.

The buffer between the Mate and his crew is the Bosun. Upon him and his ability to handle men depends much of a ship's efficiency. The *Gray* had a splendid Bosun. His name was Edward Romanin, a Hawaiian. In his early thirties, he had a particular aptitude for learning quickly. He knew considerably more about seamanship than those under him and although, in our case, this bestowed no particular merit as most of the crew knew none, he would have been an asset to any ship.

The others were a colourful band. But so few were of any experience that it was some weeks before I was able to place them in roles in which they could prove of more use than in others. Some were clearly in their wrong vocation at sea at all, but I tried to make the best of them. I would find for instance so-called oilers, completely unreliable in the engine-room, but who, after a few weeks under Romanin, became quite useful deckmen. Others, lazy and disinterested on deck found a new interest in life among the engines. The voyage was to bring many such changes.

One of the most interesting personalities was Peter Ferraro, a swarthy Portuguese from Honolulu. He was only twenty-nine, but a badly pock-marked face and little moustache made him look nearer forty. He was one of my useful oilers and whenever there was a breakdown would willingly **sacri**fice his off-duty time to lend a hand below. Ashore Ferraro had another claim to fame. He was a Casanova of a very high and accomplished order. "Weemen," he used to boast, "they just fall for me, all of them." The crew, I gathered, were regaled for many a

26

dull off-watch hour by his colourfully detailed descriptions of amorous conquests in every port of the Seven Seas.

The other oilers were both Filipinos. Vicente Espinosa who came from Manila was fifty-seven but looked seventy with his iron-grey hair. He was quiet and unassuming but fate had marked him. He was the only one of us not to see his home again. Benedicto Ortiz was nearly forty and for a Filipino his skin was extraordinarily black. Stripped, he looked like a wrestler. He had signed on originally as an able seaman.

All my firemen were Filipinos too. One of them, Savarino, who had lived many years in America, I mistook at first for a Japanese. He had a smooth, bland expression, a reputation as an admirer of white women, and carried a knife. Agustin Lascano, thirty-five and good-looking, was another of the same kind. I always felt uncomfortable near him because I knew he was always watching me like a distrustful lynx. Aldo Rocca, thirty-seven, very dark and rather tall for a Filipino, like the others had probably never seen an oil valve before he joined the *Gray*. He left a job as a cook in California to sign on.

Then there was my deck crew. Salvador Guido, a thirty-four-year-old United-States-born Filipino from New Orleans who looked as if he had Negro blood in him. He was one of the laziest men aboard and was demoted finally to sculleryman. Another non-seaman was Cesar Damone. He was a dapper fifty-four, signed on as messman but annoyed me so much I transferred him to ordinary seaman. He made no pretence of the fact that he had never been to sea before. Like many of them he was a cook, seeking a passage home. Quite different was Tony Rodrigues, twenty-seven. He was a Mestizo, an American-Filipino, intelligent, widely-read and keen to make a career of the sea. He would spend much of his spare time on the bridge trying to learn navigation from Miranda.

27

His keenness earned him promotion to acting second Mate before the end of the voyage.

Among the Americans, Mark Todd, the twenty-one-year-old crew spokesman was probably the most useful. He had served in the U.S. Navy, was immensely strong and later in mid-Pacific his skill as a coxswain was to make him even more valuable. A year older was Otto Whiteman, nearly six foot, intelligent, hard-working. He came from South Carolina and I believe had been in the Navy. Gary Vincent, thirty-two, was another of the landlubbers. He had served in the United States Army, signed on as a wiper, but I switched him to able seaman.

The only other Americans aboard were both eighteen. The younger of the two and our youngest member was Franklin Martin. He had a wife back in Charleston and had signed on as an A.B. Why he ever tried to join us I could never understand; he was gloriously inexperienced. But he compensated in another direction. He was imperturbably and continuously happy. As a morale-builder—and there were to be times when we could have used a company of them—he was worth ten times his 250 dollars a month.

George Cooper had never been to sea before either. There were occasions when he certainly must have wished he had never tried. He never really found his sea-legs and was to be seriously sea-sick for days on end.

We had two Filipino cooks, one for the officers, one for the crew. The Chief Cook was thirty-seven-year-old Willie Dominguez. He was a naturalized American and had an American wife. He was an excellent cook and said to be a handy man with a gun, but he kept it so well hidden it wasn't discovered until the Philippines Customs searched us at the end of the voyage. The biggest point in his favour as a cook was to be the astonishing ease with which he could produce the most nourishing meals when we were strictly rationed and desperately short of food. He would have made a first-rate conjurer.

Second cook Pedro Casas was forty-three and was promoted to the position from messman. Easy-going, and hard-working, he had during his life been everything from a chef to a cowboy. He replaced a Mexican cook whom I paid off in Balboa at his own request. His cooking was so atrocious I feared for his safety if he had remained aboard!

Finally there was the ship's carpenter, Raul Diaz, one of the nicest old Filipinos I ever knew. His carpentry wasn't anything wonderful, and he was dreadfully slow. Jobs I gave him which I expected would take him a couple of hours, I would find him still patiently tapping away on two days later. But he was conscientious and worked desperately hard. Nothing was ever to ruffle his calm.

After we had been in Balboa a few days we began to pay the penalty for a prolonged stay at a port so close to Panama City. It was not every day that the local marine department had the opportunity of scrutinizing vessels benefiting by the latitude of its regulations. They were quick to take advantage of our delay.

I was called up to the marine department's office and a polite official pointed out to me a clause in the Panamanian Marine Regulations which stated that all ships under the flag of the Republic must employ at least ten per cent Panamanian crew. They looked at me with a well-what-are-you-going-to-do-about-it? look. I quickly told him—nothing. It would have meant replacing three of my crew and putting the company to the expense of flying them all back to the States. The idea was absurd. But the marine authority was adamant.

I knew that as we were in Canal Zone waters I could probably successfully ignore them and sail with my crew unchanged. But in the end I agreed to take five Panamanians. In any case I would need that number to replace those I was paying off.

A motley assortment of so-called Panamanians was sent down to the tug from which to make my selection. The farcical feature of the whole business was that few of them looked even remotely like Panamanians. But nevertheless to humour officialdom I chose what I judged to be the most likely five.

The first was Luis Ritter. His mother was Panamanian, his father German and somewhere a little Negro blood had crept in. He was twenty-eight. He told me he had been to sea as a wiper so I signed him on as one. He became successively oiler, fireman, ordinary seaman and finally able seaman, a job which seemed to suit his temperament better. He used to sing a lot, and before he joined us had been a cabaret crooner in Panama City. He later taught me several Spanish songs, writing out the words in peculiar phonetics of his own. He turned out to be an excellent helmsman, and I preferred him at the wheel whenever we entered or left port and whenever first-class steering was necessary.

Of the five three were Negroes. One, Nicaraguan-born, was Sammy Jones whom I made an able seaman; he had sailed in American Army tugs during the war and was to be one of the few men aboard with any knowledge of seamanship. He worked like a slave always with a perpetual grin on his face, and was the only man I was ever to have to discourage, for his own good, from overworking.

The second was Paul Bennett. He was stocky, heavily built and quite the blackest man aboard. When he came he told me that he had pawned his watch in Colon on the other side of the Isthmus to raise his train fare to join us. "Look, boss, that's where it was," he said indicating what might have been the impression of a watch strap on his wrist. I think he'd probably taken his watch off just before I saw him. I made him a wiper. But the engineer found him so lazy I had to put him on deck under the Bosun's eye to get any work out of him. But he was even too much for Romanin and was returned ignominiously to the engine-room for the little use he ever was.

Of similar calibre was Pablo Brown, a twenty-nine-year-old West Indian Negro. He was tall and thin and wiry and had been a waiter in Panama City. I made him officer's messman but he became dissatisfied with the pay, and was later to serve successively as ordinary seaman, oiler, fireman and finally wiper. He was brazen and impudent and quite the cheekiest of them all.

Last man to sign on was a tall, gangling Swede. His name was Frederick Jacobsen. He was twenty-one and six foot three. He claimed to be a fireman but was no more a fireman than I was. A normal engine-room and stokehold would have been cramping enough for his great height, but ours with its chaotic web of extra pipes must have been hell for him. He seemed to have very little control over his tall frame and there was nowhere on the whole ship where he could move without injuring himself. I wasn't going to take him at first. I was suspicious when he couldn't produce his papers to prove he had been, as he insisted, a fireman. But he said he had left them on his last ship and now he was stranded in Panama. In the end as in the case of all the others I decided to risk him even though I suspected he wanted only to come as far as Manzanillo to get back to his wife in San Francisco.

That was my crew—thirty-two including the Towmaster, the rawest, most mixed team who ever signed articles under me. Even in my days in sail I couldn't remember a less promising crowd. I said that was my crew. It wasn't quite. I omitted one very important member. Her name was Butch. She was a bitch of very assorted origin who got aboard in Charleston and stayed with us to the bitter end. She was big, had a brown and white body that reminded one of a hunting hound but her head was obviously fox terrier. She made a splendid watch dog and seemed to attach herself to Guido. I would never allow her near the bridge and for this to the last day of the voyage she never forgave me, snarling whenever I approached her. Apart from one or two parakeets which the crew kept in their quarters she was the only livestock we carried, although a startling assortment of bird life was to join us later.

A few days later the Towmaster having seen the mine-sweepers repaired to his satisfaction, came through from Cristobal to Balboa and rejoined us. Meanwhile I was getting the tug made shipshape. I ordered Romanin to get his men busy cleaning her down and instituted daily deck scrubbing, something they had not been made to do before. I made them clean off and red-lead every spot of rust. Few of them had handled a scraper before, but within a few days the *Gray* was beginning to look more like the sort of ship I liked to live in.

At the same time I started regular boat drills. I could see no record in the log of any having been held up till then and Romanin confirmed that in fact there had been none. I told him also to see that sufficient of the men could row. It transpired that few even knew how to hold an oar. So under Romanin's guidance they began rowing lessons around Panama Bay. It was a comical sight and would have given a rowing coach apoplexy. A week's practice, however, developed a certain limited efficiency among some of them but unfortunately the seas on which they were later to put their newly acquired skill into practice were far more tempestuous than the calm water of Panama Bay.

I checked the ship's inventory. One quick glance through it told me that the *Gray* was badly understocked. With the exception of the engine-room stores we were inadequately equipped for a harbour tow let alone a trans-Pacific voyage. There was not a solitary fathom of spare towing gear, insufficient deck stores, carpenter's tools, medical supplies, chartroom equipment, and most staggering of all, not enough food. The Bosun's locker was devoid of paint-brushes, scrapers, marlin-spikes, mallets, sewing gear; there was no carpenter's saw or claw-hammer, no wire-chisels so essential to cut wire rope quickly in an emergency, and no 10 lb. chisel-hammers. Apart from the few bandages, splints, aspirins, Epsom salts and a bottle of cough mixture the medical locker didn't even conform to the minimum compulsory sea-going requirements. I quickly set about rectifying this and ordered all the essential stores I needed. I managed, too, to get a small quantity of penicillin from a U.S. Navy dispensary ashore. We might never have made Palmyra without it.

Then I set about the food supplies. I based my calculations on stores for thirty-four men for a hundred days, confident that I had allowed a safe margin of several weeks. My bigger orders were for 450 lb. of flour, 50 2-lb. loaves of bread, 500 lb. of coffee, 28 sacks of rice for my 16 Filipinos, 150 lb. of liver, three carcasses of mutton, 6 sides of bacon, 25 cases of tinned fruit, 40 lb. of cooking figs, a ton of potatoes, ten sacks of onions, 20 sacks of corn cobs, 1,000 lb. of fresh fish, 75 lb. of dried fish, 50 lb. of cheese, 200 dozen eggs, 50 gallons of fresh milk, 250 lb. of ground beef, 1,800 lb. of boneless beef, 300 lb. of sausages, 150 lb. of kidneys, 18 fresh legs of pork. My food bill came to $3,396, which ran out at $1.26 per man per day. Most of this food was to last us the whole voyage, but I knew we could restock with fresh meat and vegetables at Manzanillo. I also got aboard some turkeys in case we were still at sea on America's Thanksgiving Day. They were to be eaten long before that. A closer examination of the list of my requisitions showed me that the Owner's Agent had struck out many of the items—including spare tow-gear and medical items like brandy and catheters.

On June 28, two tugs brought the four minesweepers

through from Cristobal and they tied up at the pier ahead of the *Gray*. It was almost time to leave so I took a trip ashore to see what progress the Towmaster was making with his towing lines. The ropes had become saturated on the voyage down from Charleston and he had laid them out on the dockside to dry in the hot Panamanian sun.

It was the first opportunity I had had of examining the tow-gear. To the landsman as it lay there strung out on the Balboa pier it must have looked just a very ordinary set of ropes and wire cables. But this same gear was destined to give us all the hardest voyage of our lives. The lengths of big 11-inch manila as thick as a man's leg would have appeared to him strong enough to tow a battleship twice round the world—and so it might well have been capable of doing. But a towing convoy is only as strong as its weakest link. Our weakest links were where the huge ropes were made fast to the minesweepers.

This is how our tow-lines were rigged. It began with a powerful electric towing winch situated immediately aft of the deck-house on the tug. Its huge drum held 2,200 feet of 2½-inch steel wire which ran 80 feet along the after-deck and out over the stern to the first minesweeper. In practice never much more than 1,200 feet of wire was run out, but the distance between the tug and No. 1 sweeper could be varied with the winch. The other three mine-sweepers were strung out in line astern, each separated by 800 feet of 11-inch manila rope. The wire from the tug's winch and the three tow ropes were attached to the sweepers by steel bridles. Their function was to spread the strain of towing evenly through the sweepers' none too robust wooden hulls. The bridles consisted of two lengths of 1¼-inch steel wire. They ran along each side about level with the main deck and met fore and aft about fifteen feet beyond the bow and stern. They were attached to the sweepers and supposed to have been held rigid by

34

two 12" × 12" baulks of Oregon timber bolted to the wooden deck fore and aft and which supported the bridle wires clear of the hull. The Oregon baulks projected through the bulwarks two feet on either side of the vessel and the bridle wires were held by these about a foot out from the side. Where they came together fore and aft of each sweeper they were shackled to the tow-lines. The baulks of timber were also supposed to keep the bridles clear of the bow and stern when the minesweepers started to swing in a heavy sea. The whole idea in theory was that the steel bridle wires should surround the sweepers without any possibility of damaging them. The whole strain of towing therefore, was taken by the steel bolts which fastened the Oregon to the deck, bolts on which, in my opinion, too much depended.

What later proved to be the weakness of this rig were the four points on each sweeper where the wire bridle was attached to the projecting beams of timber. The wire was gripped to the baulk by a U-bolt which was meant to hold it so tight that it would never slip. That was the theory. In practice we were to find the strain was so great the bridles would begin to slip backwards and forwards through the bolt after a few days at sea. No matter how tightly the bolt clamped the wire against the timber it could never prevent the wire sliding and wearing. The result was that one by one the six strands which made up the complete wire were worn through until the whole bridle was finally severed. The only minesweeper on which this was not to occur was No. 4; it did not have the weight of another craft astern of it.

On the tow down from Charleston the bridles had been chafing, but the Towmaster had managed by tightening the U-bolts from time to time to reach Cristobal without anything carrying away. The minesweepers carried no crew and every adjustment to the bridles meant sending off an inspection party in a boat. During one of these examinations out in the Atlantic swell the Towmaster and the men who were manning the boat, lost their oars and began to drift away. It was only the skilful seamanship of the other Captain who quickly steamed the whole convoy about in a wide circle to come up on the little boat from astern that saved them.

The days were slipping by. The re-rigging was taking a long time. Already we had been in Panama two weeks longer than we had intended and were well behind schedule. Meanwhile aboard the tug I was slowly getting my crew into better shape.

When I first took over they were treating the *Gray* as a sort of glorious club. They used to stroll nonchalantly about the ship, would saunter into my cabin without knocking—one even came to me about some triviality while I was in the middle of a bath—were smoking in the galley and frequently interrupting the officers' meals with shouted queries from the wardroom door. I quickly put a stop to all this.

Another firm stand I had to take concerned the Towmaster himself. I found he had installed himself in the Captain's place at the mess-table. If there is any tradition of the sea about which a Captain is more pernickety than another it is the time-honoured one which reserves him a seat exclusively his own at table. Not even the Commodore of the line has the right to occupy it. I am no exception. The Towmaster found himself another place.

The crew were thoroughly enjoying their protracted stay in Balboa. In nearby Panama City which came to life every night in traditional Latin-American style in a blaze of neon lights, they could get thoroughly drunk for a few dollars, watch pornographic cabaret turns, dance till six in the morning or find themselves a *señorita*. Most were quick to take advantage of all that Panama offered. At all hours of the morning they would reel back to the *Gray* singing riotously. One night Ferraro did not return. In-

36

quiries revealed that he was in jail, blissfully asleep. He had been picked up drunk. Later in the day he politely paid his own fine and returned to duty. Another night Ortiz, who was doing watchman's duty on the gangway necessary because of the twenty-foot tide, cleared off into the city. He disappeared for two days. I logged him four days' pay.

There were further incidents in Panama City which reminded me that my uniform was still making me look like a member of the United States Army. The city was always full of American troops off-duty from the nearby Canal zone and was well policed by M.P.s. One accosted me one morning. "Hey you, haven't you got a cap, what's it for, put it on." I turned round and asked him to whom he thought he was talking. At this he became more aggressive. "Put it on or I'll take you in charge." When I explained that I was not a hatless rookie but the Master of a tug he apologized and strode dubiously away. On another occasion an M.P. followed me into a hotel. He said I was out of bounds and he was very sorry but he would have to "pick me up". Through working with Americans during the war my speech had acquired a slight drawl and nothing would convince him that I wasn't an American officer sneaking into an out-of-bounds hotel. Even when I had been through the whole story again and showed him my papers he still didn't seem to believe me.

During our stay in Balboa Sparks and I became firm friends. Somehow although he was very much younger than me he was the only member of the crew with whom I found very much in common. We used to go into Panama City together in the evenings, for a cabaret, a quiet drink and a chat. But it wasn't always quiet. One night we went to a cabaret called the Happyland. It was a typical Central American night-club complete with sub-dued lighting, Latin orchestra, impeccably attired Negro waiters, the aroma of strong cigars, powerful perfume and

37

the raven-haired *señoritas* who exuded it. As the evening wore on, the orchestra's tempo quickened and the smoky atmosphere thickened. We noticed that several of the dancing girls, all rather beautiful, at a nearby table were toasting us with gracious and flashing glances. Then we saw why. The chits for their drinks were being courteously delivered to our table. The toasts were on us. Actually it is an old Panamanian custom for suckers and later in the evening it becomes the turn of the proprietor, who employs the girls merely to entertain his patrons, to reciprocate with drinks on the house. But this evening the traditional reciprocation seemed to have been overlooked. A substantial pile of chits was mounting at my elbow. So I left my table to look for the proprietor and remind him of his responsibilities. I was unaware of a huge, ugly-looking Negro, apparently the proprietor's bodyguard, who crept out to the office behind me. Sparks spotted him and followed us both. Just as I was about to knock on the door, Sparks told me later, the Negro had raised an enormous clenched fist and was about to deliver a fierce rabbit punch on the nape of my neck when Sparks grabbed him. Oblivious of this, I was already chatting to the suave little Spanish proprietor. We got our drinks.

It was well past midnight when we left the Happyland. We started to climb into a taxi but the big Negro driver said he was engaged. As I moved away Sparks noticed from his meter that he was not, and started to argue. In a flash the Negro smashed a ham-like fist into Sparks' face, blackening his eye and breaking a tooth. I rushed back to help, but by now the driver was threatening us both with a nasty-looking tyre lever. Other Negro drivers crowded round and held him away from us. Sparks' blood was up. Cursing and spitting blood, he was demanding vengeance. But the other drivers told us the police would certainly support the driver on principle. So we hired another cab and went back to the ship.

Sparks' face was a horrible mess. But after a coffee he felt better. He insisted we go back to look for his assailant. He had a score to wipe off. He brought a heavy belaying-pin with him and we went back to the city. We hunted for him the following night too, but honour remained unsatisfied.

Before we sailed, Sparks' broken tooth began to give him terrible pain. A local dentist capped it for him, but later at sea it was to develop an abscess, from which he nearly died.

Meanwhile I was preparing my charts and laying out courses. My dividers told me that it was 1,860 miles up the Mexican coast to Manzanillo, our last refuelling point before Palmyra in mid-Pacific, where 85,000 gallons—2,000 barrels—of Bunker C heavy fuel oil had been reserved for us by the United States Navy. The Towmaster said we would be able to average six or seven knots comfortably. With four tows I felt he was being more than optimistic.

I didn't know how skilful Cuesta was at getting the most out of his fuel and the more I went over my calculations, the less I liked our chances of making the 3,400-mile haul from Manzanillo to Palmyra even with the extra fuel tanks we carried. At the very best I couldn't see us averaging better than five knots. What a super-optimist even I was to prove.

When I mentioned my fears to the Towmaster, he laughed. "Come and have a look down here," he said, and took me on a conducted tour of the engine-room which he had pepped up when earlier he had had the double job of Towmaster and Chief Engineer. We stooped and crawled and squeezed our way through masses of hot pipes which wove through every vacant space in a confused pattern. The Towmaster was immensely proud of his supercharged engines. "It's given us more revolutions and one-and-a-half more knots," he told me. "You couldn't get another atom of power out of these pistons. I've captured every darned bit of it." I was impressed, but reassurance about the efficiency of our engines in no way lessened my anxiety over possible delays our poor rig might cause us. However I knew that if we were to sail at all, it would be with the tow-rig as it was, so I went back to the chart-room to plan a course that would take maximum advantage of following winds and currents.

The great circle route and shortest distance between Manzanillo and Palmyra was 3,400 miles. But it curved across in too high and unsuitable latitudes. From my experience in crossing the North Pacific in sail thirty years before I knew that our best route lay down nearer the Equator where we could take advantage of the north-east and later the south-east trades and the north equatorial current which flowed resolutely away from the South American coast toward Palmyra.[1] This way, I measured, was 3,580 miles, 180-odd miles longer, but avoided the often stormy and variable winds of the more direct route. Even then I had visions of five helpless ships in an empty ocean, out of fuel and still hundreds of miles short of Palmyra.

Originally we had been due to reach Palmyra on July 1, but with the delays in Charleston and now the re-rigging in Balboa it looked as if we would be extremely lucky to make Palmyra by September.

It was now already the first week in July and we had been in Balboa three weeks longer than it was ever intended. Our extended visit was becoming the subject of quite a lot of unfavourable comments from the port authorities and was piling up some hefty dues for the Islands Towage and Lighterage Company.

[1] Limits of Trade winds are as follows:
Southern Limit N.E. Trade 12° N. July/September
Northern ,, S.E. ,, 9 N. ,, ,,
Depth of area of variable winds or Doldrums would therefore, during that time, be only 180 miles.

Taking advantage of our predicament the local seaman's union secretary decided to pay us a visit. He was a swarthy little fellow of Spanish extraction, always beautifully dressed in tropical white and always unfailingly polite. He insisted that my crew would have to join the Panamanian Union. I told him none of them had any intention of joining. But he wouldn't take no for an answer. He came back to see me many times; I finally had to threaten to have him refused entry to our pier. I never saw him again.

Our delay also began to give me concern for another reason. The crew were beginning to become infected with venereal disease. The longer we stayed in Balboa the more cases I had on my hands. Several were cured once only to become re-infected a week later. I sent them all to a U.S. Navy shore hospital where the treatment seemed quickly effective, but I couldn't keep the men out of Panama City and I knew we should have V.D. aboard until we got to sea.

On July 8, the Towmaster announced that the re-rigging was completed. At last I thought, we could put to sea. But while we were taking on fuel I went down to have a final look at the tow-lines. There were several weaknesses which I insisted must be rectified. The alterations took another week.

We were ready to sail on July 15. I went ashore to complete clearance formalities with the American harbour officials. There was only one minor hitch. The Americans were baffled by the tug's registered net tonnage. It was important that this be known for correct assessment of our port dues. The registration papers described her as of 912 tons gross but only 52 tons net. Now a laconic finger was jabbing at the "52". "Can this be correct, Captain?"

On the surface of it, it certainly looked suspiciously low. But in fact it was legitimate. Net registered tonnage is the gross registered tonnage less certain deductions for machinery, crew's quarters, storerooms and spaces used in navigating the vessel. In our case, the extra space taken up by the seventeen auxiliary fuel-tanks, eleven of which were on the after-deck, two on the boat-deck and four on the fo'c'sle-head, as well as the additional steam pipes installed in the engine-room, had been measured and registered but not correctly certified.

At first the officials were all for having the *Gray* surveyed before they would accept the figure. But after an hour's tedious explanation I finally convinced them and we got our clearance.

It was about this time I discovered that the Towmaster, in addition to his other activities was also Owner's Agent.

# Chapter Three

WE sailed at midday. We were considered such an unusual convoy that the Chief Pilot himself, a former United States Navy commander, did us the honour of taking us out. He put one of his own tugs on No. 4 minesweeper to give him more control as we cleared the crowded approaches to Balboa. But trouble arrived even before we dropped the Pilot. We were steaming slowly down the long line of fairway buoys which lead out of Balboa. The minesweepers were short hauled, drawn closely up one behind the other.

As the Pilot ordered a slight alteration of course to avoid an oncoming ship, No. 4 minesweeper was suddenly caught by a set. Despite the efforts of the tug alongside her, she was swept into a fairway buoy, and the bridle carried away.

We pulled out of the channel and anchored to make repairs. It took all afternoon, part of the night and most of the next morning to replace the wires. Next morning, July 16, we were ready for sea again at eleven-thirty. The Pilot had left us on the previous afternoon but we were now clear of the Port area.

I sent a boat party to board each minesweeper in turn and stream out the full lengths of tow-rope between them. Then we reeled out 900 feet of cable from the *Gray's* tow winch and as the minesweepers streamed out behind I slowly increased speed. When the boat party signalled "All Clear" from the last minesweeper and cast off in their boat I went round in a circle and picked them up.

Then I increased revolutions gradually to 6½ knots. Strung out for three-quarters of a mile behind, the four minesweepers each looking successively smaller seemed

43

very detached from us. The two lines disappeared into the sea about twenty-five yards ahead and astern of each vessel, sagging as much as fifteen feet below the surface under their own weight in the middle.

For the first few hours we were in a busy shipping lane and passing vessels unable to see our tow-lines mistook us for a naval squadron. Our navy grey paint must have deceived them, for one after the other they respectfully dipped their ensigns in salute. Flattered, although at first baffled, we solemnly acknowledged them all. What a navy we made!

For me this was an important shaking down period. I had to experiment to discover which revolutions gave me maximum speed while imposing the least strain on the bridles. Eventually I fixed on 126 r.p.m.; it gave us about six knots. Above this speed the tow-lines began to lift out of the sea. They broke surface at eight knots and immediately smooth progress gave way to one of strain as the lines alternatively sagged in the water and snapped bar-tight ten feet above it. To ease it we reeled out another three hundred feet of wire from the tug's winch, though I knew I would have to get more weight on the tow-ropes before leaving Manzanillo for Palmyra.

When clearing Balboa for North American ports, it is necessary for all vessels to steam almost due south for some distance to clear Cape Mala before making up the coast. It was during this period I had my first trouble with the Owner's Agent. As Panama Bay faded away astern, he strolled up on the bridge and peered into the compass. "Good God!" he exclaimed. "We're steering South. Surely the correct course is North?" There is no need to repeat here what I said, but he lost no time getting off the bridge.

As we had no third Mate I was taking watches with Alonso and Miranda. Mine was 4 to 8 morning and evening; normally the Mate's watch. When I came up on to

44

the bridge just before dawn beyond Cape Mala a heavy sea was making. But the *Gray* with her 17½-foot draught was riding it well. I was developing an affection for her. It felt grand to be at sea again. If I strained my eyes hard enough I could occasionally get a glimpse of the pale pool of light thrown on the sea by the stern lamp on No. 4 minesweeper. Oncoming vessels were warned that we were towing more than one vessel by three white lights one above the other on the *Gray's* foremast.

Our second day out passed without incident. The mine-sweepers were riding a rough sea well and we were making a splendid seven knots. I was following the Central American coast up to Manzanillo, keeping close to the shore for the calmer water, hoping to avoid wear on the bridles which were causing me considerable misgivings.

The third day, July 18, when we were off the Costa Rican coast and had covered 270 miles, I decided it was time to inspect the minesweepers to see how the wires were standing the strain, and to make any necessary adjustments.

I would have liked to have gone myself but hadn't sufficient confidence in the ability of Alonso to control the tug while I was away. Alonso particularly was becoming rather a disappointment to me. As Mate he should have taken the load of handling the men off my shoulders, but the mixed crew seemed to develop in him a deep inferiority complex, which at times made him afraid even to rouse them out of their bunks. So I sent Miranda instead.

We slowed down, slung out a 16-foot Norwegian flat-bottomed pram we carried, and Miranda, the Towmaster, Romanin, Jones and three others rowed away in the swell toward the first minesweeper. We were developing what was to become one of our most important routines.

As soon as the pram was clear I moved ahead to bring No. 1 sweeper within their reach. Bobbing about like a cork they made fast and scrambled aboard. Their inspection took about twenty minutes on each sweeper. Each man had a different part to check upon. Most important, of course, was the examination of the bridle wires where they were clamped to the U-bolts. But the hull and bilges had to be carefully looked at for any sign of a leak, the propeller shafts and rudders—they had been removed and lashed to the deck—in case they were coming adrift and the batteries which powered the sun lamps which lit up automatically at dusk, required servicing.

We developed a system of signals between the tug and the minesweepers, by raising flags. Flag "S" at the signal yard, for instance, meant stop, "G" at the full hoist, "Full ahead", at three-quarter hoist "Half speed" and so on. When the boat party raised the "all clear" signal from the first minesweeper and I could see they were safely back in the pram I would move ahead 800 feet to bring the next minesweeper up to them. Then the whole procedure would be repeated until I could see through the telescope that they were clear of No. 4. I would then steam round in a mile-wide circle and pick them up. If the sea was not too rough, the whole operation would take about an hour-and-a-half. In bad weather it might take five hours.

Miranda brought disquieting news with him when he scrambled back aboard the *Gray*. It was just as I had predicted. On Nos. 2 and 3 minesweepers the U-bolts were not gripping. The bridles were eating into the Oregon. No strands had yet parted but already the wire was showing signs of wear. Under the Towmaster's directions they had tightened the bolts. It was the old vicious circle again.

Eight days and 1,100 miles out of Balboa on the night of July 24 our voyage very nearly ended prematurely. We were inside the Gulf de Tehuantepec, creeping up the coast of south-west Mexico at six knots. I had first planned to save a few miles and cut across the Gulf. The fraying bridle wires changed my mind. I didn't fancy being caught out in the exposed middle of the Gulf so had de-

46

cided to follow the coast for its protection, for in this area sudden "white squalls" known as tehuantepecs, sweep down off the land.

The weather was fine and the barometer steady when I turned in about eleven o'clock. I left orders to maintain a course of 262 degrees, until Salina Cruz light was sighted, when I was to be called.

I awoke from a deep sleep at 3.10 a.m. to feel the tug rolling strangely in a rough sea. I sensed even before I leapt from my bunk that we had both altered course and slackened speed. Mystified I pulled on a pair of trousers and a greatcoat and hurried up on to the bridge. We were running through driving rain, whipped by a strong wind which was howling round the pilot-house, and the ship was diving into an angry sea. Visibility was barely a few yards. Peering astern I couldn't even see the light of the first minesweeper. The only man I could find was the helmsman. It was Ritter, standing imperturbably at the wheel, staring vacantly ahead into the gloom.

"Where's the second Mate?" I demanded. He didn't know.

Then I checked our course. It had been altered more than ninety degrees. Instead of heading parallel with the coast we were steaming straight for the head of the Gulf.

A vision of a line of breakers flashed through my mind. I shouted to Ritter ordering the helm down. Slowly we came round on to our original heading.

"Who the hell ordered you to alter course?" I asked him.

"The second Mate," he said.

Up on Monkey Island above the pilot-house I found Miranda, the officer of the watch. He told me that the Towmaster had ordered the right-angle change of course at 1.55. At 2.18 he had ordered speed reduced from 7 to 6 knots and later to 5 knots. He had taken these steps, he said, in order to reduce the strain on the towing gear.

47

I made a rapid calculation. It was now 3.15. For more than an hour we had been steaming toward disaster. I estimated we must have had barely a mile to run when I woke up. It was the only time on the voyage that I was to thank God for our dawdling progress.

And then suddenly the rain lifted for a few seconds. Through the driving curtain of spray I had a fragmentary glimpse of a line of surf crashing on to the shore not half a mile to starboard. Then the rain blotted it from view again. Providence had woken me none too soon. Another five minutes would have seen us piled up on the Mexican shore.

All that day I couldn't get the thought of that menacing looking shoreline and breakers out of my head. My mind flashed back thirty years to a day in 1918. There had been a reef then too—nearly nine hundred miles from this spot —but we hadn't been so lucky. It was in my square-rig days. I was acting second Mate of a barque carrying a cargo of coal across the Pacific from Australia to Callao in Peru. Navigation was dependent on the accuracy of our chronometer, for few ships were equipped with wireless. The Skipper did most of it. He was a salt of the old school who kept his methods jealously to himself. To me it seemed almost as if he smelt his way safely from port to port.

Well, on this voyage we had been under way for two months and were getting a bit anxious about our true position. For several days we had been steering on the skipper's dead reckoning, though as we afterwards discovered this was inaccurate. The Old Man knew we were in the vicinity of the Archipelago de Colon but he could not have realized just how close we really were. Although this area is within the Doldrum Belt, we were lucky and had a fairly strong wind. One night when we were bowling along through the murk, the yards creaking under full sail, there was a shout from the look-out: "Breakers ahead!" But it was too late. Before we could go about we had ploughed headlong with a terrible shudder on to the outlying rocks of a small island. There was a big sea running, and it was only a matter of minutes before the old ship began to break up and the main mast went over the side. The watch below came running up on deck and the Skipper gave the order to abandon ship. Then the fore-royal-mast and yard came crashing down on to the deck hitting the Skipper and killing him instantly. Seas were now sweeping the decks from poop to bow. All our boats had been smashed to matchwood but the Mate had the head-sail down hauls thrown over the side. One by one the crew swarmed down the ropes into the sea until a tremendous roller knocked each man off and swept him like a leaf shorewards.

The cook and I were the last to leave. Waist-high in the swirling water I somehow managed to get the Skipper's personal papers from his pocket and retrieve the ship's papers, then as best I could I climbed into the surf. The sea swallowed me up. My ears roared and I stayed under so long I thought I would never surface. After what seemed an eternity I was flung up face down on a white coral beach. My cheeks were scored and bleeding but otherwise I was unhurt. I crawled up the beach and found the whole crew—twenty of them—in much the same state, but safe. Within a few hours the barque had broken up and disappeared.

As far as we could see in the darkness our haven was far from hospitable. It was little more than a bleak outlying rock of the Galapagos, barely a mile across. Not a shred of vegetation grew on it and its highest point was little more than ten feet above sea level.

At daybreak we scoured the beach hopefully looking for provisions or timber that might have drifted in from the wreck. But apart from a few isolated lumps of coal everything that could float was swept by a strong current past the island out of our grasp. We had nothing but the sodden clothes in which we stood. A tour of the rock disclosed two heaven-sent fresh water springs. They saved us. With the scant debris the wreck sent us we made a crude shelter and erected a signal mast. We lived on raw turtles, turtle eggs and the few fish we were able to catch by hand. We satisfied a craving for salt by licking the spray crystals off the rocks.

It was blazing hot during the day and often drenching rain squalls swept across the rock. Sometimes we were too wet and cold to sleep. On a clear day we could see the outline of a bigger island on the horizon, but we had no means of making even the simplest raft to sail there. Our only hope of rescue we knew was an Ecuadoran government vessel which made a six-monthly tour of these islands looking for castaways. But we had no means of knowing when it was next due. It might have been a week or five months.

The Mate and I tried at first to regiment the men to keep a fragment of discipline in our little community. We tried to keep sea watches and got them marching up and down the beach and playing games. But the futility and impossibility of escape from one another began to prey on our minds. We broke up into little cliques of our own. There were quarrels and fights over trivialities and one man went nearly out of his mind. We began to seek only our own company and would wander off to hide with our thoughts and misery. But every hundred yards there would be another man with the same object, cursing because his seclusion had been violated.

At the end of three months most of us firmly believed we would never be rescued. Our minds were decaying under the strain. I found myself writing long letters home with a stick in the sand.

One afternoon, twelve weeks after the wreck we were all sprawled out asleep on the sand. Suddenly a bedlam of hoarse shouting woke me.  Out beyond was an Ecuadoran gun-boat.  We had been found.

All our misery and ill-feeling vanished in a delirium of relief.  We shouted and cheered like schoolboys.  After what seemed an age the Ecuadoran put a boat ashore.  All twenty-two of us rushed madly into the surf desperate to be the first aboard.  If the crew hadn't beaten us off with the oars we would have swamped it.  And when it put off with only half of us, we who remained flung ourselves on the beach and wept like children so convinced were we the boat wasn't going to return for us.  But it did.  The gun-boat landed us at Valparaiso in Chile, a mule train took us over the Andes and eventually we reached Buenos Aires where we picked up a ship for Newport News.  Our families had long abandoned all hope for us.  It was like coming back from the dead.

Daybreak showed us that the four tows were still with us.  It made me feel better to see them sliding along behind.  The storm was dying away and although we were still rolling through a heavy ground swell the squalls were becoming less frequent and we could see the coast clearly now.  I kept about three-quarters of a mile off-shore and set course for Salina Cruz lighthouse.

We were abreast of it at 7.30 a.m.  There was a break-water and a small Mexican village of neat white houses.  As the five vessels loomed one after the other out of a rain shower only one thousand yards abeam of them, the light-house staff, like the ships we had passed earlier, must have wondered on what important operation this five-knot comic opera Navy was bound.  It is the usual practice to report yourself to a shore station when so close, so I flashed the lighthouse our name and number on the blinker and hoisted our flags.  Although we could plainly see a crowd of Mexicans gazing at us from the breakwater, repeated blinking brought no acknowledgment.  Perhaps they thought a neighbouring Central American state was invading them.

We were now steaming through waters that are supposed to be the haunt of the famous devil-fish, the grotesque-looking grandfather of the sting-ray family, often measuring more than twenty feet across. They are found only in a few limited areas of the world's oceans and in greatest profusion off the coast of tropical America.

One sunny afternoon I was taking my watch, standing on the wing of the bridge, watching the coast slowly sliding by to starboard. Suddenly I noticed we were passing a huge flat brown object riding like a great carpet on the rolling swell. It was quite the biggest devil-fish I had ever seen.

"Come and look at this pleasant-looking customer," I called to Alonso. He came tumbling up on to the bridge and we both stared fascinated as the horrible brown mass floated lazily by. It was so big, one side of it was often on top of one wave, the body in the trough and the opposite edge atop the next wave. We estimated it was as wide as the beam of the *Gray*—all of twenty-five feet. What made it look even larger than it probably was, was the fact that as the rollers washed over it, only parts of its wings, yards apart, showed above the water. It looked like several smaller rays. But just as it was disappearing astern a roller bigger than the rest lifted most of it high out of the water and for a few seconds we saw the whole of its slimy body, raised by the swell above the level of the *Gray's* deck. Momentarily the creature was above us. It lay there quite unperturbed, sunning itself on the warm surface, and then was lost behind a roller. It must have been sleeping, because we passed within a few yards and our bow wave lapped over it, but it made not the slightest effort to get out of our way.

Seamen's tales of fantastic and terrifying denizens of the sea with whom they have come face to face are legendary, and usually thoroughly disbelieved ashore. But to have seen a fish as wide as our own ship gave us all renewed faith in the old sailor's emphatic insistence that he hadn't exaggerated a single inch. It reminded me of the biggest sea monster I have ever seen. We were crossing the Pacific during the First World War under sail. Another hand and I were aloft furling sails when he suddenly drew my attention to the sea astern. "My God, I shouldn't care to go overboard at the moment," he said. "Look at that." Dogging us about one hundred yards astern was an enormous shadow very nearly as big as the ship. It moved effortlessly and forbiddingly along keeping perfect station with us several feet below the surface. No part of its body showed above the water to give us the least clue what in creation it could be, so we scaled down on to the deck with a little more care than usual and reported it to the Mate. But from the poop there was no sign of it. It was further below the surface than we had imagined. Anyway whatever it was, whale-shark or devil fish, it had gone when next someone went aloft.

The devil-fish we had just passed was probably the species also known as the horned ox-ray, and sometimes by the variety of terms—devil-ray, vampire-ray, sea-bat, and bat-fish. Fishermen who have harpooned them from quite big launches have often been towed at express speed for miles out to sea by big devil-fish until either the line snapped or the fish dived for the bottom and hung its ton-and-a-half weight from the craft until cut free.

Panamanian pearl divers fear the devil-fish most of all—but for no valid reason. It has never been known to attack a man and in fact lives on tiny minnow-like fish and small sea crustaceans and plankton barely visible to the naked eye. It sweeps these into its mouth with two cephalic fins which protrude, as the name implies, like ox-horns, from either side of its head. It is never found far from the warm waters of the coast and likes to bask asleep on the

53

surface. It gets along with big almost graceful flapping movements of its flat flannel-like body. Although it never attacks a swimmer, a wounded devil-fish can quickly crush or capsize a small boat, and there was the story of one that grasped a ship's anchor and towed the vessel off at great speed "to the wonder and fear of the sailors".

A smaller variety known as the Mobula which goes about in small shoals of three to five, unlike its big brother which is normally found singly or occasionally in pairs, has a rather disturbing habit. It leaps four or five feet out of the water and lands back with a resounding smack like gunfire that can be heard for several miles on a calm sea at night.

Four days later on July 29, we reached Manzanillo. We had steamed 1,816 miles from Balboa at an average speed of 5.7 knots. The tow-lines were still holding.

Manzanillo is one of Mexico's biggest Pacific ports and a naval base. Its 6,000 inhabitants live in colourful orange tiled-roof houses set on terraced slopes which climb back into hills behind the town. A glorious white sandy beach stretches for several miles in a wide bay to the north of the town. The harbour is an artificial one inside a concrete breakwater.

From the bay I signalled for a Pilot. But it must have been siesta ashore. Manzanillo was asleep. There was no reply. It was only after an hour's continuous signalling that a launch chugged out to us and a grinning Mexican pilot followed by the Port doctor and a team of swarthy customs and immigration officials climbed aboard. The Pilot apologized at length explaining that there was no room inside the breakwater. "But, Capitan," he assured me, "I vill find ze de most excellent anchorage in our beautiful leetle bay."

Dropping the anchor, we allowed the sweepers' tow-lines to sink to the bottom of the bay and then streamed a kedge anchor out from the stern of No. 4, so that the tide wouldn't swing them about. As we hove in the wire from our winch to No. 1 I went aft to inspect it foot by foot as it streamed in. It seemed to be standing up well.

Then I went off in the boat to examine the ropes and bridles on the minesweepers. My worst fears were confirmed. It was as I had anticipated. Thirteen days' towing had set every bridle wire see-sawing into the U-bolts. All were chafing badly, strands had parted and No. 3's bridle had been all but cut through. It was holding by one solitary strand. We had been exceedingly lucky to make port without a breakaway.

I sent an air-mail letter to San Francisco reporting this and pointing out the unsuitability of the rig for a voyage such as ours. This I followed up with a cable asking for spare gear for it seemed to me that even after renewals the present rig would last about a week. This estimate was to prove reasonably correct.

Immediately the Towmaster set about making repairs. Within a few hours of anchoring he was bustling round like a broody hen organizing assistance from the Mexican Naval workshops ashore. Sourly the crew were helping him. They seemed to resent working for more than one Master in the same ship.

One day a freighter came in to Manzanillo flying the Panamanian flag. It was the opportunity I had been seeking ever since I left Balboa to confirm that we were flying our flag correctly. It would have been an unpardonable discourtesy to have flown it upside down and that's what I feared we might have been doing. The Panamanian flag is divided into four equal parts. At the hoist the top inner square contains a blue star on a white background, the bottom outer a red, while the bottom inner is a plain blue square, top outer, a plain red one. It could be flown either way up. Ours had no indication. An exhaustive search through all the available pilot-house signal manuals had failed to set my mind at ease. Nor could any of the supposedly Panamanian members of the crew help me. They just grinned foolishly and shook their black heads.

As the freighter drew closer I saw that she was flying the blue square uppermost—the opposite way to ours. I shouted to Alonso: "You had better haul down our ensign and hoist it up the other way."

It was only then that I noticed the freighter's crew taking an inordinate interest in our flag. Everybody on her bridge seemed to have their glasses on it, pointing excitedly. I called to Alonso to hurry things along. Feverishly he struggled to get the halliard adrift.

He was just about to begin lowering when I yelled to him to stop. Over on the freighter a man had suddenly sprinted aft, whipped down their flag, turned it over and vigorously rehoisted it to conform with ours. So we were right after all. The mistake was theirs. I called Alonso back and we had one of the few really good laughs the *Gray* ever heard. I couldn't help wondering what would have happened had we both hauled our flags down together. It would no doubt have called for a diplomatic exchange of visits between the respective Masters. Possibly he thought we were a Panamanian gun-boat.

While we were anchored out in Manzanillo Bay the crew were refused shore leave. In any case they had no money to spend if they had gone as the Towmaster, in his capacity as Owner's Agent, was in charge of our funds and refused to make any advances until the men had finished helping him with his re-rigging operations. He was afraid that once they got ashore he wouldn't see them for a week. Perhaps he was right, but in view of the long tow ahead of us I felt they were entitled to a brief spell ashore before we sailed. Most of the crew were beginning to think that as soon as the repairs were completed they were going to sail straight out of the bay and away without so much as a taste of the Mexican fleshpots.

Their resentment began to reflect itself in their work. They sent me a "round robin" which most of them had signed.

It was a neatly typed document in a quaint pseudo-legal phraseology. I wondered who the author was. "These men," it said, "representing a majority of the crew of the S.S. *Wallace R. Gray*, feeling that we are within our rights, do ask for partial payment of wages due. Particularly in view of working conditions, excessive hours, etc. These men also feel, I believe, and so say that they will not man this ship, nor turn-to until this matter is adjusted officially through the company's agent at this port, or the nearest shipping commissioner or consul."

This was serious. I lost no time calling the crew together. "This is tantamount to mutiny," I told them, waving the petition. They stood below me scowling and truculent.

Again it was the coxswain, Todd, who sidled forward, hands in pocket. He was tall and powerfully built. "The crew really mean it, sir," he drawled. "If you want us to work we want some of the pay and shore leave due to us."

I explained that as we were anchored outside the breakwater we were still officially at sea. At any time a change in weather might necessitate an urgent move to another anchorage. It was essential that we have a full crew aboard as long as we remained in the bay. However, I said I would do my best to get them a small advance of pay and gave them my word that I would personally see that most of them got at least one evening ashore before we sailed.

After a bit of private muttering and whispers Todd said in view of my promise they would go back to work. Then they filed distrustfully away.

That night, two of the crew, Vincent and Ritter, decided to take the law into their own hands. When it was dark they went ashore in one of the Mexican bum-boats

57

which swarmed around us selling fruit and trinkets. I decided to make an example of them. So I went ashore to look for the renegades. From a taxi I saw them inside a bar, drinking Mexican beer. They were having a thoroughly good binge and from their boisterous behaviour couldn't have wasted much time when they landed.

I was on the point of going and ending their little party, but changed my mind. The local police, I decided, could do a far more effective job. I had them arrested and then I went back aboard.

It was two days before a smiling Mexican police officer clambered aboard to tell me he had "two of your men, Capitan, who are very, very drunk." The police, it appeared, had found Vincent and Ritter in an advanced state of intoxication; fantastically, they had been able still further to quench their endless thirsts, even in jail.

A few hours later a police-launch came alongside with two recumbent forms stretched out on it. Vincent, who looked as if he had been drinking continuously for a week, was able to climb aboard with assistance. Ritter was paralytically drunk and unconscious. He was rolled over the rail like a sack of vegetables and lay there white-faced looking close to death. The crew lugged him off to his bunk. Next morning both reported rather unsteadily for duty. I logged them four days' pay and reduced Ritter from Able Seaman to Ordinary Seaman. Neither seemed in the least perturbed. They considered the spree worth it.

By this time it was quite obvious to me that the situation regarding the Towmaster must be resolved as speedily as possible, for I realized that we should get nowhere so long as the crew were in any doubt as to whose orders they were to obey. That night I sent for him to come to my cabin and told him that the matter must be cleared up then and there. I expected a scene but after a few moments he said: "As a matter of fact I had already decided not to go beyond Manzanillo."

58

"What about the crew's wages?" I asked. "You aren't going to get much work out of them until they're paid and it would be wise to give them a spot of shore leave or there'll be trouble."

He agreed to both and said he would leave the ship on the day of departure from Manzanillo.

# Chapter Four

BEFORE leaving the ship, however, the Towmaster insisted on making further modifications to strengthen the tow-gear.

He had made friends with the Mexican Naval engineers ashore and they were allowing him to use their workshop. The minesweepers' anchor-chains with which he was strengthening the bridles wouldn't fit the shackles connecting them to the lines. The end links in the chains were too small for the shackle-pin to fit through.

So with the Mexicans' help the Towmaster had some big links specially forged. When they arrived I went down to the *Gray's* after-deck to watch him test them. He tapped one with a hammer. Where it had been welded it promptly began to flake away. The links had to be re-made. It took another week to get his anchor-chain bridles made fast to the minesweepers.

I used the delay to get some fresh provisions aboard. I could see that my original estimates of the length of the trip would count for nothing now. Palmyra by early October had been my earlier hope; now we would be lucky to arrive before late November the way things were shaping. It would be wise, I decided, to supplement our larder. A partly inexperienced crew was going to be bad enough. I didn't want a hungry one on my hands as well.

A shipping agent in Manzanillo told me there were no freezing chambers in the town but that he would arrange for a local farmer to supply us with all the fresh meat and vegetables we needed. Next day a launch came alongside and what I took first to be a swarthy looking Mexican gipsy came aboard. He was the farmer. He would be delighted he said, to let us have "everything, *señor*, of which you and your men have need." We had only to return with him to his delightful little farm twenty-five miles out of Manzanillo and we could select personally the beasts we fancied best.

We drove out along a dusty road, up a valley in the hills behind the coast. Proudly our provider waved his arm beneficently at his farm. It was completely at our disposal. I made what I hoped was a very professional inspection of his stock, prodding and nodding encouragingly at one animal, shaking my head regretfully at another. In the end I settled for one bullock, a heifer, three pigs, some poultry and a large quantity of eggs, cauliflower, cabbages, potatoes and carrots. The animals were slaughtered that night. Twenty-four hours later everything was aboard the *Gray*.

Ten days after we arrived in Manzanillo the Towmaster declared the tow-lines ready for sea. Before we went inside the breakwater to refuel I insisted on a trial run in the open sea. "Sure," he said. "We'll go to-night."

So we prepared for sea, hauled our anchor out of the sand of Manzanillo Bay and sailed at dusk. The lights of the town twinkled away astern and a few hours later the *Gray* was rolling in the ocean swell. We steamed all night, for I was emphatic that the rig should prove itself capable of withstanding more than the sheltered coastal swell. Next morning we were forty miles out and the Mexican hills were just a faint blur on the horizon. I headed the tug into the big rollers at every possible angle all the while looking back through glasses at the way the sweepers were taking it. Several troubles were apparent immediately. I noticed that whenever the sea was on our quarter, that is striking us obliquely from astern the minesweepers slewed around to leeward, twisting the bridles to one side, so that the wires and chains began to eat into their wooden hulls. I also found that although we had more than 800 feet of 11-inch manila between the minesweepers, above seven knots the ropes weren't heavy enough to remain below the surface once the tug took up the strain. Every time I increased speed they would pull out of the water, jerk tight as a bar, and back under again. This happened every time they hit the swell. A few days of that would have parted the lot.

So back in port I made some improvements. I found some hardwood timber and bolted it tightly to the mine-sweeper's bow and stern timbers where the wandering bridle had shown signs of cutting into it. After that I fitted "flounders" between the shackles and the bridles. These are flat triangular metal plates which I hoped would eliminate some of the swivelling and twisting I had noticed during the test. Then I turned my attention to the tow-ropes. Somehow they had to be made heavier. They must never be allowed to whip out of the water again. Anchor chain solved this. I lashed 90-foot lengths of it along the middle of the tow-ropes between Nos. 2, 3 and 4, binding it tightly with fathoms of seizing wire. Between Nos. 1 and 2 there hadn't been so much jerking, so I left the rope there as it was.

I was still not completely happy about the capacity of my towing rig to face the big test of the open Pacific. The spare gear I had asked for had never arrived, but I could not waste any further time writing again to the company. It was high time we were on our way.

It was now August 9. I told Alonso to warn the crew we would sail on the tide next day. Then we anchored the minesweepers and took the *Gray* inside the breakwater and tied up alongside the oiling dock. This was my opportunity to fulfil my promise of shore leave.

I said they could all go except one engineer and an oiler who would have to stand by while we were taking on oil during the night. Gonzalez and Ferraro agreed to stay on condition that if there was time they should be allowed just a few hours to "do" the town next morning.

Then I advanced each man 25 dollars and they streamed ashore in high spirits, joking and laughing in a way that was good to see. I told them they must be back by 6 a.m. as I intended sailing at 8. I hardly recognized my grimy, ragged band. They had shaved, slicked down their hair and climbed into their best shore-going clothes. The most fastidious minister would have been proud to have them fill the front row of his church, only I was certain they were not bound for church. Within an hour of tying-up the ship was deserted. Only Ferraro and Gonzalez still oily in their dungarees were busy about the big fuel hoses that were pulsating over our rail.

It was Saturday night in Manzanillo. An ostentatious looking band was blaring a Mexican march from a rotunda, men, women and urchins thronged the plaza and narrow cobbled streets, and everywhere there nonchalantly strolled the most enchanting looking Mexican girls. All the shops were open, curio dealers were doing their best to palm off alligator-skin products to visiting seamen, noisy bars with Latin dance music pouring from their doors were doing likewise, but more successfully, with their products of the Mexican wine industry.

It didn't take the men of the *Gray* long to find what they sought most. Seamen seem to be able to smell out the red-light district of any port blindfold. Manzanillo's was in a crooked, dirty little street tucked away under a hill that towered over the town. It offered temptation and pleasures in the best Central American tradition. The crew flocked there in a body.

Sparks and I did a spot of window-shopping, had a few quiet drinks, looked in at one or two night-clubs and went back to the ship. I wanted a good night's sleep, for I had a feeling I mightn't get much once we left port.

I was up at 5 a.m. When 6 o'clock came there was no sign of officers or crew. I was furious. There I was with the tug ready for sea, a pilot ordered for 8 a.m.

63

but no crew. Sparks, Gonzalez and Ferraro were all I had.

I set out to look for them, knowing only too well where I should find them. There were no taxis about, so I walked, clattering through the now silent, deserted streets of Manzanillo's Sabbath. The town may have appeared pleasant enough from the sea but inside it early that morning it looked filthy and smelt nauseating. Even the shutters couldn't contain the vile stench that issued from some of the houses; the streets reeked of sewage. The only life that stirred were a few lean mongrels and occasional huge rats which scampered away as I approached.

Ten minutes brought me to the "Pacific Street" of Manzanillo. Sunday meant nothing here. It was still as gaily alive as the previous evening. I pushed open the swing doors of the first so-called cabaret in the street and peered inside. The place was hazy with cigar smoke and reeked of stale alcohol. A sleepy orchestra were strumming away like automatons, and a drunken Mexican couple lolling on each other's shoulders were fox-trotting dazedly. Two drunk Mexicans were drooling at the bar. The fat little manageress told me that she thought one of my men was there. She gave a seductive wink and disappeared into a room off the courtyard.

Presently she reappeared, followed, bleary-eyed, by one of my crew. On his arm hung a mischievous-looking girl of vague nationality. Both were angry at being disturbed. But I was impatient to find the others and dragged the unwilling Filipino unsteadily out into the street demanding that he help me find the others.

"I can take you there, sir," he yawned.

He led me down the street to the biggest brothel in Manzanillo. Again a plump Mexican proprietress disappeared. My bag this time was seven more Filipinos. They made passionate farewells to their tearful comforters and followed me out into the morning sunshine.

64

Further down the street I could hear the noise of a big celebration. Some of the voices had a familiar ring. It was a big cabaret-brothel, and all my missing gang were there. They had organized a party which seemed to be at its height. The orchestra jazzed away frenziedly, castanets rattled, the men were singing, dancing and drinking. All were very drunk, all had girls, everyone was in high spirits. Their twenty-five dollars had gone a long way. By the look of things we might not have been sailing for a week.

I was greeted with a rousing cheer. There were drunken shouts of "Good old Captain Ainslie". "Have a drink, Skipper." "Come and enjoy yourself, sir." Immediately I was hustled into the heart of the bedlam, a drink was thrust into my hand, another was slopped down my trousers and amid roars of laughter a girl hooked herself to my arm. I could see it was a situation that called for diplomatic handling if I were to get my crew back aboard. I could see, too, that this crew wouldn't be capable of getting the *Gray* to sea that morning. So I "shouted" them all another drink and soon found myself dancing the samba with a redhead who cooed at me in Spanish to the jubilation of the men.

When I reminded them that they were absent without leave, that it was several hours past sailing time, and that I had had enough I was shouted down. I was told I could not possibly go without seeing the celebrated Mexican hat dance performed. A gigantic straw sombrero was produced and a shapely girl cavorted round its huge brim for ten minutes before retiring exhausted amid yells of applause. I thought the hat would make a nice souvenir and tried to buy it. But it was not for sale at any price.

The increased tempo of the party was by now attracting back to the dance floor other members of the crew who had been engaged in the little back rooms when I arrived.

65

They began to saunter back sheepishly with their women. Soon almost everybody was present. But a spot roll call showed one of the Americans was still missing. Nobody seemed willing to disturb him so I asked to be taken to the room. He dressed and followed me back grumbling. The girl seemed amused.

Now I had them all together the question was how to get them back to the docks. I felt that if we had to walk there were too many side streets up which some of them would doubtless disappear. A Mexican with a truck solved the problem for me. For a handful of pesos he agreed to take us to the tug. The vehicle was far from Manzanillo's biggest, but somehow they all clambered aboard, the Panamanians whooping, everybody singing. Some rode on the roof, the mudguards, the bonnet. As we groaned off down the street there was a crescendo of barking dogs, cheering, catcalls and whistles. All the girls came out to see us go. There were tears, husky *Adios's* and a torrent of feminine Spanish.

It was with some relief that I saw the dock gates again. Just then I noticed a taxi rattling up the hill toward us. As it went by I saw that the passenger was Gonzalez, sneaking off for a brief last-minute fling ashore. "Stop," I yelled, and my disappointed engineer climbed out, and with much muttering was hoisted on to the truck. I was sorry, but I needed his assistance in the engine-room when I attempted to take the *Gray* out into the bay. He, at least, was sober.

At the dock gates we left the truck and I made the men walk ahead of me to the *Gray*. I was afraid some of the less drunk might make a final bid for freedom. They lurched aboard singing and shouting. Little Cuesta, the Chief engineer, was babbling away to me about "the old days in Manila" and slapping me affectionately on the back. His face was lit up like the rising moon. Then Ferraro who had remained loyally at his post throughout the night reminded me of my promise and asked if he could go ashore for an hour.

Meanwhile the crew had gone to their bunks. Only an occasional burst of singing issued from their quarters. Casas, the second cook, seemed to be sobering up so I ordered him to serve all hands black coffee. Half an hour later, as the Pilot was aboard, I decided to try and put out into the bay. At least I could keep the crew aboard out there. They could recover while we were picking up the tow. But I hadn't been quite quick enough.

A harassed Alonso came bolting into the cabin. "Captain Ainslie, sir," he shouted. "The men, they have all disappeared. They've gone ashore again. Only the engine-room men are aboard." I hurried down to the forecastle. It was empty right enough. Even Romanin, my Bosun, had gone. They must have crept ashore while I was in my cabin with the Pilot. This time I really lost my temper.

"Get the police," I roared at Alonso, and he scurried off.

The police Chief said it would be a great honour to assist the round-up. He seemed almost to be licking his lips with delight at the prospect of a little rough-and-tumble in law-abiding Manzanillo. "Do anything you like, use force if necessary, but get them back here quickly," I urged him. Then the *Policia* roared off in their high-powered trucks. They knew where to go. Back in the very same cabaret where I had discovered them not two hours before the police found them. The party was under way again, the orchestra just breaking into a tango when the *Policia de Manzanillo* burst in. Secretly, the police had hoped to use their batons but it wasn't necessary. The men knew the game was up. Meekly they came. Ferraro, protesting violently that he had special permission, was dragged from the arms of *la mas bonita señorita* he had ever made love to—he lamented to me later—and herded into the police truck with the rest. They arrived back on board

67

under escort still singing. Romanin explained jubilantly that "we have just been to have another drink for you, sir," as they went happily back to the forecastle. I rewarded the police with several bottles of beer for their trouble. They bowed their way ashore well pleased.

Down in the crew's mess I could hear more celebrating. Bottles and glasses were chinking, uproarious toasts were being offered. I called Romanin to break it up but he was barely able to stand. So I dealt with it myself.

If we didn't get to sea soon I began to feel I shouldn't be responsible for my actions. It was probably only because I sensed the *Gray* was in for a long passage and a hard-working one that I showed them this tolerance. At all events, I told myself, it would be the last opportunity they would have to enjoy themselves for the best part of ten thousand miles.

By 10.15 enough of the crew were capable of staggering palely on deck to permit us to leave the dock. The Towmaster came up on to the bridge, shook hands and wished me *bon voyage*. But even then we had not seen the last of him. Later he came out in a launch to supervise the streaming of the tows.

We spent the afternoon connecting up with No. 1 minesweeper, making final preparations for sea and completing customs and emigration formalities. Inquisitive little Mexican officials bustled about the ship with bundles of passports, rubber-stamps and sheafs of documents. Once again I had to go through the exhausting rigmarole of justifying the *Gray*'s 52 tons registered net tonnage.

Then in the middle of the formalities I suddenly noticed a squall sweeping down on us from the land. As I already had the tug headed seawards with the tows strung toward the shore there was a danger they might be blown down on to us. The engine-room was already at "stand by" so I hurried on to the bridge, gave the order to the Mate to heave-up, then, with the telegraph at "slow ahead" steamed out into the bay. The port officials went frantic. They thought we were taking them with us. There was no doubt at all, they must have thought a minute later, when the squall hit us and we were too busy to give them any attention, not the least doubt they were being shanghaied by this treacherous-looking Master and crew. For several minutes there was pandemonium aboard. Our horrified friends rushed bewilderedly up and down the deck. Then the chief customs officer burst excitedly into the pilot-house.

"Capitan, Capitan," he implored, tugging my sleeve, "why you taking us with you; please stop so that we go ashore."

It took five minutes to convince him we had not the least desire to cross the Pacific with a squad of Mexican officials aboard.

Almost before we had lost way the little men were tumbling over the rails into their launch which had appeared from nowhere. They were still jabbering excitedly at the top of their voices when the launch faded back into the bay.

In another launch stood the Towmaster. He was going from sweeper to sweeper checking the lines. Then the launch came alongside to put aboard the crew who had been helping him straighten out the tows.

Saluting the ex-Towmaster with five farewell blasts on the siren, I called up Cuesta on the telephone to increase revolutions slowly. This was always essential. The changes in speed between the standard engine-room telegraph signals were too great to give us the all-important gradual acceleration that would impose a minimum of stress on our frail bridles. I called the revolutions down, "Twenty-five, thirty-five, fifty," and so on, until we were moving close to our top towing speed of 122 revolutions—slightly over six knots.

As the slack was taken up and our three-quarter mile

long convoy moved out of the bay the Towmaster stood off and waved to us. The last I saw of him as his launch became a small shape in the distance was a tiny speck still waving.

As we steamed out of the bay the other ships in port, seeing we were leaving at last, broke out in a medley of whistle blasts and siren shrieks. My arm was kept busy for several minutes answering them with our own deep siren.

It was 7 p.m. when we cleared the foreland and began to hit the familiar Pacific swell that came rolling in from thousands of miles out. From the wing of the bridge I gazed back at the blue outline of the Mexican coast slowly receding astern. And as I looked a great double rainbow formed over the land. Two beautiful curves arched themselves one above the other, reaching right down to the sea at each end. I watched it for several minutes until it began to fade with the encroaching dusk. It was the first complete double rainbow I had ever seen and I wondered if it was to prove a good omen on our long voyage to Palmyra.

## Chapter Five

DAWN next morning, Monday, August 11, saw us fifty miles out. The coast had disappeared. It was a glorious hot day, visibility was excellent and we rolled gently through a light swell.

At 8.30 a.m. we passed a Swedish freighter bound for Panama. We smiled as she dutifully dipped her ensign. She was the last vessel we were to see for forty-six days.

She was just out of sight when we had our first mishap. A buffer plate blew out on one boiler. Fortunately it wasn't serious and the engineers were able to repair it in an hour. It meant reducing speed, though, to two knots while they worked on it. By 11 o'clock we were able to increase revolutions again and at midday we had logged 104 miles from Manzanillo.

By now we had lost the pretty slate-grey and white sea-gulls that had been following us and in their place had been joined by the drab-looking "Californian Pilots" and one or two stormy petrels. Beside us in the sea gambolled the inevitable school of porpoises and now and again we could see the silver flash of a long streamlined fish, the commonly but mistakenly called dolphins. These are among the fastest fish in the water and we were to have their company for many weeks to come. They were joined presently by schools of brilliantly-hued flying-fish which began to grow bigger the further south we steamed. It has always been a fascination for me to watch the flying-fish pursued by some hungry enemy shoot out of the water in their hundreds, flying perhaps a hundred yards with the sun glinting on their silver wings and then plummeting back into the sea like a big handful of pebbles. Sometimes at night they were attracted by our lights and flew on board where we found them next morning. They were tasty eating and a friendly rivalry later developed between the officers and men to be on deck earliest to gather up the night's harvest of the delicacy for the respective messes. I was rather partial to flying-fish and Willie Dominguez had a special flair for serving them up as a particularly delicious dish.

We were a happier ship now we were under way. Gone was the sullen moroseness that had for so long pervaded the fo'c'sle. Gone were the unhappy scowls that I had almost come to regard as part of the *Gray*. Everybody, officers and men, seemed to have taken a new lease of life. The crew began to smile for a change, they joked and chaffed one another, and from their mess-room came the sound of whistling and singing and the twang of a guitar and mandolines. Even Butch seemed to sense the new atmosphere aboard. She gambolled joyfully about the deck, tail thumping, almost smiling.

The only member of the crew who wasn't happy was eighteen-year-old Cooper. He was so violently seasick he couldn't work. He just lay groaning and green-faced in his bunk wishing he had never left dry land. It was his first voyage and I am sure it was the last time he tried to go to sea. Although we were steaming through sea that was as calm as the Pacific can ever be and the *Gray* was behaving like a sedate old lady, he seemed incapable of finding his sea-legs.

I knew only too well how he was feeling. My first voyage had been a similar ghastly experience. It was just before the outbreak of the First War. I was thirteen. Against my parents' wishes I had left school for the only life I thought could make me happy—the sea. For as long as I could remember of my still tender years I had been fascinated beyond description by the sight of every tall barque that came sailing into the sparkling waters of Auckland Harbour. At every opportunity I would sneak down to the docks to drink in a little of the exciting world of salt and rum and tar and sail which I longed for. Every book I read was a sea yarn. How I yearned for the day when I would be old enough to become a part of it, to feel a rolling wet deck under my bare feet, a yard under my belly and to sleep with the creaking accompaniment of a "windbag" under full sail.

At thirteen my family relented. I left school and signed on a three-masted barquentine as cabin boy for a month's voyage to Noumea and back. With awe I staggered aboard her with my proudest possession—my own sea chest. The ship was busy loading. The Mate quickly spotted his nervous protégé standing bewildered and frightened at the bottom of the gangplank. It didn't take him long to find me a job. Ten minutes later I was at the receiving end of a slide down which huge cases of tinned food were being shot. As it arrived each case nearly knocked me into the hold ahead of it. Then one came down before I had pushed on its predecessor. It caught me in the small of the back, knocking me flat. When I stood up I felt sick. I was sure my spine was fractured. But the Mate didn't think so. "Damn poor start, lad," he told me. "Let's try you on something else." He gave me a hammer and told me to take it to the carpenter. The carpenter was working on the top-gallant yard high above the deck. It made me giddy even to look up there. Still feeling crippled by the blow I had just received I began the most terrifying journey of my young life. In my inexperience it didn't occur to me that I could hang the hammer on my belt. I just struggled on up the ratlines clutching the hammer in one hand, and with only one free hand to grip the ratlines. Every time I looked down I felt sick and dizzy; twice I was stuck—but I made it, trembling and very afraid. It took me an hour to reach the deck again and I decided there and then if I was ever to have to climb that mast again I would rather run ashore. The

73

evening before we sailed the crew got roaring drunk. A drunk man had always struck a special terror in my immature heart. Here I was trapped in a mess among twelve of them who in their cups had almost, it seemed, become animals. They screamed, swore and were ill. Whenever they saw me they lashed out at me with a boot. Nobody would give me any supper, so when the orgy was subsiding and the seamen were snoring drunkenly on the mess-room floor I crept in to salvage a few scraps from their plates. But every time my hand reached out I would see a pair of eyes watching me like a cat. I fled from the fo'c'sle. If this was the sea one day of it was enough. I wanted only one thing—to get off that ship and home.

But by now we had moved out into the harbour. There was no retreat. Then I found a kindly old seaman, paid him a gold sovereign and pleaded with him to row ashore and fetch my mother. I never saw either him or the sovereign again. We sailed at noon next day.

The voyage was a horrible nightmare. I was desperately seasick the whole way to Noumea. For thirteen days I retched bile and blood and wanted only to die. I hid from the Mate in lifeboats, lockers and cupboards; he thought I had been washed overboard. What had ever made me think this was the life for me I couldn't begin to imagine. It was just sheer hell. But on the return trip to Auckland I began, shakily, to get my sea-legs. By the time we bowled into harbour I was almost liking it.

Mother came out to see me. "I have come to take you home, Ken," she said. "I hope it has cured you once and for all of the sea." But I refused to go. Instead, I transferred to the half-deck of the barque *Louisa Craig*. When she sailed for San Francisco I was the proudest member of her crew. And so the sea was injected rather painfully into my blood. Remembering this I had some sympathy for young Cooper.

Second day out of Manzanillo, like the first, was smooth

74

and sunny. It was the Pacific at her best. Only the long lazy swell disturbed what otherwise might have been a millpond.

The crew were quickly shaking down to the routine of shipboard life. Already my confidence in them was growing. Despite their inexperience they set to work with a will. I got them busy cleaning up the ship, scrubbing down the decks and lashing down all movable equipment. For I knew the Pacific better than to believe this idyllic weather could last.

We were now making seven knots, faster than I had thought possible, and the tows were following behind like well-trained ducks. But nevertheless I decided to take advantage of the weather for an inspection.

So I slowed down, slung out the flat-bottomed Norwegian pram on the *Gray's* derrick, and Miranda took an inspection party away. Romanin, Jones, Ritter, Todd, Rodrigues and Jacobsen went with him. As a boat crew they wouldn't have claimed the wooden spoon at an amateur regatta, but they were the best I had, and as time went on were to become more experienced.

Apart from Miranda, Romanin was the only man with much real knowledge of small boats. Back in his native Hawaii he had spent a lot of time in native canoes. Jones and Rodrigues weren't quite as raw as the others. Jacobsen with his tall awkward frame was the least use. But I insisted he go because he seemed the most disinclined of any to do any work. Only in the weeks to come when the inspection team's role became more hazardous did I replace him.

They rowed away wearing Mae Wests, shorts and singlets, most of them barefooted. To help them I put the tug between the oncoming sea and their boat and, as soon as they were clear, moved ahead at low revolutions to bring the first minesweeper up to them. As soon as they had made the boat fast and were safely aboard I opened up

75

again, experimenting at various speeds so that Miranda could observe the effects on the bridles over the whole range of engine revolutions. When Miranda hoisted the "inspection completed" signal I slowed down, waited until they were back in the pram and opened up again to bring No. 2 alongside them.

When they were clear of No. 4 I made a big circuit and picked them up. These wide "pick-up" circles had to be made with the utmost care, as the length of the tow was three-quarters of a mile. To have swung round too quickly would have aggravated the bridles and brought the sea too suddenly on the "sweeper" beams. I had, therefore, to make my turn wide and gradual so that at times the circle was more than a mile across.

Back aboard Miranda reported that the bridles were settling down well, but he hadn't liked the look of the wire under the U-bolts. There were signs that it would be sliding and wearing before long. However he had tightened the bolts, drawing the wire more firmly against the Oregon baulks. It was all he could do. "I think we're in for some trouble before we're through with this lot," he said, shaking his head. There was nothing we could do about it. I just prayed that we could get well toward Palmyra before they started breaking away. At midday we had logged another 138 miles—242 miles from Manzanillo. As we were travelling west, with the sun, we put our clocks back thirty minutes. All the way to Palmyra we had regularly to retard our watches.

That night the *Gray* had visitors. Uninvited, they arrived with every apparent intention of making their home aboard. The first was a big sea bird about the size of a mollyhawk. No one aboard could identify it. It flopped on to the pilot-house soon after midnight and apart from a damaged wing was very much alive and biting. A vicious, snapping beak at first repelled all attempts at succour. Then Ferraro took command of the

76

situation and seized it by smothering it with a cardigan. It had probably hurt its wing when it hit the pilot-house but the injury didn't look too bad. We decided it should enjoy the limited hospitality the *Gray* could offer at least until it could fly again. So Ferraro carried our struggling, protesting patient down to the warmth of the engine-room where the throb and heat of Cuesta's engines quickly sent it to sleep.

Our guest must have transmitted an "All safe" message that night. Next morning a full-scale bird invasion began. And most astonishing of all—they were all land birds. Rarely before had I seen such small birds so far from the coast. They were 360 miles from land. One after the other they dropped on to the *Gray* out of the blue until we had nearly two dozen. They were completely exhausted and lay helplessly flapping their wings unable to move. For an hour the crew were kept busy rescuing them from every part of the ship from the pilot-house to the scuppers. Plainly they could not have flown very much further had not the *Gray* come providentially by. They were of two different varieties. The prettiest had attractive blue and yellow breasts, the others were a less interesting mixture of brown and grey. Both were about the size of a black-bird. Each, we discovered later when they perked up a little, had a distinctive song. During the day some died. But that evening we still had fifteen showing every sign of recovering. We presumed they had come from Mexico.

The crew took an immediate interest in our feathered contingent and each bird was quickly adopted. At first they were kept in cupboards, later in biscuit tins and finally after a lot of sawing and hammering individual cages were built for them. For some time the birds moped and refused to eat. Rice which the Filipinos offered them from their dinner plates was scorned. Then somebody tried bread soaked in gravy. It was an instant success.

77

And after further experimentation crushed wheat and sweet puddings were also added to the diet of our aviary. The *Gray* was beginning to look like Noah's Ark.

That night several more sea birds of the same variety as the first joined us. They were probably attracted by the pilot-house lights. The newest arrivals were not quite as exhausted as the others and after a meal of bread in the crew's mess-room flew away next morning.

This same night we had a further development aboard. The crew began to pay the price of their enthusiasm ashore in Manzanillo. Venereal disease broke out. First, three reported to my cabin not in the least ashamed of what they had brought into our midst. They treated the whole thing as a huge joke. But I was alarmed. Thank God for the penicillin I had taken the trouble to get in Panama, I thought. I paraded the men in the dispensary, made them drop their trousers and gave each a painful jab in the buttocks thankful of the drug. They went away a little less gleefully than they had come, and I told them to report for further injections every two hours. I cursed my luck because the full treatment takes up to forty-eight hours and it meant I would have to be wakened all through the night to administer the "cure".

The following day another five men sauntered shamelessly along to report that they too had become infected and the same evening a further four followed them. I now had twelve cases on my hands and was not a little disturbed. The two-hourly injection programme was fast developing into a full-time job. So after one sleepless night during which I had been constantly woken by knocks on my cabin door, just as I was about to fall asleep from the previous "session", I decided to delegate this distasteful duty to Miranda.

He didn't relish the idea nor did he make a very expert administrator. "But, sir," he appealed, waving his olive arms to add weight to his remonstrances, "you see, never have I used one of these things—what do you call it?—the hypodermic."

"Well, here is a splendid opportunity for you to learn," I replied unsympathetically. And I proceeded to give him instructions. When the next batch of patients presented themselves at the surgery Miranda came along to master the craft. By now I was feeling quite accomplished at it myself. "Draw the flesh firmly toward the needle, then, a quick thrust—like that"—my victim groaned—"push in the plunger, and, out. It's easy. Try it." After watching five crude attempts, five faces grimaced in agony, and hearing five protestations I felt relieved for the sake of the people of the Philippines that Miranda had chosen the sea and not medicine as his career. He had not the least notion and seemed incapable of learning. But I persisted. I was determined that I wasn't going to lose any more sleep for the indiscretions of my crew. And in the end Miranda acquired a certain unprofessional technique of his own. It involved pursuing his unhappy victim retreating from the poised, rather blunt needle, half-way round the dispensary until Miranda, panther-like, pounced. Then there was a roar, an oath, and the procedure began all over again. Day and night during the next few days we could hear the shouts issuing from Doctor Miranda's surgery. I was amused to overhear one of the crew discussing his ordeal with another on deck. "Don't go up there," he warned, "they treat you like bloody guinea-pigs." If we put in at another port while Miranda was still aboard I was sure many of the crew would have thought twice before going ashore again.

But if nothing else, Miranda's injections must have been successful. Within three days the twelve men who had done his course were proclaimed apparently V.D. free. I was very relieved.

Five days and 600 miles out of Manzanillo, on August 15, we passed the only land we were to sight between

79

Mexico and Palmyra. It was Socorro Island, the southern-most of the Mexican-owned Revilla Gigedo Group. We steamed about thirty miles south and could only see the hazy outline of its higher hills on the horizon. But some-how the birds which had become our pets sensed that it was there. All the survivors had recovered by now, and until we drew close to the island had been perfectly con-tented in their makeshift cages, often filling the *Gray* with their shrill musical songs. Now they became agi-tated. The land which possibly they had been flying to or from when we collected them was calling. It seemed cruel to deprive them of freedom and in any case I didn't particularly want to take our small menagerie all the way across the Pacific. So I ordered the men to release them. The cages were opened and one after the other they took to the air, circled the tug once, and flew off toward Socorro Island. Only two of them seemed uncertain. They came back and perched on the signal yard for a few minutes. Then having apparently reassured themselves that we were not stranding them in mid-ocean set off swiftly after the others. Our only remaining guest was the sea bird still recovering in the engine-room. It seemed to be enjoying a protracted convalescence and was in no hurry to leave, so we decided to wait until its wing was fully mended before sending it on its way. Since it was a sea bird it would not have to fly to land.

We were still maintaining a steady six knots. It was close to the limit of smooth towing. If I increased revo-lutions to seven knots the heavy, wet lines curved out of the water and we began to jerk like a line of shunted rail-way wagons. The weather was still holding good, and I prayed that it would continue. We had now had six con-tinuous days of hot sunshine, an almost cloudless sky, light breeze, and smooth, rolling sea. We were getting down nicely into the lower latitudes. Our sixth day's position was 16° 37′ N. 115° 01′ W., and at noon we were 763 miles from Manzanillo. Although no happier about our tow gear I was well satisfied with our progress. And Cuesta reported that the fuel was lasting well. We were burning from 2,800 to 2,900 gallons of oil every twenty-four hours and I reckoned at this rate we would make Palmyra easily with the 72,000 gallons still remaining in our main and auxiliary tanks. It seemed that between six and seven knots was our most economical cruising speed.

I was pleased, too, with the way our ship's routine was developing. Every man except a few who were "day men" was on a watch. They had four hours on and eight off twice in twenty-four hours. The "day men" included Romanin, Diaz, the carpenter, and also two able seamen. The helmsman and lookouts I rotated between regular watches and day work. The day men worked from 8 a.m. to 4 o'clock after which the day was their own. The others did whatever jobs they might be required for during their particular watch. The 4 to 8 a.m. watch, for instance, began washing down the decks at 6 a.m., and went off watch at 8. During the day I got the crew busy painting out their quarters. At the same time I started on my own cabin.

I was still in the process of finding competent helmsmen among my novice gang. Few of them had the least idea of steering an accurate course. During the first week I frequently became aware of the *Gray* weaving nonchalantly about the Pacific with the minesweepers following in a straggling S. At night it was worse than that. On several occasions I surprised the helmsman nodding almost asleep with his eyes closed and the *Gray* heading anything up to ten degrees off course. They seemed to have the greatest difficulty learning to allow for the several seconds' lag which occurs between the turn of the wheel and the answering swing of the bow. Sometimes a night's constant bad weaving about the ocean would have us several miles off course by dawn, and several times when we took a shot of the sun and plotted our noon position I would find we were anything up to ten miles further north or south than we should have been.

But bad helmsmanship was not the only cause, I discovered. I found one day that the helmsman was becoming the centre of a little knot of off-duty men who went up to the pilot-house to yarn and keep him company. Often the helmsman became so engrossed in the conversation he would forget all about the wheel, would stare aft instead of forward and sometimes leave the wheel altogether the better to make clear some point under discussion. I quickly put a stop to all this. "What the devil do you think the pilot-house is—a public lounge?" I roared at them. "Only one man will be permitted here in future—the helmsman; now clear off the bridge." They scampered away.

Only three really good helmsmen emerged from my weeding out. They were Ritter, Whiteman and Todd. But Ritter couldn't feel the wheel spokes in his hands without breaking into song. He had, admittedly, a splendid voice and an endless repertoire of Spanish songs. Off duty his rousing, baritone voice competed more than successfuly with the wind in the stays and reached the remotest corners of the ship. But singing at the wheel was hardly something I could allow. It was bad for discipline and I found the crew interrupting their work to listen. So I told Ritter his concerts must stop.

I was finding that since the crew had regained their good spirits I was having to be firmer with them. They were quite unused to discipline and tended at the slightest encouragement to become cheeky and familiar. Cooped up together in a small ship I was in contact with them far more than is usual for a Captain. The fact that I was sharing watches with Alonso and Miranda brought me even closer. They began at first to treat me with a "one of the boys" attitude until I put my foot down. On a

82

voyage like this to have lost the respect of my crew and the inevitable consequent effect on morale would have been disastrous.

Although we were now six days out and the *Gray* had done little more than roll gently, Cooper was showing no sign of leaving his bunk. Though he still complained he was too sick to turn to I began to suspect he was malingering. He was contentedly sleeping or reading in his bunk, but whenever I went down to see him would put on a harrowing act of agonizing seasickness, groaning and retching. The sea was never going to get any smoother than this. I decided it was time Cooper found his sea-legs on deck with a paint brush in his hand. But the young American had other ideas. "I won't go, sir," he said emphatically. "Can't you see I'm very ill? It would kill me to leave my cot."

"Just the same, you're turning out now," I told him without feeling. "The fresh air on deck will soon put you right." But Cooper lay even more firmly in his bunk. I lost patience. "Are you coming, Cooper, or do I have to haul you out?" His reply was to turn over and emit a hollow, forced groan so obviously artificial that I seized hold of him and yanked him on to the deck. Cooper lost his temper. He leapt to his feet, swearing, and let me have it with both fists. All thought of seasickness had gone. He flailed me like a punch-bag. But I just grabbed him and propelled him, struggling, out on to the deck where he stood abusing me, cursing and sobbing. He didn't go back to his bunk again, and in a few days was doing a sullen job as officers' messman. The *Gray* had no place for passengers.

About this time we had another problem on board. The fireman and oilers on the four to eight watch had supper left for them in the refrigerator. They collected it when they came off watch. Casas, the crew's cook, had a soft spot for the firemen and used to leave extra tit-bits which the crew didn't normally get. But during the first week the suppers began mysteriously to disappear before the men could claim them. The ever-hungry Filipinos were raiding the refrigerator. So I had a special lock fitted. Next morning it had been forced. The food had gone. I wasn't sure who was responsible so I took a further step. I posted a man to guard it. The refrigerator wasn't tampered with again.

At the end of our first week, on August 17, we had steamed 902 miles. And still the weather was good to us. The Pacific was certainly smiling on the *Wallace R. Gray*. I wondered how much longer it could last. Most of us went about with our shirts off and the chief off-watch recreation was sunbathing. I found time for quite a lot of reading and got through a pile of books and digests. I was also busy writing letters to post in Palmyra and preparing my report for the company. Sometimes I whiled away an hour with a pack of cards playing patience. It was almost becoming the pleasant sunshine cruise the company had enthused about.

We logged our thousandth mile in the early hours of August 18. It almost symbolized the end of our trouble-free days. Dawn that morning showed a sea that was beginning to build up. Above us, high, hard edged and oily-looking clouds told me bad weather was on the way. I tapped the barometer. It was dropping fast.

During the morning the *Gray* began to take on a more business-like roll. A chop appeared on the swell and the distance between rollers started to shorten. The day before they had been all of two hundred feet apart; now they followed one another still with the same relentlessness but at intervals of less than a hundred feet. The minesweepers began to toss about and the rougher sea buffeting them brought new stresses and strains to the tow-lines. Six knots was now too fast. When two sweepers were raised on the tops of separate rollers the rope between them was hoisted out of the water and the subsequent jerk came shuddering back so that we felt it on the *Gray*. I reduced to five knots and smooth towing resumed.

But the tug was beginning to roll heavily now, for the first time since Manzanillo. Although she was a very fine sea-boat the roll became more pronounced as the sea increased and at times she dipped her rail under. I wondered how we could lessen our roll without altering course and decided that a sail would steady her and even if it did little else would make things a bit more comfortable on board.

I searched the ship and found a few odd pieces of canvas, and, in the after-peak, an old tarpaulin. It was very threadbare and in parts rotten, but I thought it could be patched. I got several of the men to work on it and that afternoon they had fashioned a square sail of sorts. I decided to set it on the fore-mast and ordered Alonso to send a man up the mast to stretch it along the signal yard. He came back after an unconscionable time to say that no volunteer had been forthcoming. None of the men had ever climbed a mast in their lives nor cared to try now that we were rolling so badly. So I went aloft myself. The signal yard was a good fifty feet above the top of the pilot-house and so could by no means be described as lofty, but those of the crew who were on deck watched goggle-eyed as I sat astride the yard-arm. It seemed an odd task for a Captain, but then this whole expedition was becoming an odd assignment.[1]

The sail was a great success. Despite its primitiveness the tattered tarpaulin steadied the *Gray* quite a bit. We didn't roll so far now. I was well pleased. It gave me

[1] The sail was set by rigging a gantline just below the radar platform and sending the end down on deck. After the makeshift sail had been bent-on it was hoisted aloft and I then stretched it along the signal-yard and lashed the head-rope to the jackstay. Attaching buntlines and sheets we set this sail, and by hauling the lee-sheet well aft and the weather-sheet well forward we were able to trim it to the wind.

quite a nostalgic feeling to look up at those few square yards of wind-filled canvas. I never expected to cross the old Pacific under sail again.

All that night the barometer continued to drop. The weather was fast deteriorating. The north-east trades on our starboard quarter freshened and next morning, August 19, when we were 1,188 miles from Mexico it was blowing a full gale, with gusts up to fifty miles an hour. Our feeble little sail, the pride of the ship the previous day, had to be furled. By evening we were riding quite a nasty storm. Black clouds raced across the sky, torrential showers beat down on our deck and the angry and confused sea rose up on either side to the level of the bridge. As successive rollers thundered past our bows and the *Gray* heeled over, green seas crashed over both rails, gushed along our after-deck and hissed away through the washports, and the *Gray* started to swing ten degrees on either side of her course. We were pitching now for the first time, and as we dived into each sea the tug staggered as if struck, our single screw sent a thudding throughout the length of the ship as the blades came close to the surface then died away as our bow lifted, only to race again a few seconds later. From time to time the propeller would race clear of the water: but little Cuesta down below in his grimy overalls had his hand on the throttle lever. He anticipated every pitch by several seconds, shutting off power just as the stern was rising and opening up again as it sank back into the sea.

By now I had reduced speed to three-and-a-half knots. But it seemed too much to hope that the tow-lines could hold through this buffeting. I looked back through the driving rain and spray but could only see the first mine-sweeper at the end of the tug's winch-wire, 400 yards astern. The seas were so high she was sometimes riding well above us on a level with our signal yard, violently tossing and pitching. At times her entire hull reared out

of the water then a few seconds later she would disappear
into a trough to reappear, water pouring off her deck.

Then I caught sight of No. 2. She seemed to be maintaining her position dead astern for which I was thankful,
but most of the time was out of sight behind the rollers.
Between squalls I climbed up on to the flying bridge and
searched the horizon through glasses for Nos. 3 and 4.
After twenty minutes I was rewarded with a few fleeting
glimpses of the top of No. 3's mast wallowing half a mile
behind. Of No. 4 there was not a trace. I was just wondering whether I should go about and search when an
object caught my eye astern but well down-wind. It didn't
reappear for a minute and then I got the glasses on it. It
was No. 4. What she was doing out there I couldn't
imagine. She might have been part of another convoy.
But most important she was still with us. I presumed her
bridle must have slipped out of position and the gale
blown her down almost abeam of No. 3.

There was nothing we could hope to do about it in the
present sea. It would have been suicidal to have attempted
to launch a boat, so I reduced speed still further and
hoped the storm would blow itself out in the night.

I turned in after my watch at 8 o'clock. Alonso who
came up to relieve me checked our course and turned the
searchlight astern. "I guess they're all there, but only
just, sir," he said. I went below to sleep.

At 4 a.m. I staggered sleepy-eyed back to the bridge to
take my morning watch. It was still blowing a gale but
the sea had moderated a little in the night. I relieved
Miranda. "How are the tows?" I asked him eagerly.

"Still with us, sir," he replied, "but if this keeps up
they shan't be for much longer." He disappeared below.

I went out on to the wing of the bridge. The wind was
shrieking round the pilot-house and I had to grip the rail
to support myself. I looked astern and could see the mast-
head lights of Nos. 1 and 2 swinging in the darkness. Of

Nos. 3 and 4 there was no sign. Perhaps their lights had gone out, I thought, hopefully, for the sun-valves which automatically switched them on every evening had been giving us quite a lot of trouble.

I flashed on the searchlight to check. Its brilliant beam stabbed away into the blackness astern reflecting the white caps of the seas. Yes, there was No. 1, looking like a ghost ship with its portholes shining in the beam and 250 yards beyond, the grey hull of No. 2 showed up dully.

The searchlight had a range of nearly a mile. It would light up all four boats on the inkiest nights. But to-night it showed nothing but black sea behind No. 2. I swung the beam in wide arcs astern. It was in vain. We had lost two minesweepers.

# Chapter Six

FOR several seconds I just stood there on the wing of the bridge gripping the rail and staring through my binoculars, praying that I might be wrong and the sweepers only concealed in a trough. But then I noticed our engines. They had taken on a different beat. The rhythm of their throb, throb, throb, had quickened. It was almost imperceptible, but on a long voyage your brain gets involuntarily synchronized with the tempo of the engines. I realized now that they were running faster than usual. It could only mean one thing. We had lost half our tow weight.

I sent Damone, who was look-out, to fetch Miranda. Quite obviously the second Mate had been merely wishfully thinking when he reported all minesweepers safe at 4 o'clock. They must have gone some time before the change of watch.

Miranda came hurrying back to the pilot-house. I let him have it. "Call yourself a second Mate, where the hell are the tows?" I shouted at him raising my voice above the drumming of a squall on the pilot-house windows. He looked uncomfortable. "They were all there when you took over from me, sir," he stammered, upset.

"Well, if you can see more than two there now I'll gladly kiss your foot," I answered.

Miranda groped his way out on to the wing of the bridge. He came back apologetically. "Yes, sir, you're right. There *are* only two. But I'll swear they were all there five minutes ago."

"We shall soon know," I told him grimly. Ringing "Stand by" I called down to the engineer to slow down, and went about. The only way to find the missing craft

89

was to steam back along the course we had come. So we crawled round and headed back a little north of east.

It was tricky, going about in the present sea. As the rollers that had been surging in from astern began to hit us from abeam the *Gray* lurched and shuddered. Up to windward I could see the ominous black shapes of mountainous white-capped seas piled higher than our flying bridge. But the tug always managed to lift herself up the side of the roller before it could crash down on to us. I was relieved when we were round and our sturdy bows were slicing straight into the small hills, making us far less vulnerable to the heaving Pacific. I had a few anxious moments while Nos. 1 and 2 sweepers wallowed round behind us. But during that critical period while the two tows' lights came about behind us the lines held.

At 4.15 we were creeping back along a reciprocal course. I called Alonso out of his bunk and ordered more men on deck to maintain the maximum possible look-out. It wasn't going to be easy finding two tiny minesweepers in this confused sea, especially as the wind might have blown them far to leeward. In the troughs between some of these twenty and thirty-foot waves we could easily pass within half a mile without seeing them.

Soon every available man had climbed on deck. They looked almost professional in their oilskins. I posted them strategically about the ship from the fo'c'sle-head to the flying bridge, slackened speed to two knots and ordered Sparks to switch on the radar. A few minutes later the scanner atop our foremast was slowly rotating while Sparks sat peering at the screen. Although the penetrating eyes of our radar pierced the darkness for up to eight miles around I wasn't happy about its chances of picking up the sweepers. It is most sensitive to metal objects and all the wooden sweepers could present were wire shrouds, railings and steel funnels. Behind a roller even these would have been out of the radar's field.

As we steamed back without a sight of the breakaways I continued my interrogation of Miranda and Damone who had been the look-out of the watch. Under further cross-examination, Miranda began to admit dejectedly that perhaps he hadn't checked so carefully. They may not have been with us after all at 4 o'clock. In fact the last time Damone was quite sure he had seen the four lights was at 2 a.m. although Miranda insisted they were there much later. I looked at the log. It was no help. The last entry was at midnight. "Weather squally, rough sea, poor visibility. Nos. 2 and 4 lights burning, tows O.K.," it said reassuringly.

It was light soon after 4.30. A miserable, wet, grey dawn filtered in showing us a turbulent angry Pacific—but no minesweepers. If Damone had been right they should have been no further than ten miles back. We should sight them around 6 o'clock, I calculated. As it got lighter our range of vision increased to about three miles from the deck and six from the flying bridge. I altered course to starboard to bring us several miles to leeward of our original course to where I hoped they would be. With the wind and the sea that was running they would be drifting rapidly south-westward. I looked back at No. 2 behind us for a clue as to how they had broken away. Her bridle was still intact but I couldn't see any sign of the tow-rope that should have gone to No. 3. From time to time Sparks reported from the radar to say there had been a blip on the screen that might have been the minesweepers. But always it was a false alarm. The blips proved to be only heavy rain showers.

We steamed on, rolling and pitching for another hour. The crew, spray glistening on their oilskins, were staring red-eyed in every quarter. Then suddenly at 5.30 in the half-light there was a hoarse shout from Romanin on the flying bridge: "Object on the starboard bow." Everyone rushed to the starboard rail. But there was not a solitary speck to relieve the grey monotony of our rolling, limited horizon.

I hurried up on to the flying bridge. Alonso was pointing excitedly away ahead to starboard. "A light, sir," he shouted above the wind, "over there." I looked hard through my glasses. I could see nothing.

Then Alonso cried: "There it is again, sir—now it's gone." A few seconds later I saw the light. It was one of the sweepers right enough, about five miles away. I could just see the top of a mast every time she and the *Gray* reached the top of a sea together. Between rollers it disappeared. Sparks still hadn't picked up anything on the radar. He only began to get the sweepers after I had altered course to bring the *Gray* up to windward of them.

As we drew closer I was relieved to see that both Nos. 3 and 4 were there. The 800-foot rope between them had held, but its weight sagging in the sea had drawn the two vessels close together. I hoped we could pick them up before they collided and holed each other. They would only have needed to crash together once or twice in that sea to stave in their wooden hulls and sink.

I kept the engines turning just enough to keep us stationary in the face of wind and sea. The first two minesweepers were strung out nicely behind us, held there by the sea. They rode the swell, rolling from side to side, rising and falling so that one moment they were high above us, the next in a deep trough far below. Of the two drifting sweepers we could only see the masts and occasionally a glimpse of their superstructure. Both seemed undamaged.

The next job was to pick them up. I knew I should have to put men aboard both No. 2 and No. 3 and steam close by, so that a line could be passed between them. But the more I looked at the sea and felt the *Gray* heaving under me the less I liked the idea of ordering my inexperienced crew into a small boat. In fact I would have been more than dubious sending away a party of seasoned boatmen.

So I decided to stand by for a few hours in the hope that the weather and sea would moderate. The barometer was showing unsteady indications of rising, and by 6 o'clock it began to look as if the storm was blowing itself out. I knew that it would be all of a day before the sea settled down but at least the high wind was abating.

While we stood by, bucking in the swell, I called Romanin and asked him to see if any of the crew would volunteer to man the motor lifeboat. I knew by his expression that he didn't expect a rush for the job. As Bosun he knew he was expected to be the first to offer, but seemed far from keen about the operation. "I don't think you'll get many of the men out in this," he said quietly. He was right. Ten minutes later he was back to report that no one had the slightest intention of committing what they viewed as certain suicide, that morning.

I didn't blame them altogether. I wouldn't have felt happy going myself, but I should have felt bound to have done had I more confidence in Alonso's capacity to handle the tug. But the operation was going to call for some tricky manœuvring and I felt the responsibility for that should be mine.

Meanwhile I ordered Romanin to prepare the lifeboat and warm its motor so that it could be swung out as soon as conditions permitted. I decided not to press the crew then and there and instead I gave them lessons in how to lower the boat quickly without crushing it against our side.

But the more I watched their clumsy, unhappy fumblings, the less confident I felt of their ability to get safely away in it at all. I knew that the moment they began to swing it out on the davits and lower it down into the water the boat would swing with the roll of the tug, and take charge. Unless skilfully handled it would be smashed to pieces against our sides. I ordered protective "puddings" or fenders, of rope and old tyres to be lashed to our side to

93

protect the lifeboat. But the boat drills the crew had had in port counted for nothing out here. Instead of a docile, stable lifeboat to lower gently off a solid, rigid platform into a glass-like sea they had a vicious swinging boat that even with the tricing lines would swing so violently it might easily strike and perhaps kill them while they were lowering it from a deck that swayed under them, into a sea that foamed first five feet, then twenty feet below.

During one of these practice lowerings Rodrigues narrowly escaped being caught up in one of the tricing lines and catapulted overboard. And another man nearly had his skull cracked when the *Gray* gave an unexpected lurch and the boat suddenly hurtled back on to the launching party.

All this time conditions were improving. By 8.30 I decided to attempt a launching. The wind had lost a lot of its force and the sea, though far from safe for the lifeboat, was settling down to a less confused swell.

But now another ugly peril presented itself—sharks. We hadn't noticed them during the storm, although they couldn't have been far away. Now the huge swell was losing its surface chop the familiar triangular fins protruding more than a foot out of the water began to circle the *Gray*. Soon I counted twenty. Big brutes they were, all of twelve to fourteen feet in length, their jaws just waiting for any morsel, human or otherwise, that might plunge their way. The sight of them sickened me. I didn't point them out to anyone else. I didn't want to add to their fears. But then someone else spotted them. In two minutes every man on the ship knew they were there.

I sent for Romanin to make a second appeal for volunteers. But any of the crew who had had his mind changed by the improved sea conditions quickly altered it again at the sight of the sharks. "They are afraid of the sharks now, sir," Romanin reported. "I can't persuade any of them to volunteer. They think they haven't a dog's chance."

94

So I waited another hour. Meanwhile, I got Sparks to tap out a signal to the Islands Towage and Lighterage Company in San Francisco advising them of our predicament. I said: "NUMBER THREE AND FOUR TOWS ADRIFT 0300 HEAVY SEA CREW REFUSE TO BOARD TOWS MEANTIME STANDING BY POSITION 14.17 DEGREES NORTH 125.52 DEGREES WEST."

At 9.30 Romanin came to me and proudly announced that four volunteers had come forward. He himself would go and the others were Todd, Jones, Vincent and Ortiz. I ordered Miranda to take charge of the party, making six in all. I felt very proud of them. I knew that none were the sort of men to whom danger or fear meant nothing. They were six rather terrified volunteers forcing themselves to do a perilous job. I got them together and explained what had to be done. But with the exception of Miranda, Romanin and Jones I don't think any of them quite knew what he was expected to do. They were a brave but very dejected band of volunteers.

I am quite sure none of them ever expected to stand on the *Gray's* deck again. They wore shorts and singlets and Mae Wests. Some were bare-footed. I ordered the lifeboat out. But at that moment a sea bigger than the rest caught the ship unexpectedly. The *Gray* staggered and gave a long roll to port. The lifeboat was snatched out of the crew's hands and swung wildly out of control dangling on the davits beyond their reach. Amid warning shouts it crashed back on to the fenders and rebounded, snapping the tricing lines by which the crew were unsuccessfully trying to bring it under control. I was so alarmed by all this I decided it would be murderous to order a party away in the lifeboat at all. They would have been dashed to pieces even before they reached the water with such an inexperienced handling party. So I ordered the lifeboat back aboard.

The only alternative was the diminutive flat-bottomed

pram. I had decided earlier never to use it again, but now I reversed that decision. At least it could be swung clear of the tug's rolling hull on our boom. At least it would reach the water in one piece.

There were some doubtful mutterings among the volunteers at this. But nobody pulled out. I felt even more proud of them.

To give them a better chance I steamed about and came up from the opposite direction so that we could lower the pram on the lee side. This way the tug would protect them for those first vital seconds while they began rowing. I also called up Cuesta and asked him to pump out some oil on that side to help take the chop off the worst of the sea. A few minutes later a blue film of oil began to spread away from our side. It created a temporary but very effective area of almost unbroken water. Before it had time to disperse I gave the order to launch.

The six men climbed into the tiny ten-footer and we swung them out clear of the side, waited until a suitable sea swept by and quickly dropped them. Their launching was a signal to the sharks. The fins dashed in a body to surround the pram.

But the little boat, with barely eighteen inches of freeboard, was snatched away from them. As Romanin and Todd rowed feverishly to avoid being drawn under our counter, the pram was swept away astern like a twig in a mountain torrent. We caught a glimpse of it, as, high above the level of our bridge, it was momentarily perched on the top of a huge roller and then slid into the trough beyond and was lost from sight.

An agonizing minute passed during which we were sure they had foundered. Then suddenly someone gave a shout. A hundred yards astern they had appeared again skimming over another roller. A swarm of sharks surrounded them. Although we didn't know it then, once or twice their oars actually scraped the backs of the sharks beside them. Everywhere they looked in the sea around them, the huge repulsive grey forms were gliding forbiddingly, barely an arm's length away. There was more than one horrified shudder in the pram that morning.

Up on the *Gray's* bridge I had another problem. When I had gone about to help the boat party away the two minesweepers still attached to the tug had been brought round to windward. Now they were in danger of running down on top of us. The greater resistance which the *Gray's* bulk offered to the sea made her drift more slowly than the sweepers. I had, therefore, to bring them round to leeward again. At the same time I had to try to keep No. 2 as close as was safe to No. 3, the first of the two adrift. The plan was that the boat party should go aboard No. 2 and make it ready for re-rigging. Then half of them would row across to No. 3 while those remaining paid out a light line to them. Once board No. 3 they would use this line to haul across a heavier line which in turn would take over the heavy 11-inch manila rope which we presumed was still attached to No. 2. When they had finished they were to signal and I would take the whole convoy about and pick them up.

But the plan misfired from the start. From the bridge I watched the pram bobbing away, through glasses. I moved ahead a little to save them more rowing than was necessary and two minutes later when the *Gray* rose out of a big trough was able to see that they had safely reached No. 2, 500 yards astern. I saw Miranda, Romanin and Jones scramble aboard and then to my consternation, before the others could follow, the pram was swept away and disappeared behind a roller. After what seemed an age they reappeared drifting rapidly to leeward. For a horrible moment I thought they had lost their oars and when they didn't show up again for nearly a minute I really thought they must have been swamped.

Then still further down to leeward the little speck

97

popped into view and there, mercifully, were two oars rising and falling. They were trying frantically to reach one of the drifters and for a few minutes it almost looked as if they might make No. 3. But through the glasses I saw them carried swiftly past the sweeper almost within arm's length. They were now drifting quite helplessly with no possible hope of reaching No. 4. And they were getting so far away intervening rollers were almost obscuring them from view.

Quickly I swung the telegraph over and steamed away to their rescue. By now we had completely lost them and they must have been all of a mile away. Presently there came a hail from the masthead look-out: "There they are, sir, dead ahead." The flimsy little pram appeared and disappeared several times before we drew abreast. The three of them, Todd, Vincent and Ortiz were still aboard and still rowing like automatons. We steamed past them and I carefully manœuvred No. 2 sweeper with the others aboard, alongside the pram. For a ghastly second I thought they had missed the line Miranda had flung them. But they got it and were hauled aboard. I breathed again.

Now Miranda began semaphoring. How he managed to retain his balance standing on the minesweeper's swaying deck I couldn't imagine. One by one, with long pauses, the halting letters spelled out a message: "TOW . . . ROPE . . . FROM . . . HERE . . . HANGING . . . STRAIGHT . . . DOWN . . . INTO . . . SEA . . . TOO . . . HEAVY . . . TO RAISE . . . WITH . . . OUR . . . TACKLE."

The big manila rope which had broken away from No. 3 and was now dangling 800 feet vertically into the Pacific would have been difficult enough for a number of men with proper gear to raise, even if it had been comparatively dry. But ten days immersion in the sea had made it green, slimy and waterlogged. Now it must have weighed all of two tons.

I switched on the signal blinker and flashed back:

"DOUBLE-UP ON YOUR TACKLE." Although this would increase the purchase considerably I doubted whether it would be enough. My doubts were soon confirmed. After a lot of manipulating and heaving a message fluttered back, "IMPOSSIBLE."

There was only one possible alternative—and I wasn't sure *that* would work. It was to fit a large bow-shaped shackle over the rope fast to No. 2, attach a 3-inch line to it and then run this line across to No. 3 and as I steamed ahead allow the shackle to slide down the hanging rope until it jammed at the eye beyond which the shackle would not slide. Further steaming would slowly raise the hanging rope end to the surface until the men on No. 3 could heave it aboard and make it fast thus linking up the whole convoy again. I conveyed this as simply as I could to Miranda. A stream of queries came back and I elaborated with more blinkings. Occasionally the sweeper would roll out of sight and the message would be interrupted to be resumed after a reassuring wave of Miranda's flags.

The hours slipped by. Midday passed and still the six little figures struggled to raise the reluctant rope. Meanwhile Todd, Vincent and Ortiz rowed across and boarded No. 3. This time they took a line from No. 2 so there was no danger of being swept away again. A company of sharks escorted them across the hundred-yard gap. I watched them climbing aboard with some trepidation, for I was always afraid that with their fearful lack of seamanship they would get too close and the pram would be caught under the minesweeper's heaving sponson which was alternately six feet out of the water and as many below every five seconds. I saw Todd safely aboard and Vincent began to follow him. Then suddenly there was a splash.

I gripped the glasses closer. Vincent had missed his footing and fallen in. I thought immediately of the sharks that couldn't have been more than six feet away. I didn't know whether to look or turn away. But something froze my binoculars on to the little drama that was going on in the small circle of my lenses. But as quickly as he had fallen, Vincent had scrambled out again and Todd hauled him safely aboard. I have never seen a man get out of the water so swiftly. Certainly he wouldn't have come out at all if he had stayed many more seconds.

By 2 o'clock the men on No. 2 had fitted the bow shackle, and over on No. 3 they began hauling in the slack of the line attached to it and made fast. Miranda signalled me "Slow ahead" and as we moved forward the shackle went slithering jerkily off down the rope according to plan. After an hour of flag waving, blinking, heaving, starting and stopping the end of the heavy manila broke surface. Then the men on No. 3 managed to get the end near enough and re-shackled it to the sweeper's bridle where the other shackle had carried away during the night.

It was frustrating being anchored to my bridge. During the long day's operations I felt I wanted to be over on the sweepers with them. Through the glasses I could see them making a dozen mistakes but often when I flashed an instruction they were too busy to see it. I even tried the *Gray's* impressive electric loud-hailer, but although I bellowed myself hoarse my voice was scattered by the northeast wind. But in any case I dared not leave the bridge for a minute. The success of the whole operation depended on quick and careful manœuvring of the convoy. Even keeping the *Gray* in one position against the rolling Pacific entailed minute by minute alterations in revolutions.

It was nearly 4 o'clock when at last the "operation completed" signal came from Miranda. For the first time in fourteen hours the *Gray* took up the strain of four minesweepers again. The men on No. 3 cast off and were hauled back to No. 2. There they picked up the others and all together were picked up by us on the tug. Although the sea was subsiding it was still very rough and the sigh of relief that went up as the pram and its six weary occupants was hoisted safely aboard, was a general one.

They were so utterly exhausted they had to be helped out of the pram. They had been without food or water for seven hours as no one had expected them to be away half that time. Their lips were cracked and dry with salt spray; they were soaking wet and despite the latitude shivering with cold. Jones had been badly skinned; his legs and arms were a mass of raw weals.

I felt immensely proud of them. They had done a magnificent job against terrifying odds and it gave me new faith in my little band. They were almost too exhausted to talk, but Miranda, for whose part I felt especially grateful, gave me a brief report on their nightmarish day, warning me that the cursed U-bolts were rapidly cutting into the bridles. Further breakaways were imminent, he said. In fact he thought it highly improbable that we would get any of the sweepers anywhere near Palmyra.

I gave each of them a tot of our precious whisky ration. Casas served them a huge meal and they flopped into their bunks. Reviewing the events of the day I decided that under no circumstances would I permit the pram to be used again. If it was too rough to launch the motor lifeboat then we should stand by a week if necessary for suitable conditions rather than risk a repetition of to-day's hazards.

I couldn't help thinking how similar our circumstances were to one of the few marine tows that ever made real history. It was the remarkable feat of towing the 170-ton Cleopatra's Needle from Alexandria to London in 1877. The Needle was encased in an ingenious cylindrical iron pontoon, 92 feet long and 15 feet wide. It had watertight compartments and the addition of a rudder, wheelhouse and crew quarters made it a crude ship of sorts. An Englishman, Captain Carter, and several Maltese seamen manned it. The tow ship was the 1,300-ton British steamer *Olga*, linked to the needle with a quarter of a mile of wire rope. All went well as far as the notorious Bay of Biscay. Here the extraordinary tow was caught in a severe storm and the ballast of iron rails inside the cumbersome cylinder began to shift. It was night and the harassed captain of the *Olga* on receiving an S O S from Captain Carter: "Foundering. Send a boat," lowered a lifeboat with six volunteers. It was swept away astern in gigantic seas and miraculously reached the Needle which was then wallowing uncontrollably in the troughs with its decking awash. But the boat party missed the line that was thrown to them and vanished in the darkness. They were never seen again. Fearing that the uncontrollable cylinder might run down his own ship the *Olga's* captain cut the Needle adrift. Next day he searched for it in vain and finally set course for England. Meanwhile the cylinder, "plunging like a porpoise and diving like a duck", drifted rapidly south-westward toward the Spanish coast. Two days later another steamer, the *Fitzmaurice*, found it and towed it into El Ferrol claiming salvage. The cylinder was made seaworthy again and a few months later in January, 1878, the 140-horsepower Channel tug *Anglia* towed it safely into London after an uneventful six-day voyage. Widespread jubilation followed its arrival, and Queen Victoria was moved to have issued the proclamation that "the Queen is much gratified at hearing of the safe arrival of the Needle".

I wondered if any such expression of regal relief would greet our own belated arrival in Manila.

# Chapter Seven

As we rolled off westward again I wondered how many miles fate would allow us before another breakaway. All I prayed for was a night's respite in which the boat party could recover from its exhaustion, a night in which we could put another fifty miles between us and Manzanillo. But no.

At 7 o'clock, as darkness approached—barely two hours and ten miles further on—Nos. 3 and 4 broke away again. I had been on the bridge continuously since 4 a.m. and was feeling desperately weary, when Martin, who was look-out, shouted down from the flying bridge: "They've gone again, sir." I looked astern just in time to see two lights fading behind us into the dusk.

I felt so bitterly disappointed and tired I thought for a moment I would just let them go. A whole day's delay and the lives of six men had been risked for nothing. Here we were back where we started. But I knew I would have to pick them up, even if it meant another lost day or two.

It meant waiting until daylight. I couldn't risk putting a boat out in the dark and in any case the only men whom I could send would be in no state to go before morning. So I went about and gave orders to Alonso, who relieved me at 8 p.m., to keep the minesweepers in sight during the night. Then I turned in. It seemed only a few minutes later that it was 3.45 a.m. and I was sleepily dressing to go back to the bridge. During the night the weather had worsened. It was squally, overcast, and the sea had become very rough again.

Miranda told me we had lost sight of the sweepers during the night and there had been no trace on the radar. There was nothing we could do but wait for the light.

But morning, grey and bleak, showed only a rolling expanse of ocean and a sea which, a falling barometer told me, would rapidly get worse. It was a far from cheerful prospect. The morning passed with still no sign of the two vessels.

And now another matter was causing me concern. Two days earlier one of the firemen had come to me with an injured thumb. He had cut it down in the engine-room, one of the engineers had dressed it after a fashion, and he had gone back to work. But the wound had been neither cleaned nor disinfected, and oil and dirt had soaked into it through the bandage.

He complained that it was giving him great pain. I pulled the filthy bandage off it and was horrified to see the thumb had become swollen and festered.

"My God, man, why didn't you report this before?" I asked him.

"Because engineer, he say, no need to worry, cut heal up in few days," the frightened fireman replied.

I cursed my engineers for their casualness and did the best I could with the rather unpleasant mess.

I bathed it in peroxide, opened it, drained it and cleaned it, then dusted it with boracic powder and put a clean bandage on. Although he had gone back to his duties, he was still in pain and I was far from happy about it. I got Sparks to radio Honolulu, 1,800 miles away, for medical advice. I knew there was a medical shore station there which stands by to flash urgent advice to doctorless ships. Sparks said they were asking for a detailed description of the wound. I wrote it down for him and thirty minutes later came the reply: "GIVE TETANUS INJECTION STOP KEEP DRAINING STOP IF INFECTION SPREADS OR IS FELT AT ELBOW ADVISE AMPUTATE." This last drastic alternative shocked me. The only surgical instruments we carried were a few scalpels. No one aboard had the remotest knowledge of surgery. So I took the first piece of advice, gave him an anti-tetanus injection and told him he was excused duty. But despite the increasing pain his thumb was giving him he refused to go to his bunk and went stubbornly back to his post in the stokehold.

But now as we scoured the Pacific for the missing tows the pain became too much. He reluctantly went to his bunk and lay there groaning.

At 8.45 that morning we sighted the sweepers, still held together, wallowing on the southern horizon. But the sea was becoming so rough and visibility so poor we lost them in a squall at 1 o'clock and although they showed up inter-mittently on the radar during the afternoon we did not sight them again until nearly six. A screaming nor'easter, and a huge swell which I imagined was the result of a violent storm several hundred miles north-east of us, put any attempt at launching a boat out of the question. Be-sides, it was nearly dark again. So once more I decided to stand by until morning, hoping we should be able to keep the minesweepers in sight this time.

Meanwhile from the fo'c'sle came reports that the fire-man's thumb was getting worse. He was almost delirious with pain. Distasteful as the thought of such an operation was I realized that amputation was now probably the only possible means of saving his life. I knew that once gan-grene set in it would spread swiftly through the arm tissues and he would only live a few days. We were far from regular shipping lanes where a passenger liner with a doctor might be able to help us. The nearest possible route, that from New Zealand to Panama, was nearly 2,300 miles further south. And Sparks told me he could hear no other vessel for more than a thousand miles. It was up to the amateur surgery the *Gray* could offer.

I realized I would have to do it, but looked forward to the task with considerable misgiving. Once when I had been Mate in a steamer approaching Cape Town I had attended the delivery of a passenger's baby, and earlier in sail I had cut a huge Oregon wood splinter out of a seaman's foot. But never anything approaching amputation. No Captain is expected to be able to carry out more than the usual fairly simple first aid.

During the day, as the *Gray* rolled drunkenly and her engines throbbed quietly, just sufficiently to keep the two sweepers in sight, I prepared for the operation. I decided the dispensary was unsuitable as it had no useful table so made the officers' wardroom my theatre.

Then I pored through the solitary medical guide the *Gray* carried. It was no help. Amputation wasn't mentioned. I opened our tiny surgical case. It contained a couple of scalpels but little else of practical use. The scalpels, which I had ordered in Panama, had arrived blunt. I thanked God now, that I had sent them back to be sharpened up. But I still had no instrument with which to cut through bone. The nearest approach was an engine-room hacksaw. So I asked Cuesta to bring me a new one out of his stores. The smallest he could find had an 18-inch blade with a set wide enough to cut through our main mast. It was quite unusable.

But after a fruitless search for an alternative instrument I decided it was the hacksaw or nothing. I asked Cuesta to heat it up and try and hammer the edge down to make the serrations finer. When he brought it back for my inspection it was far from satisfactory. He had merely dented the blade and blunted half the teeth; one stroke would have shattered the biggest bone. So I told him to get another blade, make it white hot and smooth the edge down with a steel roller and then to temper it again. He did this and the result, though still far from professional, was a much more likely-looking implement. Together with scalpels, needles and catgut we sterilized it in boiling water.

Next I prepared the wardroom table. I got Diaz to drill several holes through the top near the edge. I planned to lash my patient's arm firmly to the table with ropes passed through these. Then I had a small wooden block nailed near the edge of the table on which I proposed laying the offending thumb.

When I turned in that evening the patient seemed a little better. His thumb, he said, was giving less pain. But at 2 a.m. I was awakened by an agitated engineer shaking me violently and burbling: "Sir, sir, come quickly, the thumb it is worse. Savarino, he is dying."

I fell out of my bunk, rubbing the sleep from my eyes and went to the wardroom. Savarino was already there and I saw at once he was in a bad way. He stood swaying there in his dirty shirt and trousers, holding his right arm. His eyes were glistening and he was muttering incoherently. It appeared the pain was now beginning to spread up his arm. When I removed the vile-smelling bandage I saw at once that the thumb had become dangerously infected and possibly gangrenous. It was blackish-yellow, oozing, and swollen to nearly twice normal size. Unless it was amputated quickly it looked as if Savarino hadn't a chance.

"It will have to come off," I told him, "otherwise you may not live more than a few days." But Savarino was beyond caring. He would gladly have parted with his whole arm if it would have relieved him of the dreadful pain. "Will you let me amputate it?" I asked him.

"Do anything, Skipper, anything, but please make it better," he beseeched.

So I decided to begin the operation. Several of the crew were peering in at the door. I told them to clear off and emptied the wardroom except for Miranda whom I asked to help.

Together we helped Savarino into a chair and bound his elbows to the arm rest. Then we laid his wrist on the table edge, lashing it with rope through the prepared holes so that the thumb rested on the block. He took it all with admirable stoicism, although by this time he was close to tears.

When I suggested a general anæsthetic he looked terrified. "Please no, Skipper, it does not matter; you just make thumb better," he pleaded. I was a little relieved because although we had a small bottle of ether I am no anæsthetist and I was afraid I might overdose him, burn his face, or even put Miranda and myself right out into the bargain. To deaden the pain I gave him a morphine injection in the hand and handed him a couple of stiff glassfuls of whisky which he swallowed gratefully. When I thought the injection had had time to act, I began the incision. Actually I learnt later that morphine is not a local anæsthetic, and he must have felt everything.

I steadied myself on the table against the roll of the ship, for we were still standing by the drifting sweepers, and every roller heeled the tug far over. I knew the incision would be fairly easy, but I wasn't any too sure how much of the thumb should come off. At first I thought it looked so far gone it would be wise to take it off below the knuckle. On the other hand, I didn't want to leave the poor fellow with not even a stump. And with my experience of carving a chicken I knew the knuckle might be difficult to locate. No, far too risky, I decided. Far safer to go for the point between the knuckle and the joint as this seemed to be clear of infection.

Savarino winced as the scalpel sunk in. But he made not a murmur. It was very sharp and in a few seconds I could feel hard bone all the way round. There was surprisingly little bleeding. Then I picked up the hacksaw. This was the part I had been dreading. Miranda took a firm hold on our patient and I began sawing. At the first stroke of steel on bone Savarino screamed, his face twisted in agony and fear and he struggled like a tiger. But fortunately our preparations had been well made. The ropes holding him down didn't budge, and little Miranda, looking as green as a Filipino can, was gripping grimly.

It was some time before I could pluck up courage enough to continue. I decided that the best method was to saw through quickly. So gripping the hacksaw in my right hand and the top of the thumb in my left, I started again. At first I had difficulty making our improvised instrument bite into the bone at all and when finally it began to make some headway the clumsy blade drew the flesh with it at each stroke. Sweat was pouring off me and I felt nauseated by the whole thing but I pressed on. Savarino was alternately screaming and swearing in his own tongue, and Miranda was trying desperately, but with no success, to comfort him. By now the screams had brought half the crew from their bunks, but I was unaware of the sea of horrified faces peering in every porthole. The scene in that swaying wardroom was every bit as stiff with tension and drama as a one-in-a-million-chance operation performed by a famous surgeon before a gallery of awed colleagues.

To Savarino the sawing must have lasted half an hour. In fact it was over in less than two minutes. I said to Miranda: "For Christ's sake give him another shot of whisky." But there was no reply. When I looked round I saw that Miranda had gone. He had staggered out on to the deck and fainted. And then I realized that Savarino wouldn't need the whisky. He too had fainted. He lay slumped over the table, breathing heavily and quietly groaning.

Rather unsteadily I examined my surgery. I saw that the makeshift saw had splintered the bone stump. It looked as if it had been chopped with a blunt axe. Otherwise it looked reasonably workmanlike. Then I realized what I had omitted to do. There was a bare stump of raw bone and no flesh to cover it. In my initial scalpel work I had completely overlooked the very necessary flap of flesh to fold back over the stump. For a minute I stood there, weakly, surveying my ghastly mistake, quite at a loss to know how to rectify it.

Then it came to me. Why not a little plastic surgery? I picked up the amputated thumb. It was rotten and soft except for perhaps half an inch of the base. The stench was nauseous. But in that half-inch of sound flesh I saw a cover that would fit the open bone end. Quickly I fashioned a flap of sorts with the scalpel, cleaned the wound of bone particles, fitted it over the stump and secured it with several stitches. Then I bathed the wound with disinfectant, sprinkled it with boracic powder and tied a new bandage on. Altogether it was a very crude piece of surgery, but it probably saved the man's life.

Five minutes later he came to. I untied his bonds and he flopped back into the chair dazed and very shocked. I gave him a whisky and someone helped him to a settee. Then suddenly the reaction of the last thirty minutes hit me. Feeling sick and faint I reeled out of the wardroom, pushed through the throng of spectators and was violently ill over the rail.

Savarino didn't sleep that night, but next day when I examined the wound I was glad to see that it had bled little and looked like healing. He was feeling much better, the pain had gone from his arm and although the stump must still have been giving him hell he didn't complain. "You saved my life, Skipper," he said. I wondered if it would make him any more loyal to me, for up till now he had been one of my most troublesome men.

The minesweepers had now been adrift for a day and a half. For thirty-six hours we had burned up precious fuel and gained not a mile. Many more delays and we wouldn't have fuel enough to make Palmyra.

By 8 a.m.—it was now August 22 and our twelfth day out—I decided that the sea had moderated sufficiently to risk picking up the tows. It was still squally and quite a strong wind was blowing but the sea had gone down a lot. This time we lowered the steel motor lifeboat. It was 28 feet long, could hold thirty men and was capable of seven or eight knots. I felt a lot happier about it than the frail little pram. And now the *Gray* wasn't rolling so badly it wasn't such a dangerous job swinging it clear of our sides.

Miranda, Romanin, Todd, Vincent, Jones and Ortiz, the gallant crew of two days before, went again. But to lighten their load I called for two more volunteers. Whiteman and Ferraro joined them. They warmed the motor before launching, loaded it with tackle and the little spare tow-gear we had and were hoisted out. The moment they hit the water Whiteman opened the throttle to get away before the tug rolled back on to them, and they sped away scattering the sharks with the flurry of their propeller.

The lifeboat revolutionized pick-up routine. It meant that more gear and men could be carried and eliminated the need to manœuvre the whole convoy to pick up the boat party. All I had to do on the bridge now was to keep the *Gray* headed into the sea and bring Nos. 1 and 2 minesweepers round when they were ready to join up.

Miranda signalled back that No. 3 had broken away in almost the same place as before. Once again the 800 foot tow-rope was dangling down into the Pacific from astern of No. 2. For eight long hours the boat party worked to join the breakaways to us again. For eight hours they struggled on the rolling minesweeper to raise the sodden tow-rope. But by 5 o'clock in the afternoon they had only raised six hundred feet of it and Miranda signalled, "IM-POSSIBLE . . . RECOVER . . . MORE." I signalled him to try the sliding bow shackle procedure. Again it worked and we raised the last two hundred feet of sodden rope and joined the convoy up again. The boat party chugged back riding the rollers like a switchback railway and were swung aboard without incident. They were far less exhausted this time and there had been no real fear of the sharks.

Miranda solemnly reported on the day's work, adding that all the bridles had now begun to chafe and, as he saw it, we were soon going to be spending more time searching for and recovering tows than in steaming. In view of the fact that in the last few days we had only covered thirty-one miles I began to think he was right.

We set course for Palmyra again at dusk. But I couldn't recapture our former five to six knots as, to make matters worse, the main engine started to give trouble.

During my watch that night I switched on a small radio I had installed on the bridge to pick up news and weather reports. I had just tuned in to San Francisco and the day's news was booming in when Sparks rushed in excitedly and began twiddling the knobs. "Leave the damn' thing alone, can't you hear I'm listening to the news," I said, annoyed.

"But this is far more important, sir," he said, bringing in shrill tuning squeals and a deluge of deafening static. "I've just picked up another station on my set and they're talking about us."

"The devil they are," I said, leaping over to the set beside him. "Let's hear it then."

"That's just what I'm trying to do, sir——" He was interrupted by the voice of an American announcer, distorted and weak, which came suddenly crackling through. "This is station KLP2 calling," it drawled. "Here is the news. Across the Pacific at this moment a tug and four minesweepers are struggling. Her gallant crew are battling against odds of——" and here the reception faded away to an unintelligible hum. By now I was as excited as Sparks had been. I had my ear to the set straining desperately to hear what the world was being told about us. But although Sparks juggled professionally for five minutes he couldn't locate the station again.

"What a damn' shame," I said. "But I wonder where the hell they got news about us." The more I thought about it the more puzzled I was.

By next morning the duty helmsman had passed the story on. The whole ship was buzzing with it. But during the day I talked to Sparks about it again. "I'm surprised we haven't been in the news again to-day," I said. "You know, you young blighter, if you hadn't been on the bridge at the time I would have sworn that it was a hoax of yours." I thought Sparks looked at me a little queerly. Suddenly he burst out laughing. And then he spilt the beans. It *had* been a practical joke. He and Johnnie Stephens, the third engineer, had rigged a line from my set to the radio room. Stephens, his voice disguised by a handkerchief, had read the phoney news. Their only worry had been that I wouldn't switch on, as they didn't want to excite my suspicions by asking me to. It was a good joke, but I told Sparks not to tell the crew. They would have been thoroughly disappointed had they known. And morale was becoming an increasingly important factor aboard. To this day most of them firmly believe they were "national hook-up" news that evening.

Saturday, August 23, saw us 1,387 miles from Manzanillo. Dawn also showed us chaos in the convoy. During the night No. 4's bridle had slipped, the sweeper had veered away to port, a hundred yards out of line so that it was riding almost abeam of No. 3. I didn't like the look of it at all. And worse, the barometer was dropping fast and by the look of the high mares' tail clouds stringing out above us we were in for a dusting from the north-east. Unless we adjusted the twisted bridle quickly we should almost certainly lose No. 4 in the approaching storm.

The boat party got away at 8.30. They were getting quite proficient now and seemed to have lost their initial fears. They had now hung knotted lines which trailed in the sea from each minesweeper. These could easily be picked up and avoided going alongside several times before a man was able to scramble aboard with a line.

By 10 o'clock the lifeboat was back aboard and No. 4 had been coaxed back into line. Then off went 2 and 3.

Miranda reported that the severed ends were hanging down into the water from each of the two minesweepers. Although we should have to retrieve these the first thing to be done was to recover the two drifting sweepers and try to hold them to No. 2 by means of the *Gray's* mooring lines. The weather was rapidly getting worse, and by the time the sweepers had been secured I could see we should have to move quickly to recover the severed tow-lines, or the sea would be too rough for us to do anything.

There was one coil of 10-inch manila aboard, so I decided to use this, but instructed Miranda only to try to get the bridles out of the water and leave the severed ends hanging down. While he was tackling this difficult job I had the coil of manila brought on deck and mustering all the available deck and engine-room hands had it stretched along the deck in an attempt to free it of turns and kinks. Even in normal conditions this would have been difficult enough and present conditions were very far from normal. However, to the accompaniment of much colourful language the job was eventually finished.

After a great deal of struggling we managed to coil half of this big rope down into the lifeboat. Being new and dry the remaining half would float as we paid it out and the lifeboat towed it towards No. 2 minesweeper. At each end of the spare tow-line there was an eye-splice around a large, heavy iron thimble. These of course would not float, so I ordered the Mate to make the end still on board the *Gray* fast to an empty oil-drum before casting it into the water. With very little freeboard the lifeboat got away after a bad moment when the *Gray* heeled over so far I thought it would be pressed under. The rope snaked after them towing the black, bobbing oil-drum. It was probably the biggest swell the boat had yet been launched in, but it rode it beautifully. The tops of the rollers were level with half the height of our masts so that when the boat party had crawled up the long green smooth slope and over the foam-flecked top they disappeared for a whole minute. All we could see was the tiny drum slithering up to the crest behind as though it was driven by some mysterious motive power inside itself. And then it too disappeared and we were alone, swaying like a pendulum between the green walls. Then slowly the *Gray* was raised on to a crest and away astern I saw the lifeboat, also on a crest. But something was wrong. The oil drum was no longer obediently following them. It had broken loose and was rushing rapidly away to leeward. And then I realized with dismay that the 15-lb. steel eye had sunk. Not only was it dragging the big rope under; it was actually hauling the lifeboat rapidly astern.

They had its seven-knot engine roaring at full power in a desperate effort to hold the rush of rope, but it was as useless as a clockwork toy. Fathom after fathom of our brand-new rope, gathering speed as it went, was drawn under. For several seconds tug and lifeboat reached a crest together and I saw that the weight of rope was in danger of dragging the whole boat under. The gunwale was down close to the water and the propeller was racing ineffectively.

A roller separated us for a while; then I saw that the boat party had cut the lashing and was frantically paying out the rest of the 400-foot rope which was coiled down in the boat. It whipped away in a few seconds and briefly allowed them to make some headway. When next I saw them between rollers they were wallowing low in the water. It was pointless signalling to Miranda. He wouldn't have seen the blinker. But he did the obvious thing. He steered the almost unmanageable lifeboat down to No. 3, passing astern of No. 2 high on the crest of a wave. When next they were in sight I saw through the glasses that they had succeeded in making the end fast to a mid-ship bollard on No. 3 minesweeper.

What a situation! There we were with our only spare tow-line hanging 800 feet down into the Pacific. Sea and weather were really dirty by this time, so I signalled Miranda to double up as best he could with the mooring lines between Nos. 2 and 3 minesweepers and bring his crowd back to the *Gray*. After a few more moments during which the lifeboat cavorted beside us, alternating between our Plimsoll line and a level with the boat-deck, we snatched them and the lifeboat back aboard.

It had been an abortive mission and now we had not only the two 400-foot broken tow-lines, but another dragging 800 feet to hold us back. It would have been madness to have got under way again with Nos. 2 and 3 joined only by short mooring lines. So I hove to to await an improvement in the weather.

Already our very unprofessional square sail was doing yeoman service, helping to steady the *Gray* in the heavier seas. Now I ransacked the ship for more sail material. My idea was to bend a trysail between the derrick and the main-mast. After doing this we also bent the lifeboat's mainsail to the mainstay abaft the funnel.

The two extra sails made quite a contribution, not in extra spread, but in stability and general comfort.

All that night we rolled through a heavy swell. It was the forerunner of even heavier weather of which our ominously falling barometer continued to warn us.

Next day when we were still hove to, our big sea bird, who had been slowly regaining strength in the engine-room, left us. His wing had now quite mended, and I decided his convalescence should end. In any case he seemed restless and whenever he was brought on deck tried to spread his wings. We had become quite attached to him despite his vicious manner and everybody lined the

116

rail to see him go. Casas had fortified him with a gargantuan meal before take-off and he looked eager to be away. But if we thought his launching was going to be a simple matter we were wrong.

Two of the crew tried first, holding him up by the rail, letting him smell the sea breeze and inviting him to take off voluntarily. But he refused to take the hint. Next they tried hurling him into the air, but he made no attempt to use his wings and flopped squawking on to the deck. More drastic measures followed. Our guest was gently flung far out over the rail. The breeze caught him, his big wings unfurled and he flew round the *Gray* in wide, graceful circles. He stayed with us all that day. During the night we heard him occasionally calling. Next morning he had gone.

Instead of abating, the weather got steadily worse and we were hove to for a further two days while the storm came howling down on us from the north-east, bringing a deluge of warm, stinging rain. I had already ordered all loose equipment lashed down, had the ventilators removed, the holes plugged and all weatherside doors screwed down. Within a few hours mountainous seas had risen round us and the wind was shrieking in the rigging at seventy-five miles an hour. The *Gray* rolled and pitched more violently than we had yet experienced, and even moving about the ship became quite a perilous adventure. Our high bow never quite dipped under, but every time we rolled green seas swept over the rail and up through the scupper holes; most of the time we were awash fore and aft.

I was very anxious about the fate of the tows and when I looked astern I could see, through the driving rain and spray, the sweepers rearing up and taking a great deal of water. Like the *Gray* their decks were continuously awash. I thought it would be a miracle if the gear survived this lot. But for once it was not the tow gear that at 8.20 a.m.

caused me grave anxiety. I was startled to see that No. 2 minesweeper was down by the head. She was rising sluggishly to the seas and looked as if she had made a great deal of water. Here was a nice mess. If we did nothing about it she might founder. And if that happened her weight on the tow-ropes would bring Nos. 3 and 4 crashing into No. 1. They would very quickly hole one another and the *Gray* would be left with a single wire disappearing over her stern, on the end of which would be dangling four shattered wrecks. It would certainly have been an easy way out. All that we should then have had to do would be to cut the wire adrift and let the four sweepers slide to the bottom of the Pacific.

But it would have been a disappointing end. Having sailed so far with this troublesome convoy I was not going to abandon a single minesweeper without a struggle. Not for nothing had I risked my crew's lives. To have washed my hands of them at this stage would have made the worries and struggle of the past fortnight meaningless.

I wasn't very happy about ordering a boat party out in the teeth of a gale but when the first force of the storm had spent itself there was a lull. The sea was still angry and mountainous but the wind had ceased. So I called for volunteers. There was not much doubt about the response. My old boat party—Miranda, Romanin, Jones, Vincent, Todd and Whiteman agreed to go. Their confidence in the lifeboat seemed to be growing daily. They took a portable motor-pump and were quickly swept away astern and out of sight.

For what seemed ages I didn't see them again. But several minutes later when No. 2 climbed drunkenly out of a trough and staggered momentarily on the crest of a big wave I saw six tiny figures safely aboard her. They were there three hours! When finally they cast off and started making back for us I was glad to notice that the sweeper was no longer so far down by the head.

When we had plucked them out of the boiling sea, Miranda told me they had reached the sweeper none too soon. She was leaking badly and had six feet of water in her. They pumped out four feet, couldn't find the leak, but when they left she wasn't making any more water. I suspected she had either started some timbers or that the water might be coming in where the stern glands had been plugged; I determined to give her a more thorough inspection as soon as the weather permitted.

That night the storm had another lash at us. The *Gray* bucked like a horse, but the minesweepers stayed doggedly with us. Through the flying spray, between torrential squalls, we could see their lights describing large arcs with never more than two in sight at any one time.

All next day the wind screamed and the Pacific heaved. It was difficult to do much more than retain one's equilibrium. Despite loud crashes of crockery and pans from the galley Willie Dominguez continued to serve us with regular and surprisingly well-cooked meals.

By this time we were well off course, but by next morning the storm had blown itself out. Only a long, heavy swell remained. At 9 a.m. Nos. 3 and 4 celebrated the calmer weather by breaking away again. Now I was faced with the dual task of recovering them and retrieving the dangling 800-foot tow-rope for which I knew hand-operated block and tackle would not be enough. The only alternative power we had at our disposal was the after-capstan on the *Gray* herself. It was located on our after-deck and meant backing in astern to within a few yards of No. 3 sweeper. It would be a tricky operation but I decided to give it a try. The manila was too valuable to abandon. It was our only spare 10-inch rope and we were going to need it badly long before we reached Palmyra.

I called the crew together and held a conference. Carefully, and as simply as I knew how, I explained just what I proposed doing. I gave every man a particular job and impressed on them that one slip-up might lose us the whole convoy. The plan was quite simple.

After the lifeboat party had joined up the two drifting sweepers I was going to steam slowly round in as wide a circle as I could make. Then before the minesweepers had time to drift in to the centre of the circle I would quickly go astern and back inside the circle to get my steam-driven capstan as close as was safe to No. 3. Meanwhile the boat-party would attach a 3-inch messenger to the end of the hanging tow-rope and run it across to the *Gray* when the capstan would take up the slack. The men on No. 3 would then cut the lashing on the hanging tow-rope and we would steam out clear of the sweepers before reeling in the whole 800 feet. All this would need to be done very quickly for there was always the danger that the sweepers might begin to run down on to us. I briefed Alonso to prepare a couple of empty oil drums and told him that if I had to steam out in a hurry he was to lash the drums to the end of the messenger and throw drums and messenger into the sea clear of the propeller. Everybody nodded very intelligently. Yes, they understood exactly what they had to do.

The first half of the operation went off with naval precision. Miranda took the boat away and an hour later signalled that Nos. 3 and 4 were attached to us again. I made a wide circle and when in position rang the telegraph for "Half astern" and while our propeller churned the Pacific, edged slowly back toward No. 3, now less than a cable's-length away. Closer and closer we crawled, 300 yards . . . 200 . . . 100—then at 70 yards I saw that Nos. 1 and 2 sweepers were rapidly bearing down on us. I slammed over the telegraph, the *Gray* shivered and came to a stop. Again I circled, again we backed in. This time the sweepers held their positions better. The lifeboat picked up the messenger from No. 3. But again we were defeated.

The lifeboat motor chose this critical moment to splutter temperamentally and finally stop. Two minutes later Whiteman had coaxed it to life again but the opportunity had been lost. Already the *Gray* was making her third circle. And this time they got the messenger across, the capstan wheezed and the wet, slippery line reeled aboard. But we were still not quite quick enough. The sweepers influenced by the weight of the tow-ropes between them began to sweep quickly towards us. I had to get out again quickly; I prayed that Alonso would remember his emergency role. But our hurried departure precipitated chaos. Alonso panicked and flung the drums overboard amidships. Then in his confusion he let go our end of the messenger. He had forgotten to attach it to the drums. At the same moment the men on No. 3, assuming that we had made the line fast and were towing it away clear, cut the lashings holding the end of our precious heavy tow-rope to the minesweeper's bollard. We might still have saved it, but when Alonso had dropped the messenger it was promptly drawn into our threshing propeller. I rang down "Stop" but it was too late. The line was cut like cotton; messenger and tow-rope sank silently to the bottom of the Pacific. All that was left of the carefully planned operation were two battered oil drums bobbing in the swell. If any more tow-lines carried away now, we had not a fathom of replacement.

If Nos. 3 and 4 were to be joined to us again there was now only one way by which it could be done. Somehow the two dangling halves of tow-rope hanging into the sea from Nos. 2 and 3 would have to be raised and rejoined.

It took Miranda and his assistants the rest of the day. But they did it. They found that several yards of both rope ends had unravelled—they had to be cut off before the lines could be linked with two big bowline knots. By evening we were under way again.

Midnight that night we were more than half-way to Palmyra. Manzanillo was 1,850 miles astern. But the Chief Engineer had bad news for me. We had used more than half our fuel, he said, not enough remained to get us to Palmyra with continuous steaming, let alone stoppages and manœuvring to pick up breakaways. Now I was really worried. Once more the temptation to slip the minesweepers came to me. But having struggled with them half-way I was not going to abandon them now. So I decided to steam on as close to Palmyra as our depleted fuel would get us, and in the meantime review the situation.

Dawn, Saturday, August 30, brought us our best weather since the first week out of Manzanillo. The sun shone in a cloudless sky, a light breeze caressed the gentlest lazy swell we had yet seen. The Pacific was certainly smiling on the *Gray* this day. I looked up at our two sails proudly doing their bit. Then it struck me. Why not more sail. If our fuel could not take us to Palmyra perhaps the north-east trades might.

I called Romanin. "Search the ship," I said. "Collect every yard of material that will hold wind; anything that we can make into a sail."

Romanin took me at my word. An hour later he had accumulated an astonishing pile of oddments. There were parts of old tarpaulins, the lifeboat cover, vegetable locker covers, small pieces of canvas, denims and spare blankets. Then I told the elderly Diaz to get busy with his needle and sail thread. Sparks popped his head out of the radio shack. "Are you starting a laundry, sir?" he inquired with a grin. Five minutes later he, too, was wielding a needle. During the afternoon the first of the sail factory's products began to come off the assembly line. The first looked like Jacob's multi-coloured coat. It comprised some denims unpicked at the seams and sewn on to bits of canvas. It was a splendid piece of improvisation. By the end of the day no less than ten make-shift sails had been produced and set.

They billowed courageously from both masts, the derrick, the stays, and the railings. Then I had several blankets sewn together and set them between the shrouds and the mainmast. But they were so threadbare the wind blew straight through them. So I doubled them. It worked.

But still I wasn't satisfied. We could do better than this. The following morning I appealed for more spare clothing and had the sails we made from it strung round the framework of the tug's disused gun emplacement abaft the funnel. Then I asked the crew to hang their laundry where it would best catch the wind. I told them to peg the ends of their trousers when they hung them out so they could fill out like windsocks and make a small contribution. The crew must have thought I had taken leave of my senses. But they co-operated willingly enough. Soon the *Gray* looked like a cross between a pirate and a carnival ship.

Someone else must have thought so too. Because next morning Sparks came to me with a big twinkle in his eye. "Have you seen the forepart of the square sail, sir?" he asked.

"Why? What's particularly unusual about it?" I said disinterestedly.

"Just you come and have a look, sir," he persisted, grinning like a schoolboy.

So I went down, grumbling, on to the fo'c'sle-head with him, and looked up at our biggest sail. Neatly painted in bold white paint was an enormous skull and crossbones.

"Good God!" I exclaimed. "Who the devil did that?"

But Sparks pretended he didn't know. My first impulse was to have it removed immediately. We looked near enough to a pirate ship without the traditional emblem. I was concerned about the repercussions it might bring should we pass another vessel. But Sparks persuaded me to leave it there. "We're well off the shipping lanes here, sir," he insisted. "It can't do any harm and the crew are tickled pink." So grudgingly I let it stay. The only condition I made was that it should be hauled up immediately we sighted another ship.

Already our galaxy of sail was helping the *Gray* along. I estimated it gave us another half knot, but equally important, it steadied the tug quite a lot and eliminated much of the jolting we had experienced earlier on the towlines. I never dreamed I would ever cross the Pacific under sail again. My last "wind-bag" had done a proud twelve knots in the trades.

But our fantastic rig would not help us to anything like that in this modern tug.

# Chapter Eight

FOR two days we rolled on without a breakaway. With the help of the sails our speed crept back to four knots. No longer did we reckon our position from Mexico. It was only of a small group of atolls ahead of us—Palmyra—that we thought now. Midday, August 31, we were just 1,545 miles from it.

Still concerned about our precarious fuel situation I began to consider possible nearer islands where we might pick up oil. Honolulu, to the north, was one. But I ruled it out because it meant steaming up into temperate areas where more boisterous weather might be encountered. It would have spelt disaster to our weakened tow-lines.

I thought of Fanning Island, 200 miles south-east of Palmyra. It is a lonely British cable station and according to the Sailing Directions had a good anchorage and a workshop. But it would have taken us further south than I wanted to go.

The only other alternative was another speck on the ocean, Washington Island, also British. It lay 130 miles south-east of Palmyra. The manual told me that holes in its coral shelf anchorage had claimed numerous ships' anchors; not a very encouraging prospect as we might have no power to save ourselves in a sudden storm—assuming we did get there. Nevertheless I decided to risk it and call for a tanker to take fuel to us there from Palmyra. So we altered course a few degrees south for Washington Island. It was just 1,485 miles away, only 60 miles nearer than Palmyra—but 60 miles meant a lot to us now.

September was just four hours old when trouble came again. It was a superb moonlight night. The moon shone on the four little ships behind us and their bows set up four sparkling cascades of phosphorescence as they rode a gentle swell. When I relieved Miranda at 4 a.m. the scene almost made me feel poetic. Not for long. At 4.5 the ominous familiar change of pitch in the *Gray's* engines made me look quickly aft. I was just in time to see Nos. 3 and 4 dropping away astern. Almost rebelliously they seemed to roll away, the moonlight glinting on their portholes.

We stood by until daylight. The boat party which went away at 7.20 reported that No. 3 bridle had carried away at the fatal U-bolt and that the chain preventers had also snapped. We had used all our spare bridle wire now. They repaired it with a few inadequate fathoms of anchor-chain which they found in the minesweepers' lockers. I made Jacobsen join the boat party this time. Romanin had complained for so long he couldn't get an ounce of work out of the tall, lazy Swede, I decided to put him in a position where he would be compelled to pull his weight. But he proved a bigger menace than a help. His clumsy, awkward disinterestedness very nearly upset the boat. Later Miranda pleaded with me never to imperil the boat with him again.

I was beginning to notice through the glasses that much of the repair crews' earlier efficiency was fading. This day I saw them make a thoroughly lackadaisical and very impermanent repair. Angry, I told Romanin when he came back, that if I saw any further examples of this I would send him out again. He looked at me, and as he walked sulkily away I heard him mutter: "Son of a bitch."

This sort of thing would not do. I told him to go to my cabin. Drenched with spray and still in his life jacket he stood in the doorway, breathing resentment. But I couldn't allow this blatant piece of insubordination to pass. I knew the wearing routine of breakaways, delay and hazardous, exhausting lifeboat sorties were beginning to have their effect on the crew's spirits. But I knew too, we had loads more trouble ahead of us. If I overlooked minor demonstrations of revolt like this it would be the beginning of the end. So I demanded: "Did you call *me* a son of a bitch, Romanin?"

"No, sir," he said fiercely. "I *did* say son of a bitch, but I was referring to the possibility of having to go back, not to you, sir." I could only accept his word and he went defiantly away toward the mess-room.

Next morning the boat party paid the price of the previous day's slovenliness. Nos. 3 and 4 broke adrift again. It was 3.30 a.m. Again we waited for dawn. Thankfully the sea was still moderate. But this was no ordinary breakaway. The entire line between Nos. 2 and 3 had gone. We had not a fathom of spare manila. This almost certainly, I thought, was where we said good-bye to our two most reluctant tows.

Then I remembered several lengths of 3-inch steel wire which were held in brackets round the *Gray's* after-bulwarks. The U.S. Navy had probably left it there. There were four 98-foot lengths of it. It might get us a few hundred miles nearer Palmyra. I told Alonso to have it laid out on the after-deck and two lengths joined together. But nobody, not even Alonso, knew how to splice wire. So I left the bridge and did it myself. The bewildered crew watched, intrigued, all except Romanin who helped me turn the wire as required.

By 1 o'clock the boat party had connected the 196-foot wire between Nos. 2 and 3 and we resumed our voyage. But now even three knots was a departed luxury. The shortened tow-line between Nos. 2 and 3 forced me to reduce revolutions still further and, to prevent the short length of steel wire carrying away, brought our speed down to $2\frac{1}{2}$ knots. What an all-time low it was!

And now the wind was freshening again, the sea making. I radioed San Francisco that night: "MINESWEEPERS BROKEN AWAY NINE TIMES LAST TWELVE DAYS ALL SPARE

Back in the company's office 2,800 miles away there
must have been some anxious conferences over the Pacific
chart. Although I didn't know it then Colonel Gray had
returned to Manila. My signals were being relayed to
him through San Francisco. So it was several hours before
Colonel Gray sent a long reply piping back to our radio
shack. We must hang on to our troublesome charges, he
urged, for as long as was humanly possible.

By now we were so desperately in need of towing wire
that I seriously considered using the mainmast shrouds,
even if it meant letting the mast topple overboard. But in
the end I thought better of it.

September 3, our twenty-fourth day out, was trouble
free. We crawled sixty miles nearer to Washington Island.
The other event of note was Savarino's return to duty. It
was now a week since his thumb had been crudely amputated. But in that short time he had made a most remarkable recovery. The plastic cap I had stitched over
the stump had taken, the wound was healing rapidly and
almost all pain had gone. Down in the stokehold he soon
learned how to use his thumbless right hand.

Soon after daylight next morning we had our tenth and
biggest breakaway to date. This time No. 2's bridle broke
at the U-bolt and she joined the usual truants—Nos. 3 and
4—wallowing away astern of us. The 800-foot rope aft
of No. 1 hung down in the sea posing us an all-too-familiar
problem. I could see we were in for at least an eight-hour
delay. I decided to use it to transfer to the *Gray* some of
the diesel oil which the minesweepers were carrying as
ballast. The oil we burned—Bunker C—it was called—
was far heavier, but the engineers told me that by modify-
ing the injection jets which fed the oil into the furnace
they could safely burn a mixture of Bunker C and diesel.

Our first task was the recovery of the tow-line hanging

The most familiar sight of all: two minesweepers drifting away astern of the *Gray*

*Left*: Two of the crew go aloft to untangle a twisted sail. *Right*: The *Gray* as she looked to the

from the stern of No. 1. This was made relatively easy by hauling her in close up to the stern of the *Gray*, running a messenger from the dangling rope to our capstan, then winding it up out of the sea on to the minesweeper's deck.

Sluggishly, foot by foot, it came, almost grudgingly, out of the blue depths, green with slime and festooned with sea growth. Then I slacked off No. 1, chased after the three renegades, the boat party passed a line from No. 1 to No. 2 and the heavy, sodden manila was hove across by hand.

Meanwhile I winched No. 1 up almost to our stern rail and we ran an oil hose across to milk her of the little diesel she carried. We pumped it into the big cylindrical auxiliary tanks which lined our after-deck and which had long ago been emptied.

The operation was interrupted for an hour when the sweeper, rolling violently in the swell, began bumping alarmingly into our stern.

Quickly we paid out on the winch, and she floated clear. We used a longer hose after that and were able to keep the vicious little minesweeper at arm's length. By dusk we had transferred 1,500 gallons, almost all she held. Mixed with our own fuel it meant, perhaps, an extra day's steaming.

We had intended replacing the diesel ballast with sea water. But now it was almost dark, it would have to wait. We streamed out the tows, and set course again with No. 1, lightened of her ballast, pitching and rolling high out of the water.

As I called down the revolution increases to the engine-room to pick up our paltry safe speed of three knots, Cuesta's agitated voice, comically distorted by the telephone, appealed to me not to give the revolutions so quickly. "Please, we cannot keep up with you, sir," he wailed, almost tearfully.

"What the devil," I blurted back. "Haven't you got a ruddy rev. counter down there?"

But poor Cuesta was too upset to involve himself in long explanations. The full story had to wait until he came off duty, washed, changed, and smelling of soap, to the wardroom.

It appeared that the revolution counter had been unserviceable since soon after leaving Panama. But the conscientious Cuesta, afraid to tell me lest I thought it a reflection on his ability as an engineer, had sought alternative means of gauging his engine speed. He had drilled his staff to count the number of strokes of the big connecting rods to the minutes of the engine-room clock on the bulkhead above. This awkward procedure used two men. One stood with his eyes glued to the clock, the other beside the pounding connecting rods, counting the beats with his arms like a campus cheer leader. Across three thousand miles of Pacific calm and storm this astonishing pantomime had continued unknown to me. Cuesta didn't seem to appreciate my amusement at his reluctant admission. Even when I explained that the actual number of revolutions didn't matter a ha'porth of tar, it was merely careful acceleration I wanted, he continued to look miserable and crestfallen.

For nearly a week fate took pity on us. The weather held fine, the tows stayed dutifully with us and we wallowed towards Washington Island at a steady 70 miles a day. I almost found myself forgetting that we didn't have enough fuel to make a landfall. Just so long as the *Gray*'s engines rumbled away and all four minesweepers kept with us we were at least getting somewhere. We had all got into the way of living only from one day to the next.

September 7 gave us an incident that was a change from our routine of breakaways. And it very nearly left the ship without her mascot. Butch, who seemed more at home on the *Gray* than any of her crew, had developed the habit of sleeping on the foot-wide wooden rail above the bulwarks. She would make the four-foot leap from the deck, narrowly escape over-balancing into the sea, brace herself against the roll of the ship, and settle comfortably against a bollard. Even in the roughest sea some unconscious muscle control kept her there, dozing blissfully, for hours. When I had first spotted her rail technique in port I had wondered how far out to sea it would take to discourage the practice. But nothing the Pacific could let loose, we soon saw, could dislodge our independent-minded bitch.

But this day Butch's faculties must have been dulled by the tropical sun. Willie Dominguez came out of his galley with a bucketful of potato peelings, just in time to see an extra long roll catapult her overboard. I was on the bridge and as soon as I heard Dominguez's yell, slowed down and swung the convoy round. None of us thought she had a chance. If she wasn't sucked into the propeller she would be lucky to last a minute among the sharks which swarmed along beside us. There was a big rolling sea running which didn't help any either. But I decided Butch's loyalty had earned her the full humanity of a "Man overboard" search. I alerted the crew with the accident signal on the siren, posted look-outs and ordered the boat party to stand by.

Fifteen minutes later there was a jubilant shout from the masthead. The lookout had spotted the familiar brown and white head bobbing in the swell some yards off. But if the sharks, of which there seemed to be many more now we had stopped, had spared Butch so far there was a good chance the boat might reach her in time.

I couldn't see the little speck in the rollers from the bridge but the lookout directed us toward her. Hands more willing than usual launched the motor lifeboat in record time and a few minutes later they caught up with her, swimming strongly in the direction of Australia.

Wet and shivering Butch was brought back to the *Gray*. Tail thumping, she gambolled proudly from man to man as if to say, "It wasn't too bad, chaps, really, but I'm sure glad you didn't leave it much longer." For several days she basked in the glory and latent affection her ditching earned her, but kept well away from her old post on the rail. But dogs must have short memories. Before the week was out the lure of the rail was too much for her. Soon she was happily re-ensconced there as if nothing had happened. That dog had more lives than a cat.

The following day we had our first serious accident aboard. Strangely enough it came to the laziest man aboard—the unfortunate Jacobsen. He was lending his questionable assistance to a gang that was moving a pile of heavy oil drums. One slipped and crashed on to his foot. They carried him to me groaning with pain. His foot was badly swollen and although I wasn't certain, it looked as if it had been broken, but it was too painful to allow a proper examination. In the meantime I dressed it and put it in splints. Jacobsen, very sorry for himself, spent the rest of the voyage to Palmyra a casualty. Later he managed to hobble painfully about the ship, but his relief at being removed from the sphere of work must have more than compensated him for the pain he suffered.

830 miles from Washington Island on September 9, our thirtieth day out, events took a more serious turn. It began with something I had been dreading most—engine trouble. Several condenser cooling tubes blew out. The engineers feverishly tried to repair the damage. The tubes were a vital part. They took in sea water, distilling it to give us fresh water essential for the boilers. It was not a job that could be attempted while the engines were running.

By evening we were under way again, but Cuesta had

more bad news. The engines were deteriorating rapidly, he said, and unless we hove to for several major repairs very soon we would be without power altogether before long. Things looked black. And worse was to follow. Next morning No. 4 sweeper broke away. It was our eleventh in three weeks. And this time it wasn't the bridles. The tow-rope between Nos. 3 and 4 had finally parted in the middle.

We lost half a day retrieving her and used our last 120-foot length of wire to replace the now useless rope. The loss of our last full 800-foot span of rope between tows whittled the overall length of the convoy down to barely 300 yards. We were a thoroughly ragged flotilla now. The perfect stations the minesweepers had so proudly held as we steamed out of Panama Bay six weeks before were gone for ever. A harbour dredge wouldn't have dipped her ensign to us now.

Again I used the delay in picking up the minesweeper to get more diesel oil across to the *Gray's* perilously low tanks. We couldn't get alongside No. 2 to take out the 1,500 gallons she held, so pumped it across in two stages through No. 1. When the oil was safely in No. 1's tanks we short-hauled her and ran the hose across to the *Gray*. After No. 4 had been recovered and was again part of the convoy I steamed round and coming up on her from astern took some of her oil too. It was rather like a dog biting its tail. No dog was ever as desperate as the *Gray*.

The circle was now so tight with only 300 yards of tow-line I had only a few minutes before the four sweepers drifted in on us and I had to steam out and come round again. In all, the operation gave us another 2,500 gallons of diesel—perhaps two more days' steaming—at best another 150 miles. But even mixed with our own dwindling heavy oil we hadn't enough. Insufficient, that was, to last at our present dawdling two-and-a-half to three knot progress. Free of her troublesome burden the *Gray* could have opened up to her economical cruising speed of more than sixteen knots and reached either Washington or Palmyra Islands, comfortably. The temptation to do so took a lot of resisting. But again a dogged determination to drag my crippling charges as long as there was fuel in our tanks and wind to fill our sails, prevailed. And now it was certain we should be out of fuel in a few more hundred miles, I had second thoughts on my Washington Island decision. If we were going to need rescuing in mid-ocean better to be nearer Palmyra which was closer than Washington Island to Honolulu, the only possible course of rescue craft. So once again we headed for Palmyra. It was 860 miles away. In her Navy days the *Gray* could have done that in just forty-eight hours.

That night I did some desperate thinking. At all costs Cuesta's engines must be kept going. Even if it meant burning wood. Wood? Why hadn't I thought of it before? There were gratings, bulwarks and even cabin doors if necessary. It had been done before.

I sent for the Chief Engineer and put my suggestion to him. Thinking wistfully of his once-splendid engine he agreed, glumly, that if necessary we *could* convert to wood. It would have to be cut into one-foot lengths and the engineers would have to remove the oil injectors, he said, dolefully.

Next day, September 11, was overcast, sultry and squally. I made a survey of our timber situation and decided that the gratings were the least indispensable. That morning Romanin had them chopped up into neat foot-long sticks. They were never used. The engines themselves gave out before the fuel.

And now the minesweepers gave us a new problem. Apparently tired for the time being of breaking away they tried new tactics. They began filling with water so rapidly it looked as if the *Gray* might well be left alone very shortly. Their long immersion together with the stress the towing bridles had imposed on their hulls was straining their timbers.

At daylight on September 12, all but No. 1 were quickly settling down by the bow. We slowed down and rushed the motor boat away with our portable pumps. They were only just in time. Eight feet of water swished about inside their hulls. It was rising fast. Another twelve hours and they would have gone for ever. It took the best part of the day to get most of the water out of them and the heartbreaking feature of the whole tedious business was that with the exception of No. 2, Miranda couldn't find the least trace of a leak. The misleading thing was that they all began to go down by the head first. The boat party naturally concentrated their search forward, but in fact we later discovered the water was coming in aft through the supposedly sealed stern glands. Pumping out now became an irksome new daily burden.

For some days now Sparks had been trying to raise Palmyra radio station. I was anxious to know what rescue and oiling facilities were there. But although he was in daily contact with both Sydney and San Francisco, both thousands of miles away, there was not so much as an answering squeak out of Palmyra, less than 750 miles away. It was a mystery we were not to solve for another week.

It made us feel lonely and cut-off from the outside world. Daily our plight was becoming steadily more and more desperate. And with the latest shortening of the tows the highest speed I dared risk now was two knots. With the help of the current and our makeshift sails we were making barely fifty miles a day—on bad days less than twenty miles. At this rate it would take more than a fortnight to cover the distance to Palmyra, but on the 13th Cuesta reported he had only eleven days' steaming left in his fuel tanks. In fact they were getting so low any excessive rolling was starting to swill the oil about the bottom of the tanks away from the out-feed pipe to the boilers. The result was that every time a roller bigger than the rest heeled us the oil spray to the fires was interrupted.

And now another more ugly trouble was showing itself. The crew were getting restless. It had probably been boiling up slowly for some time, and, too concerned with our latest problems, I hadn't been aware of it. But now the full impact of a fo'c'sle full of men who didn't really understand or have any interest in the sea began to hit me. I knew they had been regularly terrified by the numerous hazardous lifeboat excursions in dangerous seas to recover lost tows. But apparently many of the men I had ordered to join the boat parties had come back from each launching among the sharks gripped with fear. And now word had spread that we hadn't enough fuel to make Palmyra there was a lot of disquieting talk in the men's mess-room.

The spirit of three weeks back had gone. Our misfortunes were beginning to prey on their minds and I began to hear whispers that some of them never expected the *Gray* to see land again. There was only one thought in most heads now—self-preservation before all else. And to a crew in this frame of mind the extreme lengths to which I was going to keep four minesweepers with us to the bitter end just didn't make sense. To their way of thinking, the sweepers were just four millstones not worth balancing against thirty men's lives.

Although I knew many of them were loyal to me there were elements I couldn't trust. I became more acutely aware of the feeling in the next few days. I noticed little cliques forming. For the first time the Americans and the Filipinos seemed to be mixing less. I became conscious of suspicious-looking discussions among little bands who got together at every opportunity and always broke up guiltily when I approached. At one stage I wondered if they were planning mutiny or even cutting the tow-lines, but they must have known that either course would certainly have meant a long stretch in a Philippines prison. In any case mutiny wouldn't have helped them much. My officers were still behind me and not a man among the others could sail and navigate the *Gray*.

Once a week I used to open the crew's "slop chest" a sort of miniature canteen from which they could buy anything from clothing, soap and cigarettes to chocolate and writing material. It had always been the signal for wild skylarking, bantering, and good-humoured leg-pulling. But now the slop chest was opened in surly silence. There was bitter rivalry to buy its little remaining stock.

During the day there were several near-fights. Where words had settled an argument a fortnight ago, fists wanted to do the job now. Even on duty there were quarrels. Only my presence prevented what would have been half a dozen savage slugging matches. On one occasion Todd jumped in ahead of Rodriguez for the job of controlling the electric winch which hauled up the lifeboat. Although exacting, it was a relatively easy job; Rodriguez guarded it jealously and no one had ever dared dispute his right to it. The two leapt toward each other arguing with their faces a foot apart, fists clenched. Tensely the whole ship stopped work to watch. Openly, everybody wanted to see a fight. If nothing else, it would have relieved the tension. But in the end they sorted it out among themselves with stinging, bitter words, and the crowd dispersed, disappointed. I was glad. There are times at sea when it is as well to let a fight go on. It can clear the air. But although I wouldn't have stopped Todd and Rodriguez, it would have been bad for morale for the Filipinos who outnumbered us all to see two Americans fighting.

There was nearly another scrap between Whiteman and Martin—again, two Americans. Whiteman was warming the lifeboat engine as it hung on the davits. Martin accidentally let the tricing lines holding it slip, nearly shooting

Whiteman into the sea. Cursing, "I'll get you for that, you bastard," Whiteman leapt back on to the deck brandishing his fists. But eighteen-year-old Martin, muscular and well-developed for his age, was ready for Whiteman. "Come on then, you big lug, I'm ready for you," he swore back. The two really looked like business. But again something, probably my presence, seemed to stop them. They slunk away cursing each other. But it wasn't forgotten. For days after that the two carried on a personal vendetta until eventually time healed the matter.

I noticed too that Romanin was becoming bitterly jealous of the negro, Jones. The big, jet-black six-footer was the only man aboard unworried by our predicament. He worked on like one of his slave ancestors, so hard I had often to stop him, I was so afraid he would break down. But he wasn't happy unless he was doing the toughest job on hand. Romanin seemed deeply resentful of his growing efficiency. I knew he felt I was letting Jones show him up in front of the crew, but it is hard to keep a good man down. Fortunately Romanin's bitter feelings developed into nothing more serious.

September 17, 445 miles from Palmyra, our noon position was 9° 30' N., 155° 26' W. and although we weren't to know it at the time, this was to be an historic day for our ill-starred voyage. We had our thirteenth and last breakaway. It was just after 1 o'clock in the morning when No. 4 made a lone break for freedom. This time it was the bridle that carried away. There was a moderate sea running and we had her back at the end of the line a few hours later.

The afternoon brought more misfortune. I discovered from my noon position that we had been caught in an easterly set that was knocking more than a knot off our already snail-like progress. I am not a fatalist but it began to seem that the *Gray* and her four minesweepers were just not meant to reach their destination. So near to Palmyra this latest setback seemed the cruellest blow fate had yet dealt us. I altered course 25 degrees to the southward to get out of the progress-destroying current, but for several days it slashed our daily mileage by nearly a third.

Now food and water began to run short. We had been nearly forty days at sea from Manzanillo. Our stores and drinking water tanks were running alarmingly low. So I introduced rationing. The men had been grossly extravagant with water in their showers despite numerous warnings. Now I was forced to have it turned off completely for several hours a day. At the same time I told Dominguez to cut down our food. Previously fishing had been a sport aboard. Now it became a deadly serious priority to fill our depleted larder.

Everybody was encouraged to try. New types of harpoons were invented, trolling gear was developed, and soon a wide assortment of fish from nine-foot madly flailing sharks to dolphin and other tasty tropical fish of all the colours of the rainbow, came aboard. Easiest to catch were dolphins. Three to six feet long, they were harpooned and hauled aboard in such profusion Dominguez had to start stocking his refrigerator with them. Willie himself became one of our most expert fishermen. At first he found the sharks were just straightening his steel hooks. But he quickly manufactured bigger ones. The deck outside his galley after that became a thoroughly perilous spot. It was rarely free of huge, ugly-jawed sharks snapping viciously and threshing their life away, capable of snapping off an arm or a leg up to a few seconds before they finally expired. But as food most of us ranked shark pretty low. It was tough and strong-flavoured. It reminded me of my sailing days when sometimes we had had to stomach it or eat nothing. Even the memory of it made my stomach twist. Dolphin made a far tastier meal, as did bonito. Lightly fried both made excellent eating. We didn't abandon shark catching altogether though. Sharkskin makes an excellent medium for cleaning wooden rails. I told Alonso to get the men using it on the *Gray*. But it was not a very popular order, and after I had watched a few half-hearted attempts to revive the shine on our grimy woodwork I didn't mention the subject again. I rather think most of the sharkskins were mysteriously dropped back into the Pacific.

September 18 took us another painful sixty-seven miles nearer Palmyra, which we still couldn't raise on the radio. Feeling among the crew was running high and manifested itself in many ways. On the 19th it looked as if it was all over. The engines after a convulsive splutter died out altogether. Thoroughly fed-up I seized the telephone and called up the harassed Engineer. "It is the fuel pumps, sir," he said. "Something is blocking them. It will take us half a day to fix."

If he had said it would take a week there would have been nothing I could have done about it. It was in fact a relief to hear that there was still life in our sorely tried pistons. For a moment I had imagined the engines had given up the ghost finally and for ever.

For ten hours we drifted westward with only our sails to help us. The *Gray* sounded uncannily silent with only the whirr of her generators, the hiss of steam, the creaking and flapping of the sails. The crew exchanged meaningful glances. Those who were within sight glanced up at me as if to say: "Now get us out of this mess if you can." But the *Gray's* own very efficient bush telegraph soon told everybody that it was not quite the end yet.

During those ten hours while Cuesta, asthmatical Gonzalez, Schmidt and Stephens worked like fiends down below in the swelter of the engine-room, the *Gray's* sails gave her just half a knot. We made a little over five miles. It was just enough speed to give us steerage way and to keep the tug ahead of the four minesweepers. To amuse ourselves we checked the speed by timing the progress of pieces of wood which we dropped over the side. Miranda would stand on the fo'c'sle-head with a good supply of timber and I would station myself aft on the stern rail with my stopwatch. After a warning yell from the fo'c'sle-head I would watch the wood, starting the watch when I saw the splash. At first it didn't look as if the wood was going to move. It just rose and fell on the lazy swell without any apparent movement. But after half a minute had ticked slowly by I saw it was coming aft and several minutes later it went sluggishly past the stern. A quick sum told us it was just over half a knot. A further calculation showed me our sails would take us to Palmyra in just over a month at this rate. It was a course I preferred to see on paper only.

Late in the afternoon there was a rumble from the bowels of the *Gray*. A few seconds later our engines thundered to life again, and we moved off into the dusk at our former two knots. When Cuesta poked his weary face out of the engine-room hatch for the first time in twelve hours that evening it was to bring further bad tidings. The repair job they had just done was only the least of our engine troubles. Within three days we should have to heave to for a much longer overhaul he told me. It was with some relief that I saw my elderly engineer loping off to his cabin. The sight of him and the news he almost invariably brought up out of that fetid oily world of his were beginning to prey on my mind.

# Chapter Nine

JUST 375 miles—less than 90 minutes by air—separated us from Palmyra Island on September 20th when the engines gave up. I was stretched out on my bunk, trying to get some sleep, but with a hundred problems tearing through my mind, I was incapable of more than a fitful doze. One minute we were vibrating with the rhythm from the engine-room, the next minute there was an ominous silence.

I reached the deck just as Cuesta's oily, panic-stricken face popped out of the engine-room hatch.

"It is terrible, sir, the oil, it is not reaching the bearings, they are not getting the lubrication. The bearings they are so hot the whole engine may seize up. It is terrible. What are we going to do?"

"You've just got to get them started again," I told him. "I don't care how long it takes, but do something, improvise, anything, but for Christ's sake give me power for a few more days."

Then Stephens and Schmidt climbed grimly up out of the silent engine-room. Schmidt was very excited. He looked more like a German than I had ever noticed before. Through his thinning sandy hair he ran his oily hands. "It is very serious, sir. We have driven and driven those engines all these weeks. But this time it is going to be a big job to repair them. We have so few spares. It will take days."

I looked despairingly at Stephens, searching for just a ray of hope in this moment of utter gloom. Tall and lean he stood there, thoughtfully drawing on a cigarette. His eyes were on the white caps of the Pacific. "I reckon we can do something with them," he drawled. "Give us a day and a half."

For the second time in three days the *Gray* reverted to her only alternative means of propulsion—her sails. Without them we should have been lost. A little tattered they were becoming, but still proudly wind-filled, dragging a reluctant, sluggish half-knot out of the Pacific. For thirty-six hours we drifted engineless, while the blazing-hot equatorial sun beat down on our decks. At 7° 18′ N. we were only 438 miles from the Equator and verging on the doldrums. Our staunch friend, the north-east trade, no longer blew with such unfailing vigour. The wind came in fits and starts and its direction began to veer through as much as sixty degrees in an hour.

Between its spasms light breezes which just gave us steerage way saved us from complete stoppage. I felt like Coleridge's Ancient Mariner, only far less picturesque. We were a crippled, hapless convoy of five, alone, hundreds of miles from the nearest shipping lane, at the mercy of the biggest ocean in the world. Had another ship sighted us, its officer of the watch would have had apoplexy. Approaching us from ahead, first he would have seen, rising out of the Pacific, a set of patchwork sails, followed quickly by a huge skull and cross-bones, then the grey hull of a streamlined modern tug adorned with blankets, tarpaulins, and weird, flapping bits of canvas. And beyond he would have seen strung untidily away astern, four small grey vessels, like some mysterious fishing fleet.

But we knew from the crackling signals that Sparks sat sifting hour after hour, that there wasn't a ship for at least five hundred miles.

The engines had stopped at 9 a.m. on the 20th. All that day, all night, and all next day we drifted. The only sounds were the creak of the yard, the sigh of the wind in the shrouds, the gentle swish of the swell idling past our bows, an occasional shout, and from time to time the metallic clank of repairs from deep down in the engine-room. When Miranda shot the sun and plotted our position at noon on the 20th he was able to announce that we had crept exactly fourteen miles.

One of my chief worries was that during the lulls in the wind the *Gray* would stop altogether and the sweepers would drift down on to us. But fortunately the weather held good and although I had several bad frights we always managed to move ahead in time. With negligible forward speed to keep the tow-lines taut the sweepers began wandering crazily out of line. Once No. 2 set off on a pilgrimage of her own. She drifted down past No. 1, came alongside us, sat there for an hour or two then rolled away ahead of us. It turned the straight line of the convoy into a chaotic zig-zag until the wind freshened and we were able to overtake her. It was a narrow escape. For had No. 2 decided to drift across our bows we had insufficient steerage way on the *Gray* to have headed her off and the tow-lines would have been so inextricably tangled we would have had to cut them adrift.

Once again we amused ourselves by clocking our speed with pieces of wood. The answer was still the same —half a knot. But for our stopwatch and driftwood calculations none of us would have believed it. A vegetable box which Dominguez flung over the rail at midday was still alongside at 2 o'clock, had in fact drifted ahead by 3.

Our thirty-six hours under sail introduced us to another world of which we had been unaware while steaming. It was the fascinating realm of the dark, rolling sea under us. We knew that the *Gray* was being accompanied by a small band of sharks and dolphins who hadn't left us for one minute in the forty days we had been on the way from Manzanillo. But now as we lay virtually stationary with our bow-wave reduced to a pathetic ripple we saw that the *Gray* was a far greater centre of attraction than we had imagined. It was as though every fish for a hundred miles around had been summoned to our side. The sea on all sides seethed with everything, from sharks and dolphins

*Left*: Looking aft from the bows.   *Right*: The exhausted boat's crew return to the *Gray*

No. 4 minesweeper in Palmyra

down to tiny schools of hundreds of brilliantly coloured fish which seemed to spend most of their time avoiding the jaws of their ugly big brothers. Most intriguing of all were the pilot and sucker-fish which religiously accompanied each shark. The pilots—they were less than eighteen inches long—fussed about almost in the sharks' jaws, blissfully confident that they were immune from their masters' big mouths, while the smaller suckers clung in handfuls along the grey bellies like limpets. Whenever one of the crew hooked a shark and whipped it madly threshing on to the deck, its pilot fish would be left bewildered and lost rushing in all directions, desperately looking for their employer. But he would return in due course only as a chunk of bait on another hook. After several minutes' fruitless search the pilots would disperse in confusion, probably to join some other shark.

By now we had several harpoonists of considerable skill. In fact they were landing dolphins so fast Dominguez's refrigerator could hold no more. We had evidence too that the same sharks had been following us doggedly for several weeks. They came aboard with half-healed scars on their backs which our harpoons had inflicted weeks before. Probably some of the more persistent among them had come the whole way from Mexico.

Thirty-six hours after the engines had stopped, a weary but now grinning figure emerged from the engine-room. Cuesta had good news.

"We have done it, sir," he said quietly, but with intense pride. "Sorry it took so long, but it was a slow job. You can have power again in ten minutes."

I felt like kissing his wrinkled old cheeks. "Well done, Cuesta," I said. "I shan't forget what you and the others have done down there in the last two days. You have got us out of a tight spot. Now you'd better go and get some sleep before you pass out."

Gratefully, he thanked me. There were tears in his eyes

as he stumbled off to his cabin. Poor old Cuesta. For a long time now I had known that the complexity of the *Gray's* engine-room was frankly too much for him. All his experience had been in far smaller, easier-to-manage craft. The men who really understood our engines were Stephens and Schmidt. Without them Cuesta would have been hopelessly out of his depth. Then, of course, there was Gonzalez.

We all felt sorry for Gonzalez. His ability and usefulness as Cuesta's first assistant was continuously over-shadowed by the dreadful handicap of his ailment. Knowing how acutely aware the other officers were of the likelihood of infection I had insisted he use his own eating utensils at meals. Gonzalez, painfully sensitive of the feeling toward him, was hurt. And since the first week out he had taken to collecting his meal and carrying it down to the engine-room there to dine alone, an unhappy, lonely figure among the huge shining cylinders he loved.

It was a relief to be under power again. As we throbbed away at two splendid knots I looked back in the darkness at the four mast-head lights scattered in disorder astern. Then as the slack lines tightened, the lights shuffled back into line and soon we were a relatively manageable convoy again. Our noon position 7° 16′ N., 157° 48′ W. was just about 270 miles to Palmyra and a little over 210 miles to Washington Island. Our tanks had 7,150 gallons of mixed oil and diesel, so it looked as if it would be Washington after all. At this time we were consuming around 1,800 gallons a day against the normal 2,800.

The atmosphere on board was becoming increasingly tense. And it didn't help any that Sparks still could not raise Palmyra radio. Apart from the very real need of rescue I wanted to confirm that the heavy oil fuel the company had ordered was, in fact, being held there for us.

It was all thoroughly unsettling. And worse still, the crew who kept up by some remarkable means with every fresh development, almost as quickly as I knew myself, were giving me fresh fears.

That night Alonso came to me looking very mysterious. He brought the most alarming news of the voyage.

"There is a lot of whispering among the men, sir. They are getting restless again. But worse, there is talk of arms aboard. I thought you should know."

"How long have you known about the arms," I asked, looking at him closely. I was half-wondering if perhaps Alonso had any sympathy for the mutinous inclinations of his compatriots, although I should have known that he was staunchly loyal to me.

"Two days, perhaps three, but I did not tell you before. I was not sure. But to-night I have heard more boasting about hidden revolvers. At first I did not take it seriously. To-night I realized that some of the men might mean business."

I thanked Alonso. "Don't tell any of the others," I warned him. "I think I can handle this."

This was an ugly development. I decided to search the ship at the first possible opportunity. But it was a difficult thing to do openly without exciting suspicion.

Fortunately the next day was a Sunday. Every Sunday I inspected the crew's quarters.

In her Navy days the *Gray* had had a crew of more than forty-five. The result was that the fo'c'sle where the men slept had a lot more lockers than they used. Fo'c'sle by the way was a misnomer. Their quarters were not under the fo'c'sle-head—their showers and toilets were—but were on the deck below the officers' cabins and wardrooms. It was into these I made some excuse to look this Sunday. I found nothing. And as I could give no good reason for prying into their private lockers I had to let my inspection stop there for the time being. But just as I was leaving I noticed Espinosa's locker half-open. I glanced casually inside. There gleamed a shining .45 revolver.

After that I decided to waste no further time with pretences. I made a snap check at 6 o'clock next evening. This time the gloves were off.

When I walked into their quarters only three men were there. They were darning socks and reading. Most of the others were still eating in the mess-room. But they weren't there long. One of the three slipped out as soon as I began searching the first locker. Before I was half-way through nearly the entire angry crew had tumbled into the fo'c'sle. I turned to face them.

"I will be quite honest with you," I told them. "I have come to search every man's locker for weapons of any description." And then I lied: "It is a precaution I am taking in your own interest. The ship will be searched by the Palmyra authorites when we arrive. If you are found to be concealing any weapons there will be serious trouble."

I then said that I proposed collecting all the arms aboard and keeping them under lock and key. "It would be far wiser," I added, knowing I was convincing nobody, "if the Master declared the whole lot. I will give a receipt for any gun or other weapon I take custody of."

A loud buzz of murmuring met this. It rose to an indignant chorus as I continued my search. Savarino, whose locker it was, thrust himself angrily to the front and stood defiantly beside it.

"You can't search this, sir," he said. "It is private." Here was a very different cocksure Savarino from the pain-wracked seaman who had beseeched me to tend his thumb three weeks earlier. I felt sorry he had such a short memory. But his fear that I might examine his locker had so convinced me he was hiding something I decided that this must be a test case.

"Stand aside!" I ordered him and rummaged quickly through an untidy pile of clothing, shaving gear, curios, and stockings and scarves he was taking home possibly to his wife in Manila. There was no weapon. I turned to his

148

bags. Savarino said they were locked and he had lost the key. "You'd better find it quickly," I told him and started on Vincent's locker.

Its owner appeared from nowhere. "You can look through all my bags, sir. I've got nothing," he said. I searched. He was right.

Whiteman was next. He was waiting for me. "I served in the Navy. My private effects were never interfered with then. I see no reason why *you* should," he said bitterly.

"Look, Whiteman," I said. "I wouldn't be doing this if there wasn't a damn good reason, so stop arguing." He too, had nothing.

By now the mumbling and protestations behind me were assuming more serious proportions. The crew weren't in a very pleasant mood. But I ignored them. In Ritter's grip I had my first haul. It was a wicked looking, long, thin stiletto. He said nothing when I took it.

I was searching the next locker when I saw a man make a sudden dive towards the *Gray's* store-room which was below the fo'c'sle. It was Ortiz. I didn't let him know I had seen him by following. Instead I whispered to Dominguez, one of my more loyal stalwarts, to see where he went.

A few minutes later when Dominguez hadn't returned I walked to the top of the companion ladder down which the two had disappeared and called. Dominguez and Ortiz came up together, the latter looking decidedly sheepish. I didn't want the crew to think I was using Dominguez as a stooge so, at the time, said nothing to either.

Later Dominguez told me he had surprised Ortiz furtively moving a pile of flour sacks under which were fifty rounds of revolver ammunition hidden there.

When I went down it had gone. Ortiz had been back. I said nothing to him but later I found where he had re-concealed it—in a hose locker under the pilot-house.

Concluding my fo'c'sle search I collected Espinosa's revolver and an ornamental, though nicely lethal, knife, belonging to Diaz, the carpenter.

By now the crew were crowding round me, almost breathing down my neck. The atmosphere was tenser than I usually care for. But despite all the fuss I knew somehow they were still afraid of me behind it all.

When I left the forecastle I knew too that they had beaten me. Half of them at least had revolvers, ammunition or knives which they had been clever enough to conceal from me. However I had another card to play yet. It was a silencer-equipped .45 revolver. Up until now nobody knew of it. I decided that every man aboard should know not only that I had it, but that I knew, too, how to use it.

Next morning I produced the revolver with its squat, sinister silencer, and strolled out on to the wing of the bridge. Then I began shooting at sharks. The shots made a muffled sort of phut. It was inaudible more than a few yards away. But it did the trick. One shark I bagged leapt convulsively six feet out of the water and sped off frantically skidding along on its tail with three-quarters of its streamlined body high out of the water. After that I tossed some jam tins overboard and methodically riddled them. Before I finished my little exhibition I had a thoughtful audience. It must have had the right effect among my troublemakers, because the rising truculence of the last few weeks almost subsided after that. But I like to think that it was not thoughts of mutiny which was upsetting the crew, but rather the frustration of all the troubles we had been through.

At noon on September 22 we were 224 miles from Palmyra, and 192 miles from Washington. We had made 26 miles since the previous noon. A hazy, watery sky melted into the massive grey rollers. It was oppressively hot and sultry.

Sparks was in the radio room still trying to get an answer from Palmyra when out of the blue the *Gray* had contact with the island in another way. It was a bosun bird. At first we could only hear it calling. Thin, ghostly calls they were. Then somebody shouted: "There it is," and above the mast we saw the white body and long, thin red tail feathers of our first bird since we released our sea bird several weeks before. It could only have come from Palmyra or Washington Island. The sight of it made me cheer inwardly. It gave the crew new faith too. They pointed excitedly at it for quite a long time. Since Noah's dove brought the olive sprig back to the Ark I am sure no bird had inspired such hope at sea. "A pity you weren't a pigeon and could take a message home with you," I thought. But an hour later there was no need.

Sparks, frustrated and worried at his inability to raise Palmyra, called the United States Navy station at Pearl Harbour, Honolulu, 1,100 miles to the north. Within a few minutes the Navy had solved the mystery for us. Control of the island had recently been handed over from the Navy to the American Civil Aeronautics Commission. Both its radio frequency *and* call-sign had been changed.

Quickly Sparks tapped out the new call-sign. Palmyra answered immediately. I told him to tell them that due to fuel shortage we would be unable to make Palmyra and would they send some of the Bunker "C" which had been reserved for us, down to Washington Island by tanker, or alternatively come out and refuel us at sea and to bring a coil of 10-inch manila as well. Naturally we were delighted at contacting Palmyra at last, but our glee turned to dismay when the reply came back: "NO BUNKER OIL AVAILABLE STOP NAVY TANKER LIFTED ALL BUNKER OIL IN STORAGE HERE ON AUGUST 18 STOP ONLY APPROXIMATELY 2500 BARRELS OF SLUDGE REMAINING IN TANKS WHICH CANNOT BE TRANSFERRED THROUGH OUR EXISTING PUMPING

This was a bitter blow. Our precious oil, specially reserved for us had seemingly been whisked away, almost
under our noses. I felt particularly angry because it effectively shattered a plan which had been forming in my
mind for several days. It was to slip the minesweepers,
carefully note their position and rate of drift, then dash
with our last few gallons of fuel to Palmyra, refuel, and
return to pick up the convoy. Lightened of our four millstones I reckoned that the *Gray* could just make Palmyra.
But now there could be no fuel if we did get there. The
minesweepers would drift off into the oblivion of the
Pacific.

When I mentioned my plan to Sparks he had made a
rather gallant offer. "Why not let me take a radio and
stay with the sweepers, sir," he suggested. "I am sure
there are at least two others among the crew who would
come with me." At the time I had rejected his offer point
blank. Now I was doubly relieved I had done so. Had
we cut the minesweepers adrift taking it for granted that
the fuel was still available at Palmyra I should literally
have sent three men to their doom.

All that afternoon I paced the bridge undecided what
to do. Palmyra was not much more than two hundred
miles way. If I abandoned the sweepers here and now,
the tug had a fair chance of making the island alone. If
I kept them with us—they had now reduced our speed to
just above one miserable knot—we should run out of fuel
long before we got there. I had to decide, and decide
quickly, whether four minesweepers and their considerable value to the Islands Towage and Lighterage Company were worth gambling against the lives of thirty-one
men. There was only one answer. Although there was no
heavy bunker oil on Palmyra perhaps they had diesel. In
the disappointment of losing our bunker fuel I had quite

overlooked this alternative. Diesel had helped us once; it could do so again.

Sparks was on the air two minutes later. I stood over him, restlessly impatient for the answer. Then the high-pitched signals poured back. A grin spread over Sparks' face as he scribbled down the message. Over his shoulder I read the wonderful news, "YES PLENTY OF DIESEL BUT PERMISSION NEEDED FROM NAVY." It was enough for me. I gave vent to the biggest single cheer the *Gray* ever heard.

"We're saved, Sparks old boy, saved," I cried. "We'll get those flaming minesweepers inside Manila Bay yet," and I rushed jubilantly out on to the deck to pass the good news on to Alonso and Miranda. Their faces beamed. And then the *Gray* witnessed something she had never seen before. The men of the watch who had heard my cheer and seen me rush from the radio room had all stopped work. They stood around the deck in groups like an anxious crowd of election night supporters whose candidate is on the point of assuming victory. Then they could contain themselves no longer. In a body they rushed to the foot of the bridge to hear what had turned on the smiles above. And scarcely had the news been relayed to them than a small oily band came tumbling up out of the engine-room. Engineers, oilers, firemen, and wipers, somehow they had got wind of it. For several minutes our decks buzzed with excited conversation. All thought of work had temporarily vanished. The relief in the tension aboard was so welcome I made no attempt to restore order for some time. Not for weeks had the *Gray* been such a happy ship as that afternoon. Now we *could* slip the tows. But much more important we could make Palmyra. The prospect of land, even a tiny Pacific coral atoll, was wonderful to contemplate. It was over six long weeks since the Mexican coast had faded away astern. At dawn next morning, September 23, I began preparations to slip the minesweepers.

# Chapter Ten

Now Sparks renewed his appeal to be allowed to stay with the minesweepers. Two other Americans, Whiteman and Todd, he told me, had volunteered to join him.

Sparks said, "You know, we are getting into the shipping lanes again now, sir. As you know we are close to the Fanning Island—Honolulu Route. If you cast off those sweepers with no one aboard, the first goddam ship that happens along will jump them as salvage and there won't be a darned thing we can do about it.

"Now if Whiteman, Todd and I stayed aboard, say on No. 1 with plenty of food and water and a radio telephone which I could soon rig up, we could keep in touch with you hour by hour, you could scram over to Palmyra, and be back before we'd drifted twenty miles. What's more I can keep transmitting for your direction finder so you can steer plumb straight for us. Why! I shouldn't be surprised if you were back within two days."

Whiteman and Todd, who had come to add weight to Sparks' plea, nodded approvingly. Obviously all three were more than keen to go.

But I didn't like the plan. Although the thought of another ship claiming our charges after all we had suffered was not pleasant to contemplate, I felt the responsibility of putting three young men adrift weighed heavily with me. So before I accepted the offer of my brave trio I spent half an hour in the chartroom.

I estimated that by the time we were ready to slip the minesweepers we should be roughly 180 miles east by north of Palmyra and about 130 miles from Washington Island. Free of the tows the *Gray* could make Palmyra in a day. A day to refuel and another day back would make three days in all. Even if their direction of drift changed in that time it shouldn't take very long to find them with our radio direction finder. I said they could go.

Sparks was delighted. Although he was only twenty-five, he had the experience and wisdom of a man many years older. There was no one aboard, I felt, with quite the same ideal personal make-up to fit them for such a job. I didn't know Whiteman or Todd quite so well, but for the most part they had worked cheerfully and willingly for me during the voyage and, most important, seemed to get along specially well together and with Sparks.

All day the *Gray* was a hive of activity. Every man turned to, to help with a greater will than the tug had seen for a month. I guess everybody had the same thought: "The sooner we drop those cursed minesweepers the sooner we set foot on dry land again and the sooner this nightmare voyage is over."

I concentrated on making a big sea-anchor which could be taken out ahead of No. 1 and by its bulk and resistance act as a drag which, I hoped, would help to keep the tows apart. One of my biggest misgivings was that bad weather might bunch the ships together, batter their hulls in and sink the lot. But fortunately for once when we so desperately needed it, the weather was smiling on us. It was hot and still with only a few doldrum rain clouds in the distance. The Pacific was just a gentle, lazy swell. Most important, the barometer was high and steady. With a little luck the whole operation might succeed.

I had the sea anchor built of canvas, rope, and light wire, which I fixed to a wooden frame. It was conical, about ten feet in diameter at the mouth and roughly eighteen feet long. I added a bag of oil with a hole in the stopper: this would release a slow ooze of oil to smooth any big seas which might come up during our absence. Surprisingly little oil can have quite a calming effect on the most violent waves.

Meanwhile the Bosun had the crew collecting all the hurricane lamps, blankets, mattresses, food and water we could spare. During the day, the lifeboat was busy chugging to and from No. 1 minesweeper on which the three had decided to establish themselves. We loaded it with enough tinned food and water for ten days. But there were rations and fresh water for thirty men for more than a month in the watertight lockers of the motor lifeboat which I decided they should have too. We gave them a drum of petrol for this, a set of charts and a small compass, so that if the minesweepers did sink they could set course for Palmyra. There wasn't sufficient petrol to make the island, but with the aid of the lifeboat's sail they could have done it. What I didn't tell Sparks was that Palmyra was so small and so low-lying, they could sail past within three to five miles in a small boat without sighting it.

Sparks busied himself rigging a ship-to-ship radio telephone and connected our end to the wireless direction finder so that I could obtain a line of bearing on their position each time we were in contact. On No. 1 sweeper he made certain he had a couple of well-charged batteries and after the installation was complete he carried out several tests between the *Gray* and the sweeper, after which he expressed himself most satisfied with the result; he believed the set would have a range of several hundred miles.

When the sea-anchor was complete I ordered the Mate to heave the leading minesweeper up to the *Gray* and unshackle our tow-wire. The tows were now completely free of us. Miranda then took the lifeboat and streamed the sea-anchor well up ahead of the tows, and I was gratified to see that after a few minutes the canvas anchor appeared to "bite" the water and looked as if it would help to keep the sweepers head to sea.

Now that the tows were slipped we had a chance to try

156

and get the diesel which was aboard No. 3 minesweeper, and so I came as close to her as was prudent. An oil hose was taken across and with the portable mechanical pump we began to milk her of her precious fuel. Completing this we then came around astern of No. 4 and took the remaining few gallons still in her tanks. The *Gray* now had exactly 3,383 gallons of mixed Bunker "C" and diesel. Even at top speed this should be sufficient to get us to Palmyra. Cuesta assured me it would, and I hoped his consumption figures would prove correct.

It was now September 24 and our forty-fifth day out from Manzanillo. This was the day. The crew's excitement, though suppressed, was obvious. Our noon sight was meticulous and we found the convoy was drifting at the rate of sixteen miles a day and that the direction of drift was north-westerly or, to be more precise, 315 degrees. During the afternoon this was checked and re-checked until I was certain there had been no mistake. The currents and winds in this area could not be predicted with any real degree of accuracy, but as we would be back within seventy-six hours, any change of direction which took place would not be of great moment. But I could not help feeling a little anxious as to whether the sweepers would keep their stations during any change. If they didn't there was quite a danger they might come together and damage themselves and indeed even sink each other. This was a risk I had to take.

As the tug's tow-wire was being reeled in the wire was closely inspected for possible damage. Its big strands showed signs of wear in places but nothing to cause any worry, and it had withstood the 9,000-mile voyage from Charleston very well.

As we stood up to windward of the convoy we were able to see what the long slow haul in tropical waters had done to their hulls. They were festooned below the water-line with a complete mantle of brilliant green marine growth.

It was quite thick and must have taken off some of our speed. I realized that the *Gray*, too, must have become quite a marine herbarium and craned my neck over the side to have a look. She certainly was. From the Plimsoll line down our hull was matted with a most astonishing tangled carpet of weed and barnacles. I had not seen such encrustation since my sailing days. The *Gray* was badly in need of a scrape.

For ten hours we stood by the minesweepers holding position with our propeller barely turning. For ten hours as they wallowed a hundred yards to port of us, Miranda and I kept them under observation. When I was satisfied, I prepared Sparks' chart and plotted the positions each day for a week where I reckoned they would be at each noon and then I sent for him to come to the chartroom for a final briefing. "You will drift about sixteen miles each day," I told him. "If all goes well I hope to be back within seventy-six hours. Meanwhile I want you to call us up every four hours starting from 9 p.m. to-night, and you must advise me if you think your drift or direction is changing. Your direction of drift will be along the line 315 degrees. If the sea-anchor stops functioning and the other sweepers begin to come down on you do not hesitate to use the spanner I have supplied you with and unscrew the nuts of the U-bolts and let the bridle drop clear of you, and you may be able to drift clear, but if not, use the motor lifeboat and tow yourselves clear. I have also given you an axe which may be useful. Should you have to get away in the lifeboat for any reason you must first work out on this chart where you think you should be at the time and from the compass rose you will get a rough idea of the direction of Palmyra. I do not think you will be able to make the island, but at least you will be moving towards it and I will then have some idea where to look for you if under these circumstances we lose contact with you. I think I have told you all I can, Sparks."

"But no, there are a few more things. I have also supplied you with rockets and flares and you are to take one of the Aldis lamps we have. Some time before I get to your position on my return, if it happens to be at night I shall train one of our searchlights up to the sky and you should be able to see the light-ray stabbing towards the clouds. If you do, you are to let off some of the rockets and we shall see them and be able to steer direct for you. Should you see us going by, burn some of the flares. Although right now I cannot see any reason why we should not be back within seventy-six hours, there is of course the possibility we may be delayed for some reason or other, but with our constant contact by radio-phone you will know of that. And now, one more thing. You must realize this. It could be that we may run out of fuel before we reach Palmyra and in that case Christ only knows what will happen. I must ask you whether you wish to change your mind and stay with us and we will take our chances of finding the minesweepers. Ask Whiteman and Todd what they think."

Sparks did not hesitate. "Sir, we have discussed the matter at length a number of times and none of us wishes to pull out. In fact we are all looking forward to the experience. We all think you have provided for any eventuality and are happy to go. But we would like you to mail some letters for us when you reach Palmyra."

Time was now getting on and the Chief Cook had ransacked his fast-emptying ice-box and had turned out as lavish a meal as he could. I ordered all hands to chow. The main course of that meal was the last of our turkeys which had been fated not to see the Thanksgiving Day dinner they were originally intended for. They took the cold remnants with them. Round about 1900 hours I had a final check and worked out our position to be 6° 42′ N. 159° 23′ W. and then satisfied I had taken all reasonable precautions for the safety of the three adventurous volunteers I told them they had best get aboard their new home. They stood there in the half-light, each clutching a small bag of possessions, showing not the least emotion. They might have been waiting for the Hoboken ferry. They shook hands with me and then with most of the others and climbed into the lifeboat.

The whole deck crew and most of the engine-room staff lined the rail as the boat was swung out and lowered into the swell. There were cheers and good-natured shouts of, "Good luck," "Don't get eaten," "It's been nice knowing you guys," and then the lifeboat sped off, scattering our tireless escort of sharks. The last we heard from them as they chugged over to No. 1 sweeper was Sparks calling: "Don't leave us long, fellers, these sharks look mighty hungry."

After they were safely aboard the minesweeper and their lifeboat securely in tow astern, I took the *Gray* once round the whole convoy. The crew gave them a rousing cheer but already they seemed to have forgotten us; they were busy lighting their lamps and organizing their home for the next few days: they did not even wave. With a final salute of five blasts on our siren I rang down, "Full ahead," and set course for Palmyra. It gave me a peculiar sort of feeling as I saw the minesweepers swallowed up in a rain squall astern.

It was a strange sensation being able to seize the engine-room telegraph and slam down for "Full ahead". Instinctively I looked astern for the tows and found myself picking up the telephone to give Cuesta the gentle revolution increases. But for three days there would be no more of that. For three days our only concern was the tug herself. The tinkle of the telegraph had scarcely died away when the bridge began trembling in a way that was new to me. The ship leapt forward, engines pounding. In two minutes we were making such a breeze I had to close the bridge windows, a tremendous bow wave had sprung up, the *Gray* quivered with her long-suppressed power: we were pounding toward Palmyra at 18½ knots.

It took quite some time to adjust ourselves to this startling new progress. The crew were so hypnotized by the huge, green bow-wave they just lined the rail and goggled. How wonderful it would have been to have crossed the Pacific, as I had been promised, like this, unhampered, at four hundred miles a day.

Our new lease of life had a dramatic effect in another sphere. The shark-dolphin convoy, our faithful, ever-hopeful escort for six weeks, fled. As our bow ripple fanned out into a wave they abandoned us in a body. Within five minutes there wasn't one to be seen.

We had left the sweepers at 2032 hours and as 2100 hours approached I returned to the bridge and stood by the radio-telephone, for my rendezvous with Sparks. I switched on, pulled on the head-set and tuned in. 9 p.m. came, and went, but on our pre-arranged frequency there was not a sound. I switched over to transmit and called the sweepers for several minutes. I got no answer. Again and again I tried, but in vain. At 10 p.m. I gave up and told the officer of the watch to keep listening. Then I turned in with a fresh worry on my mind. Had some disaster overwhelmed them so soon? It didn't seem possible. Sparks had tested both sets time and time again and surely if everything was all right we should be getting some signal from him. The weather was perfect and we had left them less than ninety minutes ago. At first I thought of turning back but then I remembered we were no longer crawling along at two knots. Those ninety minutes had put nearly thirty miles between us. To have returned would have meant giving up all hope of reaching Palmyra: we had to keep on. Even as it was, despite Cuesta's bland assurance that we had sufficient fuel to reach the Island, I wasn't too happy. My own reckoning told me our margin of safety was extremely small. It was true we still had the foot-long remains of deck-battens which the Bosun had got ready for burning in the furnace, but I did not want to place any reliance on them.

Coming on watch next morning at 0400 hours, I reduced our speed to 8 knots, for by now it had become clear that we were using too much of our precious fuel, but it was not long before even this rate was too much. The oil was beginning to wash away from the outlet pipes in the tanks. Then Cuesta remembered there were quite a few gallons still left in the galley fuel tank. This he pumped into the main tank and we were able to get back to 10 knots.

We sighted Palmyra dead ahead at 4.20 o'clock in the afternoon and I think that Miranda and I can be excused for the glow of satisfaction we both felt at making such a good landfall after all the careering round the Pacific we had done.

Something less than three miles by four, Palmyra is a very insignificant speck in an Ocean that is bigger than all the land masses of the earth put together. It is perilously easy to miss altogether, as many ships have done. No part of it, other than the buildings and palms, stands more than ten feet above sea-level. We were only six miles off it when the mast-head look-out shouted down, "I can see a tower right ahead, sir."

Very soon we were able to make out the tops of palm trees and the upper parts of white buildings and a large water-tower. I had never been to Palmyra before, but the chart showed it was made up of a number of atolls with a central lagoon surrounded by a coral reef. The entrance through the reef was a mile or so from the outside anchorage which was on a coral shelf. To reach the dock ships had to pass through this channel and proceed about two miles up the lagoon.

But the *Wallace R. Gray* very nearly didn't see either the

passage or the lagoon. She came close to ending her voyage as a pile of wreckage on Palmyra reef.

At 5.47 with the island less than a mile away we were coming in nicely at reduced speed, congratulating ourselves that the worst of our troubles were over. At 5.48 there was a rumble, a splutter and the *Gray's* engines stopped. Everything packed up; even the generators. We were a dead ship.

Quickly I grabbed the telephone and bawled into it before I realized that it too was dead. All our electrical power had gone when the generators stopped.

Meanwhile we were drifting quickly toward the reef. Rapidly we lost steerage way. It looked like the end. I tried the voice pipe, jerking the plug out and blowing down a piercing blast on the whistle. Back came Cuesta's perplexed voice.

"For God's sake give me some power," I yelled. "Just for one minute or you'll have us all aground."

But the wretched Cuesta was too distracted to speak coherently. He gabbled some dismal explanation then seemed to break down altogether.

I realized it was pointless wasting another thought on the engines. Clearly they weren't going to get us out of this mess. And every second the reef was looming nearer. I could hear the roar of the surf pounding on it now. It was barely half a mile away.

I yanked on the whistle lanyard hoping that some vessel within the lagoon might hear it and come to our aid. But apart from a hiss or two which died away in a thin spiral of steam, nothing happened.

Only one thing could save us now . . . sail. I shouted to Alonso, "Call all hands. Set the sails. Clap on every stitch you can."

He rushed away bawling alternately in English and Tagalog. Men came tumbling on deck from every corner of the ship. Many appeared barefooted and clad only in their trousers. In a short time all our ten patch-work sails had been set. I grabbed the wheel from the helmsman. There was no steerage way. And the offshore breeze which filled our sails was insufficient even to give us way enough to overcome our drift towards the reef.

Seven hundred, six hundred, five hundred yards. Now we could see the jagged reef top through the pounding surf—the coral gleamed white and ugly. At the most we had but a few more minutes in which to save ourselves. A hundred thoughts flashed through my mind, but uppermost was the thought of Harris, Whiteman and Todd. If the *Gray* were wrecked now, there would be no vessel to rescue them. It might be a week before another vessel could be sent out from Honolulu; by then anything might have happened to them.

It was useless trying to let go the anchor as it was a hundred fathoms right up to the reef. It was more sail or nothing. I knew it was a chance in a thousand but it just *had* to succeed. Again I roared my orders. No time for formality now and relaying my instructions through the Mate. Cupping my hands, I yelled, "Get me more sail. Anything you can find, locker covers, sacks, shirts, blankets, any bloody thing, but for Christ's sake be quick about it else we shall all be swimming."

The crew responded well; no doubt the thought of being flung into the maelstrom ahead of us and being dashed against that wicked-looking coral spurred them on more effectively than my own exhortations. Certainly I have never seen such a pile of potential sail material as was at my feet in a matter of seconds.

"Get this stuff rigged. Hang it anywhere—anywhere it will catch the wind. Set it on the forestay," I told them. But having produced the material they seemed to have shot their bolt and just milled about.

The reef was less than a quarter of a mile off by now and the *Gray* was beginning to feel its influence. "Get up that

164

bloody stay," I yelled; but the only one who attempted to do so was the Bosun so I shinned up with him with some rope yarns and we set what we could on the forestay. This extra sail was having an effect but not enough. "Get me some timber; a piece about fifteen feet along and another smaller one," I told the Mate. It was a last desperate bid.

Somebody handed me a long length of four by three. Seizing it I quickly lashed a cross-piece to it near the end, then I ran it out over the bow and furiously lashed it fast. Sweat was pouring off my forehead into my eyes. Romanin swarmed out and quickly made a boat-cover fast over the cross-piece. It acted as a sort of a scoop or water-sail with the sheets leading up through the hawse-pipes. It filled and—it did the trick. The breakers were very close and we were within an ace of destruction. My heart seemed to stand still as I waited. There was nothing more we could do. And then, miracle of miracles, she started to answer. Slowly, almost unwillingly, I saw our head creep to starboard. For a terrible minute she seemed to pause sluggishly and it looked as though she would swing no further. Then a heavier gust of offshore wind billowed the sails, everything was drawing. "Come on, you beauty, come on, you beauty," I called to this really great tug. "Come on." What a moment! The *Gray* gently heeled over and continued her swing to starboard and we had steerage way. Of the next few moments I have only a very distorted recollection. The terrifying roar of the surf, the sea around us whipped to a white, frothy cream, a deluge of spray on the pilot-house windows, and a few yards away a white wall of coral. We had averted disaster by perhaps seconds.

My next clear memory is of the *Gray* gliding along parallel to the reef, rising and falling on the rollers so that one moment the shore was obscured behind a green and white wall of water, the next, the blue lagoon inside sparkling in the moonlight deep and clear not fifty yards away. We would have to come up a bit further, and gladly did the old hooker answer to a few spokes of the wheel.

Our jury-rig sails were now really working and we moved steadily towards the buoy marking the limits of the anchorage, about two miles away. Those two miles took us nearly two hours and I prayed as I have never prayed before for that breeze to hold. It held all right and with twenty yards to spare we rounded the buoy and came to an anchor on the coral shelf. With considerable relief I called to the Mate, "Let go. Put the third shackle in the water." Never did music sound sweeter than the splash of the anchor and the rattle of the chain. Now we could all breathe again.

The post-mortem was brief. Cuesta was still too upset to give anything like a lucid account of our engine stoppage. So desperate had he been to please that he had under-estimated our scanty fuel reserves. We had simply run out of it. Maybe I was as much to blame as he for not reducing speed long before I did. However we had arrived, and that was the main thing. But we still had to get inside to the fuel dock. We couldn't sail in, that was a certainty.

So whilst we lay at anchor that night the four engineers went to work on the oil tanks. None of them wanted to go off duty or sleep until they had transferred what was left of the fuel in each tank, the level of which was below the outlet pipes, into one tank and so give us enough uninterrupted supply to get us from the anchorage, through the reef channel and on up to the fuel dock. It was a difficult job. The tank-tops were in awkward, almost inaccessible positions. But Schmidt managed, after some feverish contortions, to squeeze himself into position between the tank-tops and deck-head where he could get a spanner to work on the nuts.

Before daylight, Cuesta was able to offer me power again. At dawn we weighed anchor and steamed slowly towards the entrance buoy. Rounding this we proceeded up the channel and now had our first real view of the island. It looked a little bigger at close quarters, and after forty-seven days at sea, very wonderful. Land-hungry, the crew drank in every detail avidly. As we cleared the passage the Americans had blasted bodily out of the coral reef, we saw half Palmyra's area was occupied by the central lagoon. The land which encircled it was sprinkled with green coconut palms and everywhere was evidence of the island's wartime role as a United States Naval and Air base. There were overgrown run-ways and fighter strips, dilapidated buildings, disused tennis courts, radio towers, and dumps of rusting equipment fast disappearing under tropical undergrowth. One long runway with a control tower at one end appeared to be still in use for as we moved in, a large transport plane took the air.

Palmyra was transformed from a group of peaceful Pacific atolls into an important air-base some time before the war. American engineers had laid runways, and after Pearl Harbour it became an important staging post for American aircraft bound for the war theatre in the islands of the South-west Pacific. Only once and very briefly did the war itself come to Palmyra. A Japanese submarine stood offshore and pumped in a handful of shells. Its only victim, outside a few coconuts, was a dredge which it managed to sink.

Since the war the island had come under the control of the Civil Aeronautics Commission and boasted some workshops and a population of fifty civilians of whom ten were wives. There were no natives.

The only chart I had of Palmyra was a Restricted Navy one and according to it, it should have been a simple matter to get up to the fuel dock. But it was not so. As soon as we had cleared the reef channel I looked for the buoys as marked on the chart but there were no buoys now. However, I could see other "marks" mentioned and

I decided we would be all right if we went slowly and felt our way in. It was useless getting out the lead as no one aboard could use it, so with the Mate in the "eyes" ready to let me know when he saw shoal patches ahead we progressed up the channel and finally nosed in alongside the fuel dock. The voyage from Manzanillo was over. We had steamed, drifted and sailed many more miles than intended. We had been at sea forty-seven wearying, worrying days and our overall average speed had been a heart-breaking 3.5 knots.

As we came alongside, a jeep drew up in a cloud of white coral dust and out jumped a middle-aged, white-haired American in khaki slacks and shirt. He introduced himself as Hugo Stamm, acting manager of the island.

"Welcome to Palmyra, boys," he greeted us cheerfully. "Your signals had us worried for a bit. Can't have over-much fuel left can you? We sure were relieved to see you pop over the horizon last evening. What happened outside?"

When I told him it was only by the grace of God that he hadn't looked out that morning to see us strewn out on the reef, he was amazed.

"Well doggone it," he drawled. "Just to think here we were all standing, watching you fellers sailing in on us and not one of us thought that a blamed thing was wrong."

But this was no time for talk. I wanted only to refuel quickly and put out to sea again with as little delay as possible. Already I was concerned at the time we had lost.

Stamm was immediately helpful. "You sure don't want to leave those guys drifting out there too long. I'll send you some men at once and we will have you refuelled in no time. Permission has not yet arrived from the Navy to let you have the fuel, but in the circumstances I cannot refuse to supply you. How many barrels do you want?"

"About 51,000 gallons," I told him. He was as good as his word and within half an hour of tying up, the oil hoses were pouring diesel into our thirsty tanks. Meanwhile I let as many of the crew as could be spared, go ashore to stretch their legs. But they were warned not to wander out of earshot as we would be putting to sea within four hours.

As I watched them streaming gratefully ashore I saw for the first time what a thoroughly dishevelled gang we looked. If any of the Islanders had spotted our skull and crossbones through glasses the previous afternoon, any illusions that we were not twentieth-century pirates would certainly have been quickly banished by the first sight of us. We had not shaved for six weeks, our clothes showed plenty of signs of wear. Bearded, red-eyed and sunburned we must have looked little better than a bunch of pirates. The more I looked at Stamm and his staff, smooth-shaven and dressed in clean clothes, the more I began to feel about our own dreadful appearance. But for the moment our smartening up had to wait.

Whilst refuelling was going on, Stamm ran me up to Palmyra's radio station as I was anxious to learn whether they may have picked up any signals from Sparks. What a relief it was to learn that they had received a weak signal in morse early that morning. "Tows O.K. Weather good. All well," was all it said. It took a load off my mind. Ever since we had failed to contact the minesweepers thirty-six hours earlier, all manner of fears had assailed me. Now I assumed that either the *Gray's* radio or myself was at fault. But when one of the technicians had examined it and declared it fully operative I felt more baffled than ever. I could only assume that something had temporarily prevented Sparks using his set at the time we were listening. It was all thoroughly upsetting. I arranged with the Chief operator to maintain a twenty-four-hour watch on the same frequency and also to keep in touch with them myself by voice until we had either picked up the tows or returned to Palmyra.

At 1711 hours September 26 we had completed fuelling and at 1735 hours we let go the lines, backed out of the dock, and swinging round, started off down the lagoon towards the reef channel. Within twenty-four hours I hoped to have the four sweepers in tow again and my three men safely back aboard. But again misfortune struck. We had, it seemed, to pay a price for our deliverance of the day before.

At 1804 hours, twenty-nine minutes after we had cleared the dock and were feeling our way down the channel, the *Gray* touched a bank. So imperceptible was the grounding it was a second or two before I realized we were aground. At this spot my confounded chart stated there was 119 feet of water. If there had been any indication of shoaling I had not noticed it, but according to my marks we had come over this very same spot on the way in. Of course we had then been "flying very light", and now we were drawing considerably more water.

The engines were stopped at once and I took soundings. Aft there was 30 feet and forward only 13 feet. We were well up all right as our own draught on leaving the oil dock was 15 feet forward. Slow astern. Half astern. Full astern. Our propeller flailed the calm waters of the lagoon but we budged not an inch.

Here was a nice predicament. I gave a long blast on our siren and presently the island's picket boat chugged out to us. We passed a kedge anchor to them and asked them to drop it about a hundred yards astern. Then hauling on this and going "Full Astern" on our engines we made a further attempt to get free. It seemed we were as firmly aground as if we had been cemented to the bottom of the lagoon. Meanwhile we were stirring up so much sand I began to fear that too much would be sucked in by the intakes and damage our engine, so as the tide was on the ebb I decided to wait until next high tide before trying further. We started to take on quite a list and at one time I thought we would be right down on our port side. Setting anchor watches I told the Mate to let as many of his men turn in as could and get some badly needed sleep and I also followed my own advice.

I came on the bridge again at midnight and relieved Miranda whom I told to get a couple of hours sleep. At 0130 hours all hands were called and at 0150 I rang "Stand by," to the engine-room. Taking up the slack on the kedge anchor with the after capstan, "Slow Astern" was rung down to the engine-room and at 0205 we were afloat. I decided not to tempt fate twice in the same night, so after recovering our kedge I proceeded to an anchorage, and waited until daylight.

As soon as it was light enough I had Miranda collect anything suitable to use as beacons and launching the pram we took the hand-lead and started off to survey a safe channel. I was glad we did. We found many more shoals in the supposedly clear channel and all of these must have built up since the chart I had was last corrected. We spent all morning hammering "beacons" of bamboo and sticks into the bottom to indicate the boundaries of the shoals. During this work we could not but help admire the aquarium of beautiful tropical fish.

With the aid of our improvised beacons I took the *Gray* safely clear of the outer reef by 1500 hours and we set off for the castaways. It was now over three days since we had cut the minesweepers adrift, and I was not a little concerned that we had heard no more than the one feeble message. Already we were over twenty-four hours overdue, but I comforted myself that if they had continued to drift at the same rate as when we last saw them, it would put them just sixteen miles further towards the north-west.

I had originally intended returning to the position where we had left them, but in view of the delay I decided to make for the position I estimated they would be by the time we arrived on the line of drift. We pounded away from Palmyra at 16 knots. By 4 o'clock next morning we were approaching the area where, according to my reckoning, they should be. This was September 28. But now the weather which had favoured us for a week took a change for the worse. Low misty cloud began to creep in, and by dawn the sea was fast building up and heavy, drenching squalls beat down on us. This wasn't going to help the search. Behind a line of big rollers and flying spray we could pass unseen only too easily.

So I switched on the radar and posted look-outs to cover visually every inch of our now rapidly shrinking horizon. At 11 a.m., by which time the *Gray* had taken on a business-like roll, I doubled up on the lookouts.

Most of this time Miranda had been making exacting calculations in the chartroom. Never had quite so much depended on the accuracy of our navigation as now. As noon approached, the sun, which had been mostly obscured, showed itself as a mere faintly glimmering smudge in the mist above us. We managed to get a couple of sights and shortly afterwards Miranda triumphantly pointed to a spot on the chart. "Another nineteen minutes and we will be on the line of drift, sir." I checked his figures.

It seemed more like an hour before the nineteen minutes ticked by and then almost right on zero hour there was an elated cry from Alonso who had his eyes glued to the radar-screen. He had spotted something. For the past two hours he had sat looking at the screen to which the scanner fifty feet up the mast brought speckled indications of objects far beyond our range of vision. Even the fuzzy shapes of rain cloud were relayed as blobs of light.

But suddenly something more sharply defined had come on to the screen. "Come quickly, sir," he cried. "Looks like something here." I went over to the set. There sure enough was the unmistakable shape of something more than a cloud. Possibly it might be a ship.

Quickly we took a bearing on it and headed off in pursuit. It lay along 315 degrees, exactly along the line of drift our calculations put the minesweepers. For fifteen minutes the *Gray* ploughed through the mist with encouraging calls from Alonso: "It's still there, sir. Seems to be getting clearer. Yes, it's clearer all right and bigger, yes much bigger now."

And then as suddenly as the object had appeared, it vanished. It must have been a sharply-defined squall, one of those hanging rain curtains that can cross a ship, drenching one half and leaving the rest dry. The disappointment left me feeling flat and a bit dejected.

We came about and steamed back to where we had first picked up our false alarm. By this time I had called every available man on deck and posted them on the fo'c'sle-head, the flying bridge, the radar platform high above the bridge and on the gun platforms. The three pairs of binoculars we possessed I distributed as strategically as possible. And then Miranda and I laid out plans for a systematic octagonal search of the area we were in, working back towards the point where we had dropped the tows. Then we began searching in increasingly widening octagons around the position we had marked on the chart with that small hopeful cross.

When we started, a break in the low, scudding cloud put our horizon to eight miles on either side. That meant we were scouring a belt of ocean sixteen miles wide at a time. But as the day wore on squalls reduced this to five miles on either side. I settled on eight knots as the best search speed, and by dusk we had steamed our first complete octagon, forty miles around. In all those square miles of ocean there was not a sign of our four drifting minesweepers, not a speck of oil, not a fragment of driftwood.

All night we continued the search. Before dusk I had the searchlights switched on and directed their beams on the low-lying clouds above. They would have been visible for at least twenty miles and now we were overdue, Sparks and his crew would have instituted an all-night watch for certain. The moment they spotted the beams they had only to shoot off some rockets or burn the flares we had left them, and one of a dozen pairs of eyes would see it immediately.

At the same time I kept a continuous listening watch on the radio. It was tuned in on Sparks' frequency with the volume turned up. I gave orders that someone was always to remain within earshot. The moment the feeblest signal crackled through I wanted to be ready to swing the direction-finding loop and get a bearing. But dawn came and we hadn't heard a whisper. During the night we had completed two more octagonal sweeps and had covered every yard of ocean into which the minesweepers could have drifted in any direction of the compass, for sixteen miles.

Something was badly wrong somewhere. From our observations we knew they were only drifting sixteen miles in every twenty-four hours. If they were not within the octagons we had just searched, only one thing could have happened if they were still afloat. A radical change of current must have carried them away in some other direction.

And now I was reminded of a remark the shrewd Miranda had made to me as we had been approaching Palmyra four days earlier. "You know, sir," he had said, giving me a thoughtful look, "although we all know they were drifting north-west I would swear the set we are now in is easterly." There certainly had been an easterly current in that particular area. Hourly events were adding weight to Miranda's belief that the tows must have been carried east soon after we had left them. But I did not have a chance to dwell on the possibility for my thoughts were interrupted by a shout from the radar platform. Martin was calling hoarsely, "On deck there. Get the 'Old Man'. Ask him to come up here." I wasted no time in climbing the mast and in my eagerness I barked my hands on the ladder.

"Take a look out there, sir," said Martin who was huddled on the platform with Ritter. The soft reflection of approaching dawn painted their oil-skins an eerie pink. I followed the direction of his pointing hand. My heart missed a beat. There on the western horizon a reddish-orange glow could be seen. "By the Saints, I think you may have found them," I said to him.

Quickly I shinned down the mast and altered course towards the light. By now the glow was fainter but had not changed in direction and a reflection could still be seen at the base of a cloud on the horizon. For some time we raced at 18 knots towards that glow. Everyone, tense with expectancy, had not the least doubt but what it was Sparks and company burning some of the flares I had left them. Then the light appeared to flicker for a few uncertain minutes and finally went out. Although I kept the *Gray* headed in the direction we had last seen it, for several miles we saw nothing and the light did not appear again. It was another cruel anti-climax. Even now I am not sure what caused the phenomenon. Probably some peculiar trick of the dawn light.

Anyway we came about glumly disappointed, and continued to carve bigger and still bigger octagons out of the Pacific. By the following morning we had completed our sixth circuit of the first area of search. During the night the weather had improved a bit, allowing a greater distance between each sweep and by 8 a.m. we had effectively patrolled a large octagonal area 100 miles wide enclosing nearly 20,000 square miles of empty, rolling Pacific.

Up to now I had kept in regular contact with Palmyra, but they had nothing to report. It was now six days since I had dropped the tows, and I began to wonder if some disaster had overtaken them. Perhaps the sweepers had holed one another during the rough weather of the last few days, battered and sunk the motor lifeboat and hauled one another under before the men could cut No. 1 free. A dozen possible ends which they might have met occurred to me. More than ever I wished I had refused the volunteers permission to go aboard. But despite the blackness of the situation, something, intuition, call it what you may, told me that somewhere within 100 miles of us, four lonely craft, strung helplessly together, were drifting at the mercy of the wind and current with three anxious, bearded, sun-tanned and salt-caked figures scanning every horizon. Obviously from the weakness of his solitary signal Sparks' radio had suffered some breakdown. Perhaps it had now failed completely. However, if they were still afloat they wouldn't starve or go thirsty. But what a state of mind the three of them must be in by now. We just had to keep on with our systematic search and if we had not sighted them by the time we had worked back to the spot where we had cast them adrift, then I would move the search eastwards and perhaps ask for additional aid.

I went wearily into the chartroom to plot my next area of search. Between us, Miranda and I ruled fresh octagonal lines on the chart. Half an hour later the pilot-house door banged open. I looked up and there stood Cuesta the Chief Engineer, hollow-eyed from lack of sleep, looking more concerned than ever. I knew before he spoke that he brought bad news. It was the old, familiar, painfully anxious look, that expressed more than words.

"What the devil is it this time?" I barked.

"The condenser, sir. The intake pump has stripped. We can't repair it at sea and if we don't get back to Palmyra we shall break down completely through lack of water for the boilers."

"My God, Cuesta," I said. "Your cursed engines will

be the end of us all yet. Can't you possibly improvise? There must be something you can cook up to keep us going for a few more days. I am not going back and leave three men out here. Their lives may depend on our efforts now. Can't you switch some other pump? What about the portable motor pumps we have? For heavens' sake try something."

But Cuesta stood his ground. With his little characteristic arm gestures he insisted that no improvisation could prevent total engine and boiler failure if we didn't go back at once.

This was terrible. To abandon the search now was unthinkable, but what alternative did I have? An unserviceable condenser-pump meant we would be unable to convert sea water to fresh for the boilers. Cuesta was the Chief Engineer and he should know just what he could and could not do. If I went against his advice then what happened to the other men under my command would be entirely on my own head. What the hell could I do? And then I thought of the three brave men on the sweepers. I had told them I would be back for them within seventy-six hours. Already they had been drifting, cut off, without radio reassurance that rescue was on the way, for nearly a week. I couldn't give up the search now.

I turned to Cuesta. "We're not going back," I said. "All you need is fresh water for your boilers. Well, you shall have the blasted water."

The Chief Engineer looked a bit perplexed, and I think he thought I was talking through my hat. I wasn't.

"Listen here, Cuesta," I said, jabbing a finger towards the pilot-house windows. A heavy squall was beating a tattoo against them. "See that rain? There's your bloody water and we are going to use it. If I can catch the water can you get it into your tanks? I shall rig the best rain-catchers you ever saw and steer into every rain squall I can find and move with it. Will that satisfy you?"

Slowly a smile spread over his old Oriental face. "Why yes, yes, sir, it will certainly do." And then the worried look came back. "But what if the weather clears?"

But I wasn't prepared to argue that one. "We can worry about that when the time comes," I replied. "Now get your men busy and have the tops cut out of all those empty drums on the after-deck."

Out of some of our make-shift sails I got the crew to make rough hoses to fit on to scupper pipes, then rain-catchers of sorts were hung between the shrouds and the masts, and wherever else possible, and then I told the Bosun to organize a bucket brigade using both deck and engine hands. Leaving just a couple of men on the look-out, everyone, officers as well, was ordered to procure buckets, trash cans or anything else which would hold water and was easily portable, and to stand by. They looked at me as if to ask, "Just what is this crazy Ainslie up to now?"

When everything was ready I had the *Gray* steered into the middle of the nearest rain squall, and very soon our rain-catchers were full and overflowing. It pelted aboard faster than we could ever hope to collect it. The bucket brigade formed up. They had the idea now. Everyone entered into the spirit of the thing with heartening zest. Standing there in rows stripped to the waist, their trousers drenched by the warm, vicious rain, and clinging to their bodies, they struggled hard to send the buckets down the line. Thousands of gallons drove aboard in the first squall. The last man of the chain tipped the water into a tank and from this it was piped through temporary hoses into the boiler tanks.

All afternoon right through the night and into the next day the work went on with brief respites in between. Out of one squall and into another we went, with little alteration of course. Cuesta's tanks were filled so fast the bucket brigade was able to relax and we could afford to miss some of the squalls which came in solid curtains from the clouds above, down to the sea.

Eventually this pantomime progress took us back to the position where we had dropped the sweepers. For some hours we hove to whilst I checked again the rate and direction of drift. The answer was the same sixteen miles a day north-westward. It was more puzzling than ever.

I was considering moving down the line of drift for about thirty miles, the equivalent of two days' drift, but before I came to a decision whether to continue the search to the eastward, the weather cleared. There were no more rain squalls in sight and I realized I now had no alternative but to return to Palmyra whilst our hard-earned water still lasted. For now I had to consider the men still aboard the tug. Reluctantly, at midnight, I set course for Palmyra.

# Chapter Eleven

It took us just twelve hours to reach Palmyra. Half-way back I was again perturbed when Miranda pointed out for the second time, an east-flowing set. It was more noticeable than before and knocked a knot or two off our speed. If the minesweepers had been caught by this same current it was obvious why we hadn't been able to find them. Instead of drifting nor'-west toward Japan they would be heading quite rapidly back in the direction of Central America.

I was so concerned by this discovery I sent an immediate signal to Palmyra requesting an air search. My message would be relayed to the American air-sea rescue squadron in Honolulu, and an aircraft probably flown the thousand miles down from there.

It was midday, and low tide, when we got back to Palmyra reef. I anchored to await high water, chafing at the delay because our boiler water was being used up fast.

Before we sailed in that night—October 2—the men amused themselves fishing. The reef was alive with an interesting assortment of fish, and all morning the lines went up and down. By the afternoon when our anchor rumbled up, the decks were piled with a flapping, gloriously-hued harvest. Looking at them that blazing hot sunny afternoon I never thought they were to bring us the major calamity of the voyage.

As soon as we were tied up I jumped ashore and hurried up to the radio-shack. Perhaps there had been a further signal from Sparks? But no such luck. "I guess we have listened on their frequency without a break since you sailed," the duty operator told me. "There hasn't been a squeak. If you ask me I think that operator of yours is having trouble with his set. That first and last message we got from him was on mighty reduced power."

Feeling not a little depressed I paid a call on Stamm over at the administration block. He cheered me up a lot. "Nothing to worry about, Captain Ainslie," he said. "We'll have our Army air-rescue planes out looking for them in a day or two. The first aircraft should be along any time now. Then it'll only be a matter of hours before they spot them."

I hoped he was right. After the best meal I had eaten in three months I walked back to the *Gray*, and new troubles, big troubles.

Even as I approached the tug in the twilight I sensed something was wrong. It was 7 p.m. and at least someone should have been in sight.

Thoroughly alarmed, I ran the last two hundred yards and rushed aboard. The most pathetic sight awaited me. The decks were littered with a groaning, sprawling, writhing mass of men. No one could stand. No one could speak. They just lay there convulsing, retching and helpless. It looked for all the world as if some dreadful death ray had suddenly been turned on the *Gray*.

For a moment panic gripped me. I thought my entire crew were dying. I rushed over to Willie Dominguez. He was lying outside his galley. I knelt down beside him and beseeched him to say something.

"Willie, Willie," I cried, "for Christ's sake, what's wrong with you all?"

But he just looked like a dying sheep, looked straight through me, glassy-eyed, as though he neither heard nor saw me. And then he suddenly clutched his stomach like a man who has just been shot. His mouth lolled open, frothing, and he gave the most terrifying groan I have ever heard. Quite clearly he was incapable of speaking.

It was the same with the others. My agitated inquiries brought only harrowing, ghastly groans and more stomach clutching. I hurried into the galley assuming the trouble had been caused by something they had eaten. The only evidence was the remains of some boiled and fried fish and vegetables. So I ran to the mess-room. Yes, it was the fish right enough. On every plate sat a half-eaten portion of boiled or fried, acutely poisonous red snapper. The meal looked as if it had been interrupted by an air-raid warning. Knives and forks were scattered on the floor, upturned plates lay under the tables, cups had been shattered, forms overturned.

In the hope that someone may have been late for supper or that I might find one not so badly affected and get some sense out of him I went into the wardroom. Here the story was the same. All the officers were either groaning in their bunks or on the deck of their cabins. A quick tour of the vessel disclosed more men in the same terrible state in the fo'c'sle, but from none could I get information of any sort. It seemed that I alone out of the *Gray's* complement had escaped. Apparently all hands had eaten at the same time, and it looked as though even the oiler on watch had taken his meal at the same time as the others, for there was no one in the engine-room.

Then I saw Franklin Martin staggering along the dock. He had been to try and get me on the telephone. He too was suffering great pain and could just manage a shuffling stooped sort of walk. He confirmed that it was fish that had been the cause of their sufferings and that it was the fish they had caught whilst we were at anchor outside. The cooks had utilized it to the full. The menu had featured fish soup, fried fish fillets, fish sauce, and boiled fish. Apparently it had taken about ten minutes to act.

According to Martin, only the Filipinos had drunk the soup. The Americans had preferred fried fish, the others boiled. As a result they had on the whole been more severely stricken than the Americans who had avoided the more virulent of the poison—the juice.

"It tasted something vile," Martin told me, gripping the rail for support. "Right from the first mouthful it started to burn like hot coal, but we kept on eating. I guess we just thought old Casas had over-seasoned it. There were not a few impolite remarks as we waded through the stuff, and then half-way through our meal, it seemed to hit us all at the same time. Some of the guys just gripped their stomachs and rolled on the deck yelling and groaning, others beat it to their bunks and the rest of us staggered as best we could out on the deck just about where they are now, sir. It gave you a desperate feeling that you just had to get out in the fresh air, and the most appalling thirst. But I can't swallow." Martin showed signs of becoming worse and when I asked him to go ashore again and try and get help he said he would not be able to make it again. There was no time for me to go myself as I had to get into immediate action and try and get the fish out of their stomachs. It seemed to be so rapid in its action I was afraid some of the men might die if I wasted any more time. The burning of the throat and mouth mentioned by Martin seemed to indicate the poison must be corrosive in its effects.

First of all, with the help of Martin I made a hurried check to see whether any of the men might have wandered deliriously ashore. But I found them all aboard somewhere. It would seem all were too badly affected to more than stagger to and collapse in the places I found them.

To administer an emetic to these men proved to be easier in thought than in actual practice. Obtaining some salt from the galley I mixed two tablespoons of this with warm water in a glass, for each man, but found it impossible to get any of them to swallow the mixture. The effect or at least one of the effects of the poison seemed to have brought on what I took to be a sort of paralysis of the throat muscles, and they could not swallow. "This is a nice how d'ye do," I said to myself. "Just what the hell am I going to do now?" Somehow or other I *must* get the stuff away from them, for by now I was thoroughly alarmed. From many, the groaning had become a dreadful low-pitched chorus, but others seemed too far gone and weak to even move or cry out.

Going to the dispensary I obtained a sort of douche can and a length of fine rubber hose. There didn't appear to be time to even sterilize these so I just gave them a rinse. Transferring the salt water mixture to the can, I fitted the hose over the connection, then rubbed it with some olive oil. Now we would see whether this idea would be any better. The first man I came to I gently inserted the tube in his mouth and started to slide it down his throat. To me this was not an easy operation, but I persevered and when I thought I had inserted sufficient of the rubber tube I held the can high and allowed the solution to trickle down into his stomach. Feeling quite pleased at this initial success I then went from man to man repeating the process until finally I had administered an emetic to all the patients.

More men were showing signs of distress and I began to fear my clumsy efforts to relieve them was only making things worse. My muttered prayers of a mixture of curses and words of appeal for guidance were, it seemed, falling on deaf ears. I wasn't a blankety Doctor and the little medical knowledge I had seemed to have deserted me. "What the blazes could I do now?" An enema? Yes, that was it. Give the blighters an enema. All this time Martin was trying to do what he could to assist me so I told him to get a can of hot water and some soap. He staggered off to do my bidding and returned with the can of water and the soap. Putting the soap in the water I stirred it around until I had obtained a good foaming lather. Some of this I then transferred to the douche can and fitted a nozzle in the end of the rubber tube. Then

184

with Martin's assistance I began one of the most distasteful tasks of my career. From man to man we went administering enemas like hospital nurses. We just rolled each man gently over on his side and gave the enemas where they lay. The continuous moaning was beginning to get on my nerves, but we kept on and by the time we had finished I was ready to drop myself. The whole operation had taken three weary hours. It was now 11 p.m.

Most of the men now seemed to be a great deal easier, but the Chief Cook was still emitting horrible groans. So I went to him. He found words to whisper to me, "Please, Skipper, please don't go away. Don't leave me. Can't you see I am dying? And I want to see my Mama before I go, please, Skipper, can't you——" and here he suddenly doubled up with pain and rolled over squirming and moaning on the deck. I felt very helpless just standing there and watching him, but Dominguez was only one of twenty-nine who were claiming my very doubtful ministering. What more could I do? I wearily went to my cabin and got hold of the *Ship's Medical Guide*. I thumbed through the index, then through the pages. But it told me nothing of what I wanted to know. I flung it down and returned to my patients once more. And now I lost the only assistance I had. Martin suddenly complained he was feeling worse. Within a few minutes he was unable to speak and started to groan as badly as the rest. I helped him to his bunk and left him.

Back on deck, the hum of the generators made me realize there was no one to attend to them. Without this attention they might seize up, and then there were also the fires in the furnace. These things had to be attended to, but I personally had not the foggiest notion of how to go about the matter. One of the engineers would have to stagger down to the engine-room and show me how. So I went in turn to each of my four engineers. Cuesta, the Chief, was lying bathed in sweat, almost unconscious. It was certain he could not help me. Gonzalez was worse. On top of his suspected trouble and asthma, the poisoning had been disastrous. He had turned a sallow green, was scarcely breathing and did not even have the strength to moan. Stephens was groaning so loudly I couldn't even get him to talk. It left only Schmidt. True to his race he was taking the intense pain with stoicism, but despite himself was squirming on the ward-room deck.

I knelt down beside him. "Schmidt," I said, "I want you to help me. Can you come below and show me how to shut down the generators? You are the only man who can possibly do it." He turned his weather-beaten, pain-wracked face up to me, winced, and said imploringly, "Please no, sir, I am too ill. I cannot stand. It would kill me."

But too much was at stake. Not only his life, but those of Harris, Whiteman and Todd depended on the *Gray's* capacity to put to sea again. If the generators burned out, she would not. So, though I hated doing it, I had to order the miserable Schmidt to make the effort. I knew him well enough to know that had he had a spark of energy left in him he would need no urging. But both of us knew he was incapable. Yet somehow it had to be done.

I hoisted him to his feet, but he couldn't stand. His knees just sagged and he tottered groaning, against me. But with my support he managed to stagger the twenty yards down the deck to the engine-room hatch. This was where it became really difficult. Schmidt had almost passed out with the agony of his short hobble. He lay against the hatch gasping for breath and holding his stomach as if it would fall out if he let it go. Somehow I had to get him down those three flights of engine-room ladders to the bed-plates of the engine-room. There was only one way to do it. I would have to carry him.

Schmidt was short, stocky and heavy. Looking at him you would have thought he weighed perhaps a bit over ten stone. But now as I bent down and slung him over my shoulder I quickly realized his muscular frame concealed every ounce of twelve. It took me a minute to get him safely balanced, another two to hump him over the hatch, and then our hair-raising descent began. It was, I think, twenty-three feet to the bottom down those three flights of ladders. I went down backwards, facing the rungs, clutching the rail with one hand, Schmidt with the other. Every movement brought a sobbing cry from his lips, every step, which I felt for carefully before dropping on to, gave me the feeling that we were overbalancing. For Schmidt it must have been sheer hell. His most painfully affected part, his stomach, was doubled hard over my shoulder; his breath began to come in shorter and shorter gasps and the stifling heat of the engine-room sent sweat rolling off both our bodies. He wore only dungarees and singlet and it took half my strength preventing my arm slipping off his saturated body.

It was minutes before I felt the wonderful security of the first platform under my feet. I lowered Schmidt on to it and leant against the ladder to recover my breath and strength. Then, I went a few steps down the next flight, put my shoulder under him and edged my way down to the control platform. To get from here on to the last flight was a small feat even for the able-bodied engine-room staff. The platform was crossed by an almost solid wall of hot steam-pipes. It was part of the Towmaster's super-charging network, and one had almost to lie down and crawl for four feet to get under them. I had quite forgotten this conglomeration. Now I regarded it with dismay.

Carefully I laid Schmidt down on the shining metal platform. Below us the steam hissed and the generators hummed. The smell of hot oil enveloped us. "You'll have to help yourself here," I told Schmidt. But he didn't hear me and just lay where I had put him, eyes half-closed and close to unconsciousness. I wondered if, after this dreadful ordeal, he was going to be in a state to give me the vital instructions I needed. Clearly he wouldn't remain conscious much longer and even more clearly he could do nothing further to help himself on this mission.

As best I could I rolled him over until he was lying flat on the platform. Then I crawled under the pipes, turned round, grabbed his legs and dragged him through after me. Another pause for breath, time to wipe my sweat-plastered face and Schmidt was on my shoulder again, sagging, helpless as a carcass of meat. For a horrible moment I staggered to regain my balance and somehow I managed to find it and the descent continued.

Reaching the bottom at last I dumped Schmidt on to the watch-keeper's seat. Above the noise of the generators I yelled at him, "For God's sake try and snap out of it for a few minutes and tell me what to do." His only answer was a sickening groan. I seized him and yelled again: "Schmidt, Schmidt, can you hear me? Don't fail me now. We must turn the generators off. WE MUST TURN THE GENERATORS OFF." He hadn't heard me—but, yes he had —his lips were beginning to move. I put my ear close to them. Slowly, painfully, in a hoarse whisper, the instructions came . . . "the . . . valves . . . sir . . . in . . . the . . . stokehold . . . must . . . must turn them off . . . first . . . fires must die down."

"Well done, Schmidt," I said, "but don't I have to turn off the oil pump first?" There was no answer. So I had a look around to see whether I could locate such a pump which commonsense told me must be somewhere about. I found bilge pumps and other pumps but none were operating and then I saw one driven by an electric motor. It seemed to be the only one working but whether it was what I sought I had no means of knowing. There was no switch on it, so going to the switch panel I looked to see whether it was here. Below each switch there were some indecipherable markings so I took a chance and pulled one; by luck it was the right one. Then I groped my way to the stokehold and after a bit of trouble found some valves near the boiler which was being fired and turned them off. Returning to Schmidt I managed to get him to indicate where the valves were to our turbine-driven generator. These I screwed down and the whine started to die away and so did the lights. I had forgotten that with the generator shut down there would be no lights in the engine-room as well as the rest of the ship. The blackness down here was complete. Of Schmidt, all I could hear was his quiet groaning. Looking up twenty-odd feet through the shadowy pattern of steam pipes, I could see the faint outline of the open skylights and through these the glimmer of the starlit Pacific sky beyond. Our return journey was going to be that much harder without lights. Getting Schmidt down had been bad enough. But I had to find him first so I felt my way towards where he lay.

Once again on my shoulder, his weight seemed to have increased and my own strength proportionately weaker. The effort had left me spent, and for some minutes I could only lean against the ladder. Rung by rung I crept up towards that small square of starlight. At every step I barked my shins and swore. By the time I had squeezed both of us under the pipes, my head was swimming and my strength almost gone. The last two flights were a ghastly unreal nightmare. It had taken half an hour from the bottom to the top. Next thing I remember was grabbing the hatch, sliding Schmidt on to the deck and flopping down beside him. Schmidt just lay open-mouthed, wheezing and white-faced. Too far gone to even groan, he seemed to have collapsed completely. His eyes had sunk into their sockets, giving him a horrible ghoulish appearance. "Heavens," I thought, "he's dying." In my own exhaustion it seemed his breathing had about stopped. It was half an hour before he had revived sufficiently for me to help him to his cabin where I left him after throwing a blanket over him. If ever a man deserved a medal that man was Hermann Schmidt.

It was now well past midnight. I had to find some means of illumination and so I searched the lamp-room where I found a solitary hurricane lamp. We had given the others to the men on the minesweepers. With the aid of this I started on my rounds of my patients. They were all still in a bad way, but there was little more I could do for them. Then I discovered one of them was missing. It was Damone. I wondered where the dickens he could have got to. I doubted he had fallen in the lagoon as it would take more than the strength he had to get over the bulwarks. And then I saw something move over near the dock shed. I went ashore and had a look. Yes, it was Damone all right, an unhappy yet comical figure in his spotless white cap he had worn all the voyage and which always seemed as if it had just been laundered. I secured a blanket, covered him, and left him where he was hoping he would not contract a chill.

A renewed chorus of groans made me have a look at some of the men. They wanted water but with the ship shut down there was no flow of water from any of the taps. I would have to go ashore to try and find some, and I thought, too, I would go up to the radio-shack and ask the operators to procure assistance from some of the islanders for me. But as soon as I again started to go ashore the groans became wails. It seemed no one wanted me to leave them for an instant even to get water. Some even managed to call: "Captain Ainslie, Captain Ainslie, don't leave us; we are dying." So I remained aboard. At least my presence seemed to have a certain psychological value.

I was feeling unutterably tired. Since leaving Palmyra for the search on September 27 I had snatched only a few hours' sleep and it was now October 3. But sleep was impossible until I had found someone to look after these seriously ill men. So throughout the rest of the night I continued to attend to them as best I could. On one of my rounds I found that both Alonso and the Bosun had managed to crawl up on to the forecastle-head and both were lying down near the hawse pipes. What a dejected pair they looked, alternately moaning and crying out. Alonso particularly was in a bad way. He looked at me with eyes bigger and rounder than I could ever remember having seen before. "Sir," he said, "I can't stand this pain much longer. Please, please do something." But I could only offer him my very poor best efforts as given to all the others and a few words of comfort. I put a crude canvas cover over both him and Romanin and left them to their moans. Even as I walked away I could still hear him repeating, "I cannot stand it, I cannot stand it." I thought to myself, "I won't be able to stand much more myself." The whole business was like a lurid dream from which I could not awaken.

Dawn came at last. As its first rosy light crept over the lagoon and washed the *Gray* in pink, it lit a pathetic spectacle. Every corner of the deck had a half-naked, recumbent form stretched out inelegantly in his own filth. They were all a revolting sight, desperately in need of a bath and of hospital attention neither the *Gray* nor Palmyra could give them.

Soon after daybreak I saw a jeep passing us some distance away. By blowing a docking whistle, yelling and waving I succeeded in attracting the driver's attention. He was one of the operators going on early morning shift. As soon as I was able to tell him of our trouble he roared off in a cloud of dust to telephone Mr. Stamm.

Stamm arrived a few minutes later and came aboard. All he could say was: "My God, what a smell!"

"This is terrible, Captain Ainslie," he said holding his nose, "you need some women here. I'll try and get some of the wives down to help. These men look as if they are dying."

An hour later Stamm was back with several of the island's administrative staff and four wives. They were young, and two, rather pretty. But the sight that met them aboard the *Gray* was more than they had bargained for. The spectacle of a deck littered with these gaunt, bearded, shaven-haired men of half-a-dozen different nationalities, was almost too much for them. The most attractive of the four wives, a young auburn-haired girl, took one look at the scene, went pale and hurried ashore. She was terribly sorry, she said, but she could not stand the stench. A second girl soon followed her. I could not blame them.

The other two women stayed. They were blonde and typically American. So did all the men. But the job soon proved to be too horrible even for them. Stamm said we would have to make an urgent appeal to Honolulu for doctors and went off to the radio-shack to send the message.

Meanwhile the small volunteer band did what little they could to make the men more comfortable. The girls took them water and somebody fetched cans of fruit juices.

Then Stamm came back with the news that Honolulu had not a doctor to spare but would try and make arrangements for one to be flown up from Christmas Island which lay to the south of Washington Island. He also told me that a plane had been promised us to take up the search for the sweepers, and also that the radio-men had heard nothing further from Sparks. Then my helpers said they could not stand it any longer and went ashore.

During the day some of the men returned and we carried all the patients off the ship and laid them out in cots beside the shed on the dockside. The scene looked for all the world like a casualty clearing station in a front-line battle zone. There was one man we could not persuade to go ashore. It was Espinosa. He lay among the auxiliary tanks on the after-deck and every time we tried to get him to come ashore he became so upset, I decided to leave him where he was in the meantime. He was wildly delirious and had a temperature of 103°. I suspected he was losing his reason, but apart from the concern this gave me, I was also concerned about his rising temperature and determined to get him into the wardroom, where his chances of contracting a chill were much less.

The illness seemed to be entering a new phase now. The pain began to spread below the stomach into the bowels and bladder. It was the most vicious, insidious poison, this, I had ever known: a sort of creeping, searing pain that seemed to burn and paralyse at the same time.

I began to find difficulty keeping track of everybody and was worried at the too-easy possibility that someone might plunge off the edge into the lagoon. There was a nasty moment when I discovered Ferraro and Damone missing. I found them after a panic search. Somehow Ferraro had dragged himself into the cabin of a crane. Damone was lying stretched out beneath it. The poison's latest effect seemed to fire its victims with a strong desire to crawl away and be alone.

When I went back to the dock I was startled to find more than half the cots were empty. A search of the nearby undergrowth found them groaning and clutching their distended abdomens. Nothing could persuade them back into their cots. They were too overwrought by their own misery to realize the added dangers of a chill and pneumonia. So I just covered each man up with a sheet and left them.

As I turned round to go back to the *Gray* I saw a figure in dungarees and a singlet swaying on his feet, barely a yard from the edge of the dock. I yelled and sprinted after him. When I was six feet away he began to topple forward into the sea. With one tremendous leap I sprang, knocking him sprawling back from the dock-edge. I picked him up and carried him to an empty cot. It had been a narrow one for Damone.

Night came again. It was now twenty-four hours since the fatal meal. I hadn't slept for thirty-six hours with the worry of the search, had in fact only snatched a few hours on my bunk in the last five days. I was feeling so unutterably weary and groggy I knew that very shortly even if the crew's lives depended on my wakefulness, I should have to get some sleep. Stamm commented on it when he did his rounds that evening.

"Jumping Jimminy, buddy!" he said. "You sure look as if you could sleep for a month. Take my advice and turn in for a few hours before you drop." But a "few hours" wouldn't have worked out. I knew that as soon as I put my head on that pillow I would be good for nothing for twenty-four hours.

That night Stamm had the dock floodlights switched on. They almost turned the pierside into daylight. Under their glare I went from cot to cot. Worst of them all were Gonzalez and Espinosa. Both had temperatures of 105°, both were in a delirious semi-coma. Their hearts and pulses were fading alarmingly. On top of his other disabilities I knew it would be a miracle if Gonzalez survived. Their only hope now lay in the speedy arrival of a doctor. But still there was no definite word of one.

Once during the night when I went aboard I got a bad fright. Walking along the deck I was suddenly confronted by an apparition in white. It was the closest I have ever seen to the popular idea of a ghost. For a few seconds it had me puzzled. But when I ran after it my arms closed round a sheet with the distraught and very real form of Espinosa enshrouded in it.

Too far gone even to notice me, he was gesticulating, wandering aimlessly about the ship, and burbling weirdly to himself. I led him back to his cot among the auxiliary tanks, but no sooner had I tucked him in than he rose up with the sheet wrapped round him and walked away like some ethereal spirit. I had almost decided to tie him down for his own safety when quite of his own accord he went, muttering, to a cot in the wardroom.

By morning—it was now October 4—Stephens, Lascano, Cooper, Schmidt and Martin began to show signs of recovery. They asked for food. The islanders brought them canned orange juice, fruit salad, hot soup and ice cream. Word travelled fast that some of the *Gray's* patients were beginning to eat again, and throughout the day we had a stream of visitors bring food offerings. Even the little American children came down with gifts of candy.

Just after dawn I heard the drone of an approaching aircraft. Soon it appeared, a big four-engined United States air-sea rescue plane from Honolulu. It circled the island then came rolling in down the big runway. But when the doors were flung open only its youthful-looking crew sprang down. There was no doctor.

I was bitterly disappointed. But after a chat with the Captain, a tall Pacific war veteran, I felt better. He told me he had been sent to look for the minesweepers. No doctor could be spared to come with him, but one was being sent on a second aircraft within forty-eight hours.

The pilot said he proposed beginning the search immediately. I asked if I could go with him as an extra observer. But it appeared he had first to get authority from his base in Honolulu. That night when he got back after a fruitless search, he sent off a signal. Back came the reply: yes, I *could* go the next day.

That evening Schmidt and Stephens, though still very groggy, decided that their convalescence was complete Hoping it was the beginning of a general recovery all round I asked Schmidt to go aboard, get steam up and re-start the generators. Now the air-search was beginning, the minesweepers might be found any hour. I wanted the *Gray* to be ready to pick them up the moment they were spotted.

But before he could prepare the engines Schmidt needed the assistance of an oiler. Looking along the rows of cots I noticed Lascano. He was sitting up, talking and smoking, and looked as able as Schmidt and Stephens to undertake a few light duties back in the engine-room.

Before we took off next morning I ordered Lascano out of his cot. He got to his feet and dressed with a face like thunder. Clearly he had planned a few more days in bed. "If he gives trouble don't stand any nonsense," I told Stephens. "He's obviously shamming; a little work will keep him out of mischief."

From positions I had given him the pilot had plotted an area of search on his own chart. Despite our subsequent discovery that another current might be sweeping the minesweepers east it was decided to eliminate first the area into which they would have drifted if the observations we made before leaving them were correct. This took us east-north-east of the island to put us on the edge of a big square of ocean immediately north-west of the position where we had dropped the three men. Already on the previous day's search the aircraft had covered quite a chunk of this area.

As we roared away from Palmyra I looked back at the island and realized just how tiny it was. In ten minutes it was just a small speck in the wide blue ocean; another five minutes put it out of sight.

It took us less than forty minutes to reach the search area. The pilot handed round powerful binoculars; the navigator busied himself over his charts. I began methodically scanning the horizon. It was a glorious, hot Pacific day. Although we were flying at 8,000 feet the sun beating through the perspex transformed the cabin into a baking hot-house in which even shirt sleeves seemed superfluous.

Visibility was perfect. Below, the horizon extended for fifty miles in every direction—a smooth, sapphire blue carpet speckled with the white caps of breaking waves and the tiny, deceptive ripples of the swell I knew only too well to be all of twelve feet high. Somewhere down there, wallowing in the rollers, were four drifting, derelict mine-sweepers, three anxious, sunburned, bearded men.

Seventy-six hours I had told them. That was eleven long days ago. Since then whatever current they were riding could have carried them nearly two hundred miles. Assuming they were travelling no faster than sixteen miles a day, this made an immense area of possibility—many thousand square miles of it.

I wondered as mile after mile of sea slid by below, what Sparks, Whiteman and Todd were thinking. Probably that something had happened to the *Gray*, that she had foundered, run aground on Palmyra, or that her engines had broken down finally and completely. They were probably beginning to wonder if we had all been lost, whether we had advised Palmyra of the drifting mine-sweepers. But whatever fate they might have presumed for us, Sparks as radio operator knew that the Islands Towage and Lighterage Company in San Francisco would know of their plight. He himself had sent the message. No, even if they believed the *Gray* had gone, Sparks would know that it would only be a matter of hours before Colonel Gray instituted some form of search.

I tried to picture the three of them down there. Sparks, cool as always, probably fiddling with his radio set which we could only presume had failed them. Whiteman and Todd, shirts off, were probably fishing, reading, sun-bathing or squatting on the highest part of the mine-sweeper watching the horizon for the faintest wisp of smoke, straining their ears for the most distant noise of an aircraft. By now they would have exhausted all the stories they knew, were probably too anxious to play poker. But on the credit side they had one very big entry in their favour. They had food and fresh water for months. If the minesweeper kept afloat they could survive until Christmas.

We were away from Palmyra for fourteen hours. We flew parallel search lines fifteen miles wide for two thousand miles. But we found nothing. Occasionally the aircraft's radar picked up vague unidentifiable objects and we diverted to follow them up. But always they ended in a disappointment I knew all too well—rain squalls.

It was dusk when the palm trees and water tower of Palmyra popped out of the Pacific ahead of us. We banked in to land. Tragic and ugly news was waiting for me. Stamm came out to the aircraft to tell me quietly that Espinosa was dead. A few minutes later I learned too that in my absence there had been trouble aboard the *Gray*. Miranda came hurrying along to tell me about it. Johnnie Stephens, he said, had tried to murder Lascano.

# Chapter Twelve

Poor old Espinosa had died that afternoon. Soon after I took off, his condition had suddenly worsened and Stamm had taken him over to the administration block. But there was little anyone could do for him. He rallied for a short time during the early afternoon then became wildly delirious, raving and heaving about in his bed. Just before 1 o'clock he calmed down and lay very still with the colour draining from his face. A few minutes later he was dead. Pneumonia had taken him. Stamm said they had put the body in one of the island's spare freezing chambers. It was the only way it could be preserved in the heat. There were no implements on Palmyra capable of scratching the steel-hard coral, far less able to dig a six-foot grave. It seemed that no one had ever ended his life on the island before and the question of burial was a problem which hitherto had never arisen.

I asked Stamm to do his best to prevent the news of Espinosa's death reaching the rest of my crew. The psychological effect it might have on those still critically ill, could have hastened further ends, particularly among the more superstitious of the Filipinos. So while Espinosa's body lay stiffening in the freezer I reassured all inquirers that he was being well looked after and was "quite comfortable" up in the administration block.

Meanwhile I set out to investigate the alleged murder attempt on Lascano. From a variety of colourful and grossly-distorted stories I pieced the incident together.

It appeared that my fear Lascano would refuse to go below with Stephens had not been unfounded. As soon as I was out of the way the resentful engine-room hand had gone straight back to his dockside cot. Stephens had yanked him out and marched him, loudly protesting, up the gangway and along to the engine-room hatch. But here Lascano began to resist violently. Stephens had lost his temper, picked up a hefty pipe-wrench and struck him over the head.

Lascano had fallen to the deck swearing dreadful revenge. Blood gushed from an ugly four-inch wound on his head. "I'll get you for this, you American bastard, just you wait," he cried.

Hearing Lascano's screams those of his countrymen who were able to leave their cots, came groggily on board to see what the trouble was. Miranda, unable to walk, crawled painfully along the dock, dragging himself up the gangway and along the deck.

For several minutes Stephens, horrified at what he had done, stood there alone, still gripping the pipe-wrench, facing the enraged men. In their eyes he had done an unpardonable thing. Only Miranda's presence saved him, and that only just, for Miranda was a Filipino first, an officer second. At heart he would have liked to see Stephens get what he considered he deserved.

Swearing they would get him later the angry Filipinos finally staggered, muttering, back to their cots. Miranda dressed Lascano's wound, and Stephens and Schmidt went below to raise steam alone.

"You were a damn' fool to hit him," I told Stephens. "But anyway he asked for it. I would have done the same had I lost my temper.

"The trouble is you can't stay aboard now. You wouldn't last two nights. Those Filipinos would cheerfully hang for a murder of revenge. Take my advice and make yourself scarce. If you don't want a knife in your back go and spend a few days looking round the island. Stamm will put you up. You can come back when we are ready to put to sea again. They won't have forgotten by then—they never forget—but they are unlikely to try anything under me at sea."

"I don't fancy any Filipino's knife between these shoulder-blades," said Stephens. Tenderly he felt the back of his sun-browned neck. "I guess Mrs. Stephens' little Johnny will be out of town for a few days. Don't forget to call me before you sail, sir."

And so Johnnie Stephens went off to make himself as scarce as anyone could on a four by three-mile atoll. I waited to make sure none of the Filipinos had followed him, then went to find Stamm. It was my fourth day without sleep but the earlier desperate craving for it seemed to be fading. In a vague, light-headed sort of way I felt I could now keep going for another week without sleep if necessary.

Stamm was in conference with the air-sea rescue pilot. "Just the man we want to see," he greeted me. "We were just discussing how to dispose of the body of your Filipino fireman. Your suggestion to take him out to sea in our picket-boat is a good one, but the currents round the island are so damned unreliable he might well be washed up again. But now our Air Force friend here, has a much better suggestion. Tell him, Hank."

Hank took a long drink at the pale iced beer in his glass and said: "Why not wrap him up in a flag, weight his feet, and put him in the bomb bay of my plane. We could hold a little service and I could drop him as far out as you like."

"Good God, no," I said. "Maybe it's a good idea but if Espinosa's wife ever got wind of it we would have the wrath of the entire family on our shoulders."

Our discussion was interrupted by the arrival of a white-faced and terrified young American. He was the freezing chamber watchman and looked as if he had been badly frightened. For a minute he couldn't speak. But a whisky under his belt stopped his trembling and he recovered sufficiently to stammer, "The man in the freezer, he's come to life. I've just heard him knocking on the door. I was afraid to open it by myself."

We all gasped. This was monstrous. I looked at Stamm. "Are you sure he was quite dead?" I asked him.

"Dead as a doornail," said Stamm. "I saw him myself. Not a trace of life."

With the watchman safely in the rear we all trooped over to the haunted freezer. It was a big, solid affair with foot-thick doors covered in fine white layers of frost. Despite the balmy tropical night I shivered at the sight of it. We all stood silent and looked at each other. None had the guts to open the chamber. At last Stamm struggled with the lock. My own feelings were decidedly disturbed and not altogether devoid of fear.

As the heavy door swung slowly open none of us knew quite what would happen and, as Stamm reached for the light switch we held our breaths not knowing what supernatural spectacle we were about to witness. But instead, the light showed us only Espinosa's recumbent form on a wire basket stretcher. A little diffidently we crept over. I leaned forward and looked at Espinosa's mask-like face. He lay in his pyjamas, cold, stiff—dead. "There's only one door he will ever knock on," I said to Stamm. "St. Peter's."

I spent the rest of the night doing the rounds of my patients. Most were still seriously ill and besought me with their eyes not to leave them. Gonzalez was weakening rapidly and I began to wonder if he would see another day. But inside that tortured body of his, was a very determined streak which did not die easily. When dawn came he was still wheezing and groaning in his cot. An hour later a large transport plane arrived and landed. Although I didn't know it, that big four-engined aircraft meant that within a few hours I could slide into the oblivion of merciful sleep. It brought two doctors from Honolulu.

They came straight down to the dock. One was an American Army doctor, mid-thirtyish, the other, more elderly, a Honolulu quarantine doctor. They were astounded at what they saw. The Army man, after a quick inspection round my little open-air hospital, said, "Captain, most of these men are in a very bad way, far worse than we had imagined. It's hospital in Honolulu for them, and quickly. They are suffering from acute poisoning."

Within a few hours the twenty-one worst cases were loaded on to stretchers and put aboard the Skymaster. They were Alonso, Gonzalez, Romanin, Ferraro, Savarino, Rocca, Diaz, Damone, Jacobsen, Casas, Dominguez, Guido, Ortiz, Cooper, Ritter, Cuesta, Lascano, Vincent, Bennett, Brown and one other whose name I have forgotten. It left me only Miranda, Stephens, Schmidt, Rodriguez, Martin and Jones the negro. When they were safely aboard, we loaded Espinosa's body, unknown to them, into the cargo hatch. After an autopsy he would be given a decent burial somewhere in Hawaii.

Just before the plane roared away, the Army doctor turned to me and said, "Look, Captain, you don't look so hot yourself. Why not go with them to Honolulu and get a bit of rest."

I thanked him. "No," I said. "You see, you haven't seen quite all of my crew. Three of them are drifting on a minesweeper, God knows where, out there. I wouldn't feel really happy leaving here until they're found. Thanks all the same."

"I quite understand," he replied with a friendly pat on the shoulder. "But let me give you just one small piece of advice. If you want to be able to take that tug of yours on to Manila, get some sleep mighty soon." Then he slipped me several small white pills. "They'll help you to sleep," he said.

I stood on the runway and watched the big plane until it was swallowed up in the blue Pacific sky. Then suddenly the physical ordeal of the past four days began to catch up with me. Noises roared through my head, my ears didn't seem to hear properly, my eyeballs were prickling, I couldn't see or think. I felt as if I could sleep for a week. Dazedly I walked over to the room Stamm had given me, I took a shower, climbed in between the sheets, swallowed the pills and was asleep in a few seconds. Those pills certainly didn't leave anything to chance. They held me in their black, dreamless grip for thirty-six hours.

It was October 8 when I woke. When I had been properly convinced that it was not the 7th I went off to the radio shack for news of Sparks. But there had been none. For two weeks now the operators had listened twenty-four hours a day for the faintest semblance of the Morse letters "H.P.V.D.", the *Gray's* call-sign. But by now none of us expected to hear anything. Even if his signals were the same strength as the one weak message that they had picked up the evening we dropped the minesweepers, the four little ships would almost certainly have drifted out of range by this time.

Meanwhile the search plane had continued its daily two thousand miles, fourteen-hour searching. Its radio operator listened on Sparks' frequency throughout each sortie, the crew of eight scanned the ocean through binoculars, its radar swept the rollers. But of the minesweepers there was no trace. Not even a stick of wreckage, a tiny patch of oil.

For the moment there was nothing more I could do. Now I had lost most of my crew the *Gray* was immobilized. The search and rescue was entirely a military operation. So I took a day off. Stamm gave me a shotgun and I set off to explore the little there was of the island and to bag a few frigate birds on the lagoon. Strangely there were mallard ducks too, but I left them alone as I was sure they were only using the lagoon as a resting place on their ocean flight from somewhere to somewhere.

It was the only really lazy day I spent on the whole voyage. I swam in the lagoon, shot, and all the while kept an eye open for any equipment that might be useful in re-rigging the tows when they were found. But the Navy had left very little. All that I found was the wreckage of an aircraft that had crashed on take-off six months earlier.

Next day brought startling developments in the air search. No less than twenty-four United States' Navy P.B.Y.s and Liberators roared in. They came from Pearl Harbour, Johnston Island and Christmas Island. And just as the last taxied in, two big flying-boats landed on the lagoon. The Navy had taken over the search. Sparks, Whiteman and Todd had become the subject of a full-scale operation.

Within half an hour the aircraft had disgorged enough aircrew and ground staff to man quite a sizeable front-line base. More than three hundred of them came tumbling out. They increased Palmyra's population six-fold, and before the day was out had turned the peaceful little atoll into a noisy, clanking, chattering hive of activity. It looked for all the world as if Palmyra was preparing to defend itself from some vast invasion force.

Over at the normally quiet administration block I found that the drafting office had already been transformed into the search "Operations room". A naval Commander, short, lean and boyish-looking, was setting up his headquarters with brisk efficiency. Maps and charts were being laid out on tables, aircraft roster boards fixed to the walls, extra telephones installed, everybody was furiously doing something.

Heavens, I thought, this is going to cost the Islands Towage and Lighterage Company a fantastic sum. I was almost amused to contemplate Colonel Gray's reaction when he learned that I had hired a full Navy air squadron to find his minesweepers. It would surely cost the company many times the price of all the sweepers and the *Gray*. But the Commander's quiet voice reassured me that it wouldn't cost the company a single dollar. It was a useful training exercise which the Navy in fact welcomed, he said. They were calling it "operation H.P.V.D."

After I had given him all the information I could about the minesweepers' rate and direction of drift I asked him if he could spare operators to keep a twenty-four hour watch on the *Gray's* directional radio. "Sure," he said. "You can have a couple of men to-night."

The island was teeming with men. There were pilots, navigators, radio-operators, flight engineers, mechanics, fitters, riggers, instrument repairers and cooks. Their loud talk and laughter brought Palmyra a strange breath of the outside world.

The island administration was thoroughly overawed by the whole situation. Its chief concern was that it could offer neither adequate food nor accommodation to its unexpected guests. But the Navy improvised admirably. Many of the men slept in their aircraft; others opened up some of the disused wartime buildings. I heard too, that a tanker with the special high octane aviation fuel the Navy required, had meanwhile been diverted to Palmyra from Samoa.

At first light next morning, the new phase of the search began in earnest. All early morning the quiet of the island was shattered by the roar of motors coughing to life, the noise of aircraft being run-up and the crescendos of twenty-four take-offs. From the lagoon came a different sound. It was the swish of rocket-assisted take-offs which the two flying-boats used to get airborne in the shortest possible run.

It was 8 o'clock before all the aircraft had gone. The runway looked strangely deserted: the island sounded uncannily quiet. Over in the commander's operations' room I followed the search on his charts. Unlike the *Gray's* octagonal method, the air-search was fan-shaped and as soon as one area was covered another segment was begun, widening always in a north-westerly direction.

Leaving nothing to chance, the Navy had extended the far edge of the big triangle they were systematically scouring, to five hundred miles north-east of Palmyra. Each aircraft had been briefed to cover a different patch of ocean, making its parallel legs over a hundred miles long. Thus each plane flew over one hundred miles, turned ninety degrees, flew nine miles, then another ninety-degree turn taking it back one hundred miles parallel with the last long leg and so on.

With twenty-six aircraft out it was not long before quite a big segment of ocean had been exhaustively searched. Hour after hour throughout the day as the aircraft radioed back their progress, I watched the Commander's pencil filling in more and more of the area on his chart beyond which the minesweepers could not possibly have drifted. But when dusk brought the aircraft back one by one, like pigeons home to roost, there had been no sign of the sweepers. Just in case they had been spotted by an aircraft whose radio was unserviceable I waited until all the pilots had strolled in to report to the Commander.

One of the last brought wonderful news. His radio operator had picked up a succession of desperately faint signals. It was the call-sign "H.P.V.D." Immediately the operator had swung his directional radio loop to get a bearing on the source of the message. But before he could do so the signals stopped.

I left the search headquarters feeling a new man. It was the first ray of hope in two weeks of steadily increasing despondency. Not for one moment had I ever doubted that my three men were still afloat on one of their four craft. It was good to know that my hopes had been justified. Somewhere, only God knew where, out over that blue horizon within five hundred miles of Palmyra, they were alive and waiting to be rescued. That wouldn't be long now.

Elated I hurried down to the *Gray* to see if any of my

five remaining crew were fit to prepare the tug for sea. When the minesweepers were found there mustn't be an hour lost before the *Gray* went racing to the rescue. It was going to be a proud moment and I didn't want any other ship doing the job for me. Down at the tug I found Miranda, Schmidt, Rodriguez, Jones and Stephens, who had been able to come out of hiding. One look told me all I needed to know. None of them was in a fit condition to do an hour's work, far less help me put to sea. The poison had left them pale, thin and weak as kittens. They seemed to have no energy or interest—and clearly needed all of a week to rest and regain their strength. Schmidt and Stephens were still so run down they had been unable to cope with even the minimum of engine-room duties and had had to shut down again.

But next day there was an unexpected development which abruptly stopped the air-search and compelled us to raise at least enough steam to turn our engine for a few hours. The Navy made the alarming discovery that the aviation fuel they were using for their aircraft was contaminated and, so they thought, dangerously sub-standard. The Commander ordered all planes to be grounded until experts had examined the petrol. It appeared they had been using stocks which had been lying on the island in rusting drums for several years. Several thousand gallons of the stuff had been used before someone spotted what looked like water in it. It was a disappointing blow just when the signal had raised my hopes of an early rescue. But there was nothing I or the Navy could do about it. To have continued using doubtful fuel might have sent the best part of the squadron to its death. I could only pray that the fuel experts would be a little quicker coming than had the doctors.

Meanwhile the Navy tanker with aviation fuel was on its way to Palmyra. As she would have to discharge at the oiling dock it meant that if the *Gray* was to be refuelled and ready we would have to get our oil on quickly. The oiling dock was only half a mile from the main dock where we had tied up. Although he was obviously still a sick man Schmidt immediately offered to give me power for the short move.

Several hours later a tired voice called up on the engine-room telephone, "Ready to go when you are, sir." I stood on the bridge and Miranda, Rodriguez and Jones, my skeleton crew, let go the lines. But the steam pressure was about as strong as the two men who had so wearily raised it. It was barely enough to turn the engines; we just hissed and wheezed and the propeller gave a few lazy dispirited turns. Fifty yards out into the lagoon we lost steam altogether. I had to let go the anchor. Schmidt and Stephens tried again. An hour later Stephens' voice said, "We're ready to try again, sir, but there's mighty little power."

I signalled Miranda to raise the anchor. But as the steam windlass began slowly creaking there was a frantic call from Schmidt. "Stop the windlass, sir, it is using all our precious steam." It was a ludicrous situation. So I told Miranda to raise the anchor just clear of the bottom and we crawled over to the oiling dock with our anchor dragging below us. But even in this, the shortest of all the *Gray's* journeys, our troubles were not over.

As we were gliding in, engines gasping, Schmidt yelled hoarsely up the voice pipe that we were sinking. There was no evidence of it from the bridge. I asked him what the devil he meant. For a moment I thought we must have over-run our anchor and that it had holed us. But all Schmidt could tell me was that water was coming into the engine-room and rising fast. Fortunately his fear proved ill-founded. When we had tied up at the oiling dock I took soundings all over. The engine-room "holing" was immediately explained. Through lying idle for several days the *Gray's* bilge pumps hadn't been working.

All that had happened was that the accumulated bilge water had begun to overflow into the engine-room as we got under way. But the effort of moving the tug, coupled with his belief we were sinking had been too much for Schmidt. He staggered up on deck and collapsed.

Now I only had four men. Somehow I would have to find at least another dozen or the *Gray* would be immobilized. I appealed to Stamm for some islanders to act as an emergency crew but he couldn't spare any. Then I cabled the company. At the same time I reminded them that I would not continue the voyage from Palmyra until they sent me new tow gear, Bunker "C" fuel and provisions.

Meanwhile the Navy's fuel experts arrived. A special aircraft brought them down from Honolulu. I was expecting a team of bespectacled scientists or something. Instead four men who looked more like mechanics climbed out. It took them less than an hour to tell the Commander that his petrol was quite safe and useable. Next day the search was resumed.

October 9, 10 and 11 went by. Aircraft roared in and out all day, the search base grew, an emergency supply route was opened up to bring food, mail, and more men from Honolulu. The number of the island's disused buildings re-opened, grew daily and to entertain its three hundred men or more, the Navy flew in a mobile cinema. On the Commander's chart the shaded area of ocean searched, grew from a tiny thumbnail to a big segment half the size of the sheet. But every evening the twenty-four planes and the two flying-boats came back with the same gloomy news, "We searched from dawn to dusk, we flew more than two thousand miles, we saw nothing."

And now I had another problem. The search began to make newspaper headlines. It began with minor paragraphs in the Hawaiian papers, spread to a daily column on the front pages and finally drew banner headlines in San Francisco and throughout the States and Associated Press cabled accounts to most newspapers in other countries. And then cables began to pour in. Worried wives, mothers and sweethearts of almost every member of my crew demanded to know: was it their man I had ruthlessly cast adrift in mid-Pacific? No sooner had I sent off the appropriate replies than a Honolulu reporter arrived to get his paper an "on the spot" story. But I was afraid if I gave him an account of our difficulties and the reasons leading to the "slipping" of the tows it would affect any insurance claims the company might have contemplated. And so I refused to give the reporter his story. But it made no difference. Despite my warning, other members of the crew talked to him. In any case I was powerless to prevent the story leaking out from the twenty-one men who were now in the hospital in Honolulu. A feature was made of our skull and crossbones emblem in the papers.

By now even the Navy was getting worried. They had been given what must have seemed on the surface of it, a ridiculously simple search. Four minesweepers drifting at the most twenty miles a day; it was simply money for old rope after the fast, elusive Japanese task forces it had chased and run to earth five years before. Something was wrong somewhere.

The Commander called for me again. "Look here, Captain Ainslie," he said. "Are you sure these craft of yours couldn't have gone in any other direction?" I had already discussed this possibility with him, but he had placed reliance on my original observation. But when the Commander showed me the huge patch of Pacific they had scoured, west and north of the point we had dropped them, I said again that it was more than a possibility.

The following day the Commander began to extend the search area over new water to the east. Although charts of the currents in the area, which had been specially flown in, indicated no east-flowing current for a considerable distance, it was the only alternative left. Meanwhile at Navy headquarters in Pearl Harbour, orders went out for a stepping-up of Operation H.P.V.D. During the day a Vice-Admiral arrived to take over the search personally.

This chap quickly appraised the position. "We need more planes," he said. Signals flashed back to Pearl Harbour. The result was that the United States Navy's biggest carrier, *Valley Forge*, with more than a hundred aircraft aboard was radioed to stand by for orders to proceed to a point at the limit of the search and fan her planes out from there. At the same time, several smaller Navy vessels in the area were diverted to the search. Overnight Operation H.P.V.D. had become the Navy's biggest activity since the war.

On October the 12th, the eighth day of the air-search, and the eighteenth the minesweepers had been adrift, the Commander decided it was no longer necessary for his two signal-men to be stationed on the *Gray's* radio. To my bitter disappointment they left the ship that day. Unable to help in any other way I had regarded the listening-watch on our own radio as my only personal contribution to an operation that had developed far beyond my wildest imagination. Determined that the radio should still be manned, I went aboard the *Gray* to listen myself and Stephens kept the emergency generator going.

All that night and the following day, with brief snatches of sleep, I sat with the headset on, straining my ears for the merest crackle. After a meal ashore, I went back at 7 p.m. Two hours went by. I passed the time reading a magazine. Then at nine o'clock, I heard a series of thin, feeble notes. It was perhaps ten seconds before I realized that they were spelling out the call-sign, "H.P.V.D." In a fever of excitement, I gripped the phones to my ears till they hurt. There was no mistaking it, dot dot dot dot, dot dash dash dot, dot dot dot dash, dash dot dot came the magic letters. For half a minute I just sat transfixed, hypnotized by the wonderful message; then suddenly I remembered the direction-finding gear. I swung the loop that would give me the bearing of the signal. But by the time I had adjusted it, the signals had stopped. Fiercely and loudly I swore. Of all the blundering fools I was surely the worst. This was the moment we had waited eighteen days for and I had to bungle it. I felt like weeping. But at least it told me the minesweepers were afloat; Sparks, and presumably Whiteman and Todd too, were still alive.

I waited another long hour before Sparks began again. Several times tiny squeaks of static and interference brought me to my toes, swivelling the loop, but each was a false alarm. And then the signal came again. It was just after 10 o'clock. There were three desperately faint "H.P.V.D.s" followed by "C.Q." (calling any station), but they were all I needed. I got my bearing: 081 degrees true, from Palmyra. Meanwhile Sparks was still tapping away. Then came a message: "WAIT 20 MINUTES," then silence again. But now it didn't matter if his set broke down completely. *We had a bearing.* Somewhere—by the sound of the signals, it was a long way—down that line of bearing 9 degrees north of east, were my four little ships. I had few moments of triumph on this voyage, but that evening at the *Gray's* radio direction-finder was assuredly one of them.

I sent Rodriguez scurrying over to fetch the Commander and some Navy signal-men to confirm my bearing. They arrived breathless, just in time to hear Sparks resume his transmission twenty minutes later. Again he sent three "H.P.V.D.s" followed by a string of "C.Q.s". The Navy verified my 081 degrees. After that there was silence from the minesweeper.

213

And now as we spread out the chart, and ran a track out along the line of Sparks' bearing, the mystery of the search's failure was explained to us. The minesweepers *had* drifted east. The bearing put them somewhere along a line which stretched away towards Central America, well south of the southernmost limit of the air-search pattern. Miranda's suspicion had been proved correct. It only remained now for an aircraft to fly out from Palmyra on a course of 081 degrees true and sooner or later the tows would be sighted. Just how far down the line we had no idea. Unless a radio operator on a neighbouring island, like Washington or Fanning Islands, had got a cross bearing we had no means of "fixing" the exact position.

I was too happy to sleep that night. I just counted the hours until dawn when an aircraft could race away. A Liberator took off at first light. At first it had been suggested that one of the flying-boats might land and pick the three men up. But daylight showed the Pacific to be in no mood for this. A big sea was running and the barometer showed promise of worse to come.

Back in the emergency operations room, I waited with the Admiral and Commander, ready to devour every radio message the aircraft sent back. One, two, three hours crawled by. The suspense was dreadful. And then at 9 a.m. came the signal which for me, in a few seconds, ended the worst suspense of a lifetime and put "OPERATION CONCLUDED" to the Navy's biggest post-war search, "HAVE SIGHTED ONE SWEEPER THREE MEN ABOARD WAVING APPARENTLY ALL WELL."

# Chapter Thirteen

THE Navy didn't waste much time. Within an hour of the signal reporting that No. 1 minesweeper had been found, a fast Coast Guard Patrol vessel was dashing to the spot from Palmyra.

The solitary minesweeper was 440 miles west of Palmyra. It had drifted 364 miles eastward—quite a different direction to that on which we had based all our search calculations. Only our estimate of the rate of drift had been correct. For eighteen days it had averaged fifteen miles a day, just one mile less than we had judged.

But what had happened to the other three minesweepers? Had they stove one another in and been swallowed up by the blue fathoms or had they merely become separated and were now drifting away, each on a silent course of its own?

Slowly throughout the day, terse scraps of news flashed back from the aircraft. "HAVE DROPPED SUPPLIES," then, "HAVE SIGNALLED MEN BUT NO REPLY OTHER THAN REASSURING WAVES." At midday came, "NOW SEARCHING FOR OTHER SWEEPERS"; 2 o'clock, "STILL SEARCHING NO TRACE."

Then, an hour later, the radio began chattering again. "HAVE SIGHTED SECOND SWEEPER SIXTY MILES EAST OF FIRST NO SIGN OF OTHERS." This was encouraging news. Eagerly I stood by the radio expecting any minute word that the rest of my little fleet had been found. But when dusk brought the aircraft back to the island, there was still no trace of the other two.

I was too relieved and elated that Harris, Whiteman and Todd were safe, to be very concerned. Two sweepers

—if indeed they had foundered—was a small price for the deliverance of three brave men.

Next morning as the rescue vessel sped toward No. 1 minesweeper, the mystery of the missing two was explained. An aircraft flew out and parachuted a portable transmitter to Sparks. He told the Pilot that Nos. 2 and 3 had long ago gone to the bottom. They were all fit and well, he reported; in fact their chief concern had been for the safety of the *Gray*. The Pilot quickly reassured them about that and told them their own rescue would be only a matter of hours.

The following day, October 15, was an important one in the voyage of the *Wallace R. Gray*. The rescue ship picked up Sparks, Whiteman and Todd; the air-search ended, all the aircraft flew away, and the first batch of my crew who had supposedly sufficiently recovered, were flown back to Palmyra. There were six of them: Alonso, Gonzalez, Martin, Savarino, Damone and Diaz. They stepped out of the aircraft looking every bit as ill as the day they left. Martin had been sent to Honolulu some days after the main body of patients for observation as a suspected case of appendicitis, but it proved to be only the after-effects of the fish poisoning. Alonso looked ashen grey. Worse, he had since developed hæmorrhoids which rendered him almost incapable of any further duty aboard. Gonzalez, whom I never expected to see alive again, was a walking skeleton. Wheezing, groaning, and talking only in asthmatical gasps, he looked closer to death than ever. It was strange that my recommendation that he be sent back to Manila when fit to travel had not been acceded to. I decided to ask that he be flown home to Manila as soon as possible. In useful strength then I had gained only three men, they, weak as kittens. In view of his incapacity I decided that Alonso should continue the voyage only as supernumerary officer and promoted Miranda Mate. Miranda openly had been anticipating

216

this, but he deserved it. I had not forgotten his part in commanding the boat party on its many perilous missions. I now learned that the cause of the poison was phosphorus, absorbed by the red snapper when it fed on a type of moss growing on the bottom of the lagoon.

Now signals began to come in from the patrol vessel which had picked up our castaways and which was now standing by the sweeper. The lifeboat was past salvaging and had to be sunk. The messages confirmed, that despite their ordeal the three men were in splendid shape and in high spirits. That evening we were startled to hear a broadcast interview with each of them from a Honolulu radio station. A commentator with a portable recorder was aboard the rescue ship. Unlike the hoax he had perpetrated several weeks earlier, Sparks was genuine national hook-up news now. The interview was relayed throughout the United States and even some of my friends in Sydney and other places heard it. But, ironically, poor reception on Palmyra blotted out all but a few snatches of the conversation. One of the few remarks I picked up was Sparks telling the world: "We weren't over-much worried; we knew the Old Man wouldn't rest till he'd found us . . ."

Meanwhile at the request of the Islands Towage and Lighterage Company, a Honolulu tug, the *Shag*, was despatched towards a rendezvous with the coastguard ship. On arrival the men and the tow were to be transferred to her. This was done and then the *Shag* picked up No. 4 minesweeper some sixty miles away and steamed towards Palmyra. As I imagined that what remained of the towing bridles would be in poor condition I decided to take the *Gray* out if I could razzle up another few men and relieve her of the sweepers.

While I was preparing the tug for sea, Daley, the company's executive, who in the previous May had given me the first news of the ill-described "holiday cruise", arrived by air from Manila via Honolulu on October 17. The moment I saw him I knew something was on his mind. He wore a purposeful but somewhat distant look which fairly reeked of forbidding news. But when I questioned him he merely said that he had come in response to my ultimatum not to take the *Gray* on to Manila unless I got the gear I wanted and that he was there to see that I got it. But I knew there was more behind his visit than just that. For the moment, anyway, it seemed I was to be kept in the dark.

I went off to my cabin to complete a report for the Company. I sat down and picked up the pen. It was then I noticed a radio message which had been received by Palmyra radio and which was addressed to me. I opened it. It was to inform me that my father had been taken seriously ill and was not expected to live.

Suddenly it happened. On top of the strained, pent-up emotions, which the anxiety and horrors of the trip and of the last few weeks, had bottled up inside me, this news was too much. Something seemed to snap inside. I buried my face in my arms and was unable to control my feelings. I was unashamed but bitter and desperately, dreadfully weary. For ten minutes I just lay there sprawled across the desk, letting my sobs pour out unchecked. What my experiences had failed to do, this last personal blow had. When my misery had subsided I felt weak and sorry for myself but in a way intensely relieved. It left me with an urgent desire to get away and bury myself out of sight. I hurried off the ship, avoiding the crew, and went to a tiny, disused shack concealed in the undergrowth. There, I had things out with myself while the turbulence died away inside me and I felt at last I could face people again.

I went back and found Daley. "Look here," I said, "I've been through hell on this voyage. It's been too much and it's only just caught up with me to-day. The way I feel at the moment I couldn't take the *Gray* half-way down the lagoon, let alone to sea. Would you mind if Miranda took temporary command? He knows the passage and has a fair idea how to handle the *Gray* now. I don't want to go!"

"Why, of course," he said. "Back in Manila we have known from your daily signals just what it has been. I guess it's been no pleasure trip. Go ashore and rest for a day. I'll go out with Miranda. There's nothing to worry about."

The balance of the men had returned from hospital in Honolulu with Daley, with the exception of Romanin, Ferraro and Jacobsen. The two former crew members had their homes in the Hawaiian Islands and I did not expect them anyhow. Jacobsen's foot had been fractured all right and he was still in hospital.

So, for the first time since the *Gray* left Balboa over three months before, a voice other than mine ordered "stand by" and then nursed her storm-bleached nine hundred tons out into the familiar rolling swell of the Pacific. Fleetingly I felt a pang of regret as I watched her big grey bulk receding down the lagoon without me, but I knew inwardly I had been wise. It was not until I reached the Philippines several weeks later, that a second cable told me my father had died at the very same hour and day as my breakdown.

The *Shag* arrived next day with No. 1 minesweeper in tow. Sparks, Whiteman and Todd had transferred to the *Gray*. It was another two days before she got back. No. 4 minesweeper which the *Gray* had taken from the *Shag*, was not content after three weeks' truancy, to remain long back in the fold. Twice on the short voyage back to Palmyra she broke sulkily away. The *Gray* was in sight of the island when the bridle carried away the first time. Two hours were lost retrieving her. During the night she went again. I didn't know it then, but those two simple breakaways were a disguised blessing for me. They gave Daley a brief first-hand taste, far more effectively than could a hundred reports of mine, of the difficulties of our nightmare voyage from Manzanillo.

As the *Gray* steamed up the lagoon I saw a figure waving to me from the bridge. I waved back not knowing who it was. Then I recognized him. It was Sparks. Grinning like a Cheshire cat, he looked more pleased than a schoolboy home for the summer holidays. I could hardly wait until the *Gray* was close enough to leap aboard and grip his hand. It was a wonderful reunion. Far from looking the part one might expect of three men who had been adrift nearly three weeks, they were bursting with health, more sun-tanned and bearded than ever, and laughing and joking with one another like three circus clowns. Sparks, who had a flowing black beard Father Christmas would have envied, came along the deck to greet me with a tremendous whoop.

"It's mighty good to see you again, sir," he said. "Quite frankly, me and the boys thought the old *Wallace R. Gray* had bought it and that nobody knew we were out there."

"The three of you look a damn sight fitter than when we left you," I told them jocularly. "While I've been sitting here stiff with worry, every man of my crew prostrate with fish-poisoning and half the United States Navy scouring the Pacific for you, you have been enjoying a glorious tropical cruise, lazing in the sun and eating yourselves fat. Why, by the look of you, you have each put on fourteen pounds. Anyway, the occasion calls for a small celebration. If I remember right, there's a bottle of something up in my cabin."

Four stiff whiskies. . . . Four glasses chinked. Sparks, prompted by grunted asides from Whiteman and Todd, told the full story of their nineteen anxious, lonely days adrift.

"It was not until we saw the old *Gray* galloping away from us with a mighty big bow-wave, that we began to realize just how empty and lonely the Pacific can be. I watched you face into an old man of a squall and said to the others: 'I hope to goodness the Skipper's got enough fuel left to make Palmyra.' And then, we forgot all about the *Gray* and set to work making ourselves comfortable for what we believed would be three nights at the most.

"We checked the sea-anchor. It seemed to be doing a fine job out there ahead of us and was keeping the four sweepers well spaced. Soon it was nine o'clock and time for our first radio-rendezvous with you. I had rigged my set on the lower of the sweeper's two decks in a cabin under the pilot-house and the three of us crowded excitedly inside. But here was our first disaster. Goddam it if I hadn't gone and left the blankety headphones aboard the *Gray*. It was only a few minutes off nine and we all rushed madly about the sweeper praying hard that there might be a spare set lying around somewhere. There wasn't.

"Whiteman said, 'A prize bloody operator you are,' and he was right. Nine o'clock came and we all stared at the set, each imagining in his own mind the stream of the *Gray's* anxious signals which were pouring into that useless contraption. But at least we could transmit. We could tell you everything was O.K.

"And then came tragedy No. 2. Just as I began to tune in there was a peculiar creak from above me, and damned if a big strut of timber, seven feet long, didn't crash down smack into the middle of the set. What a mess it made. For a few seconds, we just stared dejectedly at the pile of mangled tubes, condensers, bits of torn wire, and, worst of all, a cracked and leaking battery. My biggest concern was for that battery. It was one of the two I had, apart from the weak one powering the sun-valve masthead lamp. I had no means of recharging it, and now its fluid was running away in front of me. We managed to patch it all right but it was never much good after that and gave such reduced output, I doubted if my signals would be strong enough to reach Palmyra. Fortunately, we had enough spare parts to make a temporary repair to the radio itself, and later that night I got a few signals away saying that everything was all right. To save the battery, I made only a very brief transmission. It was two days before I had properly rebuilt the set and by then the battery was hopelessly weak. So I had to bring the other into commission.

"We all slept well that first night. Todd appointed himself cook and dished up a splendid supper. He found that the boat had oil-pressure stoves but that didn't help much without power. He scouted around the ship and found enough scrap-wood to get one stove going by building a fire in the space where the oil would have been sprayed in.

"Next morning we had our first trouble with the convoy. We awakened to find that No. 4 had swung away to one side and looked as if it wouldn't be long before she drifted back on top of us. So we all climbed into the motor lifeboat and took a trip over to investigate. We found that No. 4's bridle had slipped. There was not much we could do about it so we just left it and hoped for the best.

"The sea which had been just a big oily swell the previous evening was beginning to roughen. Our craft bucked about like a rodeo steer and it was some time before we got ourselves used to the sharper, unpleasant movement after the old tug. And with the tossing about, the lifeboat started crashing against our hull. We had so little way on we just couldn't keep ahead of it and despite a great heap of fenders we hung over the side, the lifeboat began to get bashed about.

"Although we had no instruments other than the compass you gave us, we tried your trick of throwing bits of wood over the side and timing how long it took us to pass them. From these we gathered we were still drifting about

222

sixteen miles a day, as you had told us, although whether in the same direction we were not sure. From the sun we got a general idea we must still be moving roughly west.

"Todd and Whiteman spent that first day amusing themselves fishing. The sea was swarming with darned big sharks. It looked as though they had transferred their allegiance to us when the *Gray's* bow wave scared them away from the tug. They landed quite a number and we also used to get some flying-fish which had flown against the top cabins. Meantime I was working like a one-armed paper hanger making more permanent repairs to my unhappy radio.

"I thought at first of charging my damaged battery from the minesweeper's big generator. This was driven off the main diesel engine. Both, as you know, were mothballed, but it would have been simple enough to have removed the protective sealing material. But then I realized that the impulse starter which gave the engine its initial kick needed a battery. So I was back where I started. Anyway by the second evening I had made the radio as efficient as ever it would be and tapped out a few 'C.Q.s', hoping someone might read me. Then I sent a brief message saying we were still alive and kicking.

"The third day, which we then naturally presumed would be our last, brought more trouble. As soon as it was light we saw that the sea-anchor had ceased to function. Its tautening effect on the three tow-lines had gone for good. It just drifted aimlessly about on the rollers, anywhere but where it should have been—ahead of us. This was something we had been dreading. Now there was nothing to keep the sweepers apart. The big sea which was running did not help things. But then a breeze sprang up from the north-east. We rigged the lifeboat sail on our mast and it took over the job of the sea-anchor, keeping us nicely separated until the wind died out around mid-day. And then the fun started.

"Nos. 2 and 3 quickly drifted together and began smacking each other's hull with terrifying, splintering crashes. Occasionally, a roller would thrust them apart and then, Jiminy, they would roll on top of each other again with a noise like a thunder-clap.

" 'It looks bad, fellers,' I said. 'Let's get across for a look-see.' We climbed into the lifeboat—it was in a pretty low state itself by this time, what with all the bashing it was getting against our own hull—and went over to No. 2. We found her in a bad way. Her hull was breaking up so fast it looked as if she wouldn't be afloat by the evening. When we went below, we stepped into ten feet of water. She must have been holed below the waterline because she was filling up quickly. We couldn't find the hole, and in any case it wasn't too healthy with No. 3 banging against us, the lifeboat getting more and more bashed, and the sea full of unpleasant sharks. No, sir, we didn't like the look of things at all. And by now the two sweepers had got themselves so darned tightly locked, every roll brought their superstructures crashing together. Big pieces of timber were being shattered as easily as you crush a matchbox; the deck was pitching enough to frighten any man, and the noise was terrifying.

" 'There is not a hope in hell of saving them,' I yelled to the others. They looked as scared as I felt. 'This place is a bloody death trap. Let's get back while we still can. We'll have to chop them adrift, and quickly.'

"By the time we climbed back aboard No. 1, No. 2 was half-submerged, her decks were awash, and No. 3 was slowly breaking up her pilot-house. And now, No. 4 was coming in to join the fray. 'Get the axe for God's sake,' I shouted to Todd. At the time I had forgotten the spanner for the U-bolts which you had given us. Anyhow later we were unable to find it.

"Todd came back with the bluntest, most ineffective-looking tool that ever found itself on a ship. Meanwhile

Whiteman had brought a couple of even more useless hatchets from out of the lifeboat.

"Had we been joined to No. 2 by the original tow-rope, it might have been a simple cutting job. But the line was 2-inch steel wire. Our blades would never have cut one Goddarned strand of the stuff. The alternative was to hack through the heavy Oregon baulks which held the bridle. It was then that we remembered the spanner, but although we made a quick search, we were unable to find it.

"We took it in relays, sweating, cursing, and blistering our hands, with the crashing of the two sweepers in our ears. We knew that if we didn't cut her free before she sank, her weight would drag our stern down and both the other boats down on top of us; it would then be only a matter of time before No. 1 shared the same fate and we would be left among the sharks in a barely seaworthy lifeboat.

"Those timber baulks were twelve by twelve inches. It was like cutting down a lamp-post with a kid's toy tool set. Ten minutes' frantic belting had produced just a couple of shallow niches. But we stuck at it. I guess we needed no goading. The sight of No. 2 going down by the bow was enough. It took an hour to cut them free. Never have I put so much energy into sixty minutes. And just before the last baulk broke away, No. 2 took her plunge. She went down slowly, with a kind of gurgling noise. As she went, an enormous bubble of air came rushing up to the surface followed by an astonishing collection of bits of wood, gratings, hatch covers, everything that could float free.

"But she couldn't sink far. Not yet. She was still held between us and No. 3. For several minutes, she hung straight down from our stern, dangling there 120 feet below, while the steel bridle creaked under the strain and our half-chopped baulk began to tremble and crack. Around us a great blue film of oil spread. Bracing our-

225                    PO-P

selves against the roll of the ship, we went on chopping, hacking like madmen. And then, suddenly the dead weight of No. 2 hanging below us began to crack the last baulk. The baulk carried away and the whole bridle splashed free of us into the sea. We lay back too exhausted even to light a cigarette.

"My God, what a sweet moment that was! But it seemed we had merely avoided one disaster to face another. No. 2's weight began to haul No. 3 across to us—and there was just nothing we could do now but sit and wait. But I guess Providence must have said: 'You boys have had enough for one day,' for, when No. 3 was about forty yards away, the vertical weight No. 2 put on her bows began to drag her under too. But she didn't give in any too quickly. For three hours we just sat there, staring sort of hypnotized, and praying pretty hard that she would sink. Then finally, a big wave shook her, she staggered a bit, and then down she went in a swirling vortex of water to join No. 2.

"And then something happened none of us had given a thought to. It came so unexpectedly and with such darned speed, it was not until several minutes afterwards we realized just how close we had come to providing a meal for the sharks.

"As the two sunken sweepers set off on their last voyage of all, their combined weight caused No. 4 to rush head-long straight for us. One minute she was rolling idly in a big trough, next, the tow-line joining her to No. 3 was hurtling her forward at about twelve knots. She had the biggest bow-wave I have ever seen. It was pouring over her rail and drenching her pilot-house. She seemed to gather speed with every yard. I yelled to Whiteman and Todd, 'Brace yourselves; she's going to cut us in half!'

"With an awesome sort of fascination, we watched her approach. She was almost hidden by the wave she made and was making an eerie God-awful swishing noise. Ten yards away, we flattened ourselves on the deck with our cheeks hard on the timber, arms covering our heads, and held our breath. Suddenly we were deluged with water, the air was filled with spray, the deck rocked under us, and then . . . silence.

"By some miracle she had missed us by less than two feet. And as she tore past, the tow-line must have snapped. When we looked up, No. 4 was quietly lying two hundred yards away. I never want to come as close to it as that again.

"And now we began scanning the horizon for a sight of the *Gray*. It was just seventy-two hours since you had left us. Not for one little minute did any of us doubt that you would be back on time. But dusk came without a sight of you. During the night we took turns at lookout, also to see that we didn't get too close to the light that showed No. 4. When you hadn't shown up next morning, none of us was seriously worried. Perhaps you had been delayed refuelling; perhaps you had had to wait for the tide; it might have been one of many things, we reassured ourselves.

"And so the fourth day passed. During the day, No. 4 began to drift away ahead of us, and by evening we were getting only occasional glimpses of her when she rode over the top of a specially big sea. When dusk had brought no grey tug over the horizon, I guess we started to wonder for the first time if something hadn't gone wrong. At the end of the fifth day, I must say we were getting seriously worried. By the sixth, we had decided that the *Gray* must have wrecked herself on Palmyra.

"But I still continued to send out my signals. I must have tapped out 'H.P.V.D.' a thousand times. I knew they weren't getting any too far; the battery was almost dead, but we hoped some ship might be near enough to get a bearing on us. By now, No. 4 had disappeared over the horizon. We were following her, drifting, we imagined nor'-west. If we believed the chart of our day-to-day noon positions which you had left us, we would be passing within 110 miles of Palmyra in another five days. There was fuel enough in the lifeboat, but the boat itself was so badly damaged, none of us had the tiniest inclination to risk a dash in it to the island or anywhere else for that matter, even had we been sure of our position.

"Slowly the days went by. At the end of the first week we lost count of them. I guess we had kind of come to accept our position. The first disappointment and feeling of anxiety had given way to a feeling in which we resigned ourselves to drifting, searching the horizon, waiting, hoping, sunbathing, fishing, reading, eating and sleeping. Physically we were far from being badly off. We had plenty of food, sixty gallons of fresh water, which we supplemented just in case, from rain squalls, more than enough sunshine, and, above all, our own companionship.

"We instituted regular watches so that at least one man was on lookout twenty-four hours each day. The night watches were particularly important as I remembered you having told me you would shine the searchlight up in the clouds and we knew we would be able to see this even if you were miles away. But except from flashes of lightning from time to time, we never saw a light of any sort.

"As time wore on and a week became ten days—we were never very sure just what day it was—we became more and more hard put to it to find something new with which to occupy ourselves. Most of the books we had brought with us we had already read aboard the *Gray*, we soon exhausted every story we knew, and after a time even landing large man-eating sharks got to be a bore. There was always the card pack of course. We played that to the bitter end—always poker, and always either Todd or I won. We must have won hundreds of dollars from poor old Whiteman, but no money ever changed hands, and never will.

"We used to lie out in the sun, stripped to the waist, staring up at the sky and the clouds, talking about our homes back in the States. They seemed an awful long way away. I thought of my wife in Washington and wondered if she knew and was worrying herself sick. Todd talked of his wife in Charleston and Whiteman, who is single, about his mother in South Carolina.

"By now the weather was ideal. Blue, hazy sky, big fluffy clouds, and we rolled kind of sluggishly over the swell from one trough to the next. After a time—it must have been about fourteen days, when the novelty of floating aimlessly across the Pacific had properly worn off—depression slowly settled over us. We talked less and turned more often to our private, silent thoughts. Whiteman took to climbing the mast and sitting up there on the signal yard, peering at the horizon. He could see further up there, but there was never even a false alarm to raise the smallest spark of hope.

"Several times I was tempted to dive over the side for a quick swim. The water looked so darned inviting. Then a nasty-looking grey fin would glide quietly past and I would think better of it.

"One afternoon we were sitting on deck absorbed in our own thoughts when Whiteman, who seemed to have Asdic ears, suddenly jumped up and started staring at the clouds. 'Listen, can you hear it?' he cried. 'Hear what?' we chorused. 'It's an aeroplane or I'm a Panamanian,' yelled Whiteman, quite excited. We all strained our ears. The only sound was the gentle slap, slap of the swell against our hull and the gurgle round our stern. And then, we all heard it. It was a plane right enough. We couldn't see it, but it was getting closer—must have been above the clouds we thought. And then, about five miles away, a silver speck appeared between two anvil-topped clouds. It looked like a Dakota, or C 47. We leapt up, grabbed our shirts, waved like maniacs, and shouted ourselves hoarse. But the pilot did not see us. Thirty seconds later he had gone behind another cloud. He didn't appear again. We did not even have anything to flash to him but tried the Aldis. The battery was too weak. Despite the bitter disappointment, it gave us something to talk about for the rest of the day, and God knows we needed it. Perhaps it was an air-search, we said. Perhaps there will be others soon. Always it was 'perhaps'.[1]

"By now the lifeboat had been so bashed about that it was full of water and was only prevented from sinking by its buoyancy tanks. We salvaged all the provisions and varied our diet for a few days with pemmican, malted milk, meat extract and biscuits. We certainly had plenty of food. I reckon we could have kept alive out there for three or four months.

"Toward the end we were getting to thinking we might never be rescued after all. What worried us was that although we could only have been a couple of hours' flying distance from Palmyra, no further aircraft, if there was indeed a search in progress, had come near us. If there was going to be an air-search our bit of ocean should have been covered long ago, for we still thought our drift would be in the direction you had told us. Perhaps too, we thought, they had assumed from the absence of signals from us that we had already foundered and been drowned. But there was nothing we could do but wait. Waiting, hoping, praying. Yes, we had each of us been praying pretty frequently and quite fervently by this time. And I think those prayers were listened to. All around us the scene never changed—just one great mass of heaving water, sometimes calm, sometimes spray whipped and choppy.

"Again and again we pored over the chart you left us.

---

[1] This was a plane on its way from Christmas Island to Honolulu and which had been told to keep a lookout and to go off course a bit for the purpose.

Long ago we had exhausted the estimated noon positions you had projected for us. So we ourselves extended our supposed line of drift to see what land we might eventually reach. It was a little encouraging as it showed we should pass quite close to Johnson Island below the Hawaiian Islands, and from that we assumed we should also cross nearby steamer lanes, but afterwards it stretched away towards Kamchatka. That was not so encouraging. But in any case we knew that before very long we would get into other currents and possibly be swept in any direction.

"But I never let up on trying to get a message out, pathetically feeble as our transmissions had become. I was now using the battery which powered the sun-valve lamp but it, too, was very weak. Every evening I would switch on and tap out those magic letters 'H.P.V.D.'. There was always a chance a ship just over the horizon might pick them up. But without a headset I never knew if a single dot had been heard.

"And then, rescue came. It was a cloudy, sultry kind of morning. The sea was making and by the look of things we were in for a bit of a blow. It was our eighteenth day, but as far as we were concerned it could have been our thirtieth.

"We had just finished breakfast. Todd was washing the dishes in the galley; Whiteman was in his favourite position up on the signal-yard; I was tinkering with the radio. A yell from Whiteman brought us both flying out on deck. We didn't need any telling why he was shouting. Coming straight toward us, flying at less than a thousand feet, was a big Liberator. Boy! what a wonderful sight she made. And this time there was no mistake about it, that aircraft was looking for us all right. For a few minutes we went crazy as she roared over us. We jumped up and down, waved till our arms hurt, yelled and whistled, and shook each other by the hand a dozen times over.

"The Lib. was now circling at a few hundred feet. We could see the pilot clearly. He was waving too. Then he flew away and came at us in a long shallow dive. A yellow package came flying down and splashed into the sea fifty yards away. He made three more runs, but each time the yellow bags missed us and went into the sea. We couldn't get them as the lifeboat was full of water. But on his fifth swoop he dropped one smack aboard. In fact it damn' near went down the funnel. Like kids on Christmas morning we ripped open that pack and found it contained food and medical supplies. We needed neither but we thanked the pilot with more furious waving and I tried to call him up on the radio. We learnt later he heard me very faintly. Then the Liberator flew away.

"We were delirious and hysterical with excitement now. We laughed and joked and pulled one another's legs. WE HAD BEEN FOUND. Life felt good and sweet and worth living again.

"An hour later another plane arrived or maybe it was the same one, and began showering us with more survival packs. One big one hit the side and fell into the sea but we managed to fish it out. In it was an emergency wireless set, one that *worked*. I rigged up the aerial and while Todd cranked the generator handle, I made contact with the aircraft. I'm afraid that operator didn't have a chance to get much information out of us for half an hour. We had too many anxious questions we wanted answered ourselves. 'Where was the *Gray*, were the crew safe, what was the date, how soon were we to be picked up?' And while Whiteman and Todd squatted over me demanding, 'For Gosh sake, Sparks,' what the aircraft was telling me, I learnt about the poisonings, how the *Gray* had gone aground, that most of the crew were in hospital, that Navy aircraft had been looking for us for about ten days, that we had drifted east and not nor'-west, that a rescue ship was on the way from Palmyra, that we were front page news in America and that the day was October 13—we had been adrift eighteen-and-a-half days.

"We told the Liberator they needn't look any further for Nos. 2 and 3, but that No. 4 sweeper, as far as we knew, was still afloat somewhere. For the rest of the day we weren't without an aircraft overhead for five minutes. As fast as one left it was replaced by another, until they all flew away at dusk. None of us slept that night. I guess we were too darned excited. We just sat up talking.

"And next morning over the horizon came the Coast-guard cutter from Palmyra. She sent a boat across to us and took us aboard and we were told she was standing by until a tug from Honolulu arrived. One of the first persons who spoke to us on the cutter was a Honolulu radio commentator who produced a microphone and began shooting a lot of questions at us. We hadn't realized how much interest the world had been showing in us till then. It was rather overwhelming and we tried to say as little as possible. I guess you know the rest. Here we are safe and sound—the men they could not drown."

"There's not much I can say to you," I told them, "except that I haven't felt quite so proud of any three men for a very long time. You've suffered what must have been nineteen very worrying days. Had there been no one aboard, No. 2 almost certainly would have taken the whole convoy to the bottom. Even if she hadn't, without signals we might never have searched in that part of the Pacific. The company should be intensely grateful to you."

I then offered them as a reward, an immediate air passage each, back to the States. But they shook their heads. "Just you try and sign me off here," said Sparks with an impish grin. "Doggone it, sir, I didn't sit out there looking after your blamed sweepers for eighteen days for nothing. This boy, for one, won't take his discharge one day before those sweepers are safely tied up in Manila Bay, no siree."

"Nor me," echoed Todd.

"Not bloody likely," confirmed Whiteman.

So they stayed, and glad I was to keep them. I sent them ashore for a couple of days' leave and Stamm lent them a jeep and a shotgun.

That evening Daley came to see me. "I've finished my investigation," he said. "I've seen and heard all I want. Your voyage seems to have been dogged by the darnedest of luck. I think you have improvised in the face of impossible odds magnificently, and I've already cabled this to Manila. I hope you won't give up here."

I looked at Daley. There were a lot of things I wanted to say but they could wait. "No," I said quietly, "I shan't give up here."

With a few exceptions all the crew had now returned from their convalescence in Honolulu. The exceptions were Ferraro whose home was in Hawaii, and whom I never expected to see again, and Jacobsen, whose injured foot was confirmed fractured, and Romanin, the Bosun. He, too, lived in the Hawaiian Islands. The others arrived looking none too cheerful and complaining that the poison had left them unfit for any but the lightest duties. The red snapper seemed to have effectively reduced my crew to a shipload of invalids. Clearly new blood was going to be necessary if we were ever to reach the Philippines. I cabled Manila. A few days later a young American engineer climbed out of a plane and introduced himself as McCarthy. An ex-United States Air Force pilot, he had a certain knowledge of marine engines and was a friend of Colonel Gray. As he was trying to get to the Philippines, Gray had suggested he come along with us. From the moment he joined us, McCarthy was a tonic. A fresh face in our midst and a cheerfulness untainted by the bitter memories most of us held, gave the *Gray* new life.

Soon after we reached Palmyra I had cabled the company refusing to go further if I wasn't sent new tow-gear. I

234

now got a refreshing response. A converted landing-craft, the *Baracuta*, came in from Manila and Guam with a splendid pile of heavy steel wire, Manila rope, shackles and even a quantity of badly-needed heavy Bunker "C" fuel oil. The *Baracuta* supplied another urgent need, too—men. Her Filipino skipper lent me six of his Filipino crew—two messmen, two able seamen, an oiler and a fireman. I confirmed Miranda as First Mate, Schmidt as first Assistant, Stephens as second Assistant Engineer and Jones as Bosun.

The crew's return from Honolulu had one unpleasant repercussion. It revived the feeling against Stephens. Their stay in Hawaii had, if anything, stimulated the Filipinos' thirst to avenge the pipe-wrench incident. Stephens, now back aboard, felt more and more uneasy about the feeling which hung over him like the sword of Damocles. Everywhere he went, Filipino eyes followed him, watching, waiting an opportunity. It got to the stage where Stephens was openly afraid to leave the ship for fear that he would be followed ashore and assaulted. So obvious was it that I called for Miranda, seriously concerned.

"Look here, Miranda," I said. "It seems your countrymen are out to get Stephens. I don't want to be drawn into this obnoxious revenge business, and let me tell you this; I need Stephens aboard, and I want him alive. The sooner you spread that round the crew the better. And you can tell them from me that if there is any trouble the Skipper will shoot first and make his inquiries later!"

# Chapter Fourteen

THE next ten days were fully occupied fitting the new tow-gear to the two minesweepers and preparing the *Gray* for her 5,000-odd-mile voyage to Manila. I was impatient to get to sea again, but the crew were still so weak and washed out, the re-rigging took twice as long as it should have done. I had to drive them to it, had to stand over them, bullying, wheedling, to get the simplest job finished. The poison had left them listless, dispirited and depressed. They seemed to have lost all interest in the *Gray*, and on several occasions I caught some of them just wandering off round the island. Our morale was as low as ever it had been.

At the end of a week when we were no nearer ready for sea I decided it was time for a little strong-arm tactics. I called the crew together and told them straight that any man who refused to work would immediately be put under arrest and Stamm would arrange to have him flown to Honolulu and dealt with in an American court. This seemed to work. It produced a surprising resurgence of activity and by October 25 we were ready to go. I think the men were beginning to appreciate that the sooner they had the tows ready the sooner they could get away from this uninteresting, but hospitable, little island that offered none of the traditional diversions a sailor expects to find and enjoy in port. The island had no cafés, night clubs, nor a solitary woman to comfort the *Gray's* restless hearts. Palmyra's ten wives had been warned to give the ship a wide berth and the men likewise were forbidden near the married quarters. I regarded it as a very wise precaution and saw to it that it was rigidly enforced.

Meanwhile down in the stifling engine-room, unknown

to me, friction was boiling up between Stephens and Schmidt. Although they were both splendid engineers their personalities were as different as rum and rope. Stephens had a perpetual easy-going, nonchalant, "what-the hell" attitude to life, Schmidt an inflammable, highly-excitable, nervous temperament that had to be carefully handled. But Stephens refused to do any handling. He began to annoy the little German in many trivial, but to Schmidt exasperating, ways. Despite Schmidt's repeated pleading Stephens would never bother to clean up the engine-room when Schmidt was succeeding him on watch, he never replaced the tools he used, and worst of all, he began accusing Schmidt of being "just a ham engineer". That did it.

First I knew of it was when Schmidt, pale and angry, came to my cabin with a grimy letter. I opened it. It was his resignation. In thin spidery writing it went:

To K. Ainslie, Master,
from H. Schmidt.
Subject: Transfer of duty.
In view of the fact that my ability as an engineer has been questioned I request transfer to another department. I have no special preference as to assignment; duty on any company ship in any capacity is acceptable by the undersigned.

H. Schmidt,<br>First Assistant Engineer.

"What the devil, Schmidt," I exclaimed. "What does this mean?" He stood there looking sick and unhappy. "People keep saying I am incompetent," he said. "I have had enough. Therefore I wish to resign on the spot or be transferred somewhere else."

It took ten minutes to talk him out of it. "You can't just walk out on me here," I said. "I have never complained. Damn it, Schmidt, I have always thought you were a first-class engineer, and we would never have got here without you. When *I* start criticizing you, then's the time to worry, not before." In the end I promised to talk to Stephens and he reluctantly agreed to withdraw his resignation. He went back to the engine-room, forlorn and dissatisfied, clutching his oily envelope.

For the first time I was able to rig the two lines as I wished. From here on I didn't intend there to be a single breakaway, a single mid-ocean boat party, a single broken strand. And what's more I planned a speedy eight-knot voyage all the way. I had one overwhelming desire—get this crazy outfit into Manila Bay, sign off, collect my money, and get as far away from the *Wallace R. Gray* as possible.

No. 4 minesweeper gave us our biggest headache. She had been towed in with her superstructure badly damaged from the battering the other craft had given her. But fortunately she was still sound and seaworthy below the waterline and that was what counted most. I reinforced her stern post, passed a wire bridle along each side of her deck, and ran it round her stern below the surface between the stern post, through the screw apertures below the tuck. This meant that all the towing strain in future would be taken squarely by her whole stern. I then ran the bridle wires out forward through the hawsepipes and shackled them as before to 800 feet of manila rope. No. 4 now became No. 1. No. 1, which became No. 2, I linked direct to the *Gray* with 1,800 feet of 2½-inch steel wire. This was attached to the tug's winch, and at sea would run away astern to No. 2 in a long bight below No. 1. Its weight would always keep it far below No. 1's keel and both sweepers would be held independently and without the burden of another craft in tow behind. We worked until 9 o'clock most evenings to hurry the work along.

Two days before we sailed, the islanders turned on a

party for the *Gray's* officers and a splendid dinner for the men. And on the evening before departure Stamm came down to the ship with a great aura of secrecy and invited me to another party he said they were having. I couldn't think what excuse he had found for a second celebration, but told him I would naturally be delighted to come. It was not until I arrived at the administration block, shaven and clean-shirted, that I realized what the party was in aid of. It was in honour of the *Gray's* skipper.

We sailed soon after noon next day, October 26. Every man, woman and child on Palmyra came down to see us go. Stamm came aboard to say good-bye. "You know, Captain Ainslie," he said, "you've turned this little desert island upside down, you've given us more excitement and more to talk about than we've ever known before, you've put us to a hell of a lot of trouble, splashed us across the newspapers, yet damn it, despite it all, I wish you weren't going. In a few hours you will have gone over the horizon for good, but, believe me, all of us here will be thinking of you and your boys and all they've been through for a very long time." He shook me warmly by the hand. "*Bon voyage*, and don't forget, if ever you need another air-search sometime, the old runway will still be here."

I watched his big, cheerful face go down the gangway. Then I called up Cuesta on the telephone. "How are those dreadful engines of yours?" I asked him. "Think they'll manage another 5,000 miles?" His thin voice came back, "Oh yes, sir, no need to worry. We'll get you there, certainly we will."

I was just about to order the lines away when I became aware of a commotion ashore. Butch, whom we had scarcely seen since the day we arrived a month before, appeared on the dockside followed by a hoard of at least twenty dogs. Palmyra carried a dog population grossly out of proportion both to its size and population. There was roughly one to every three inhabitants, an extraordinary assortment of every shape and size, ranging from "Doctor", a short-legged Labrador and self-appointed leader of the pack, down to bedraggled collies, spotted terriers, and a company of shaggy half-breeds. Butch's was obviously the first feminine company any of them had enjoyed as long as they had been on the island. Her arrival was the answer to the lonely dog's dream. And Butch, ignored aboard, had not been slow to take advantage of her new-found popularity. For just over four weeks she had roamed the island, a conceited queen, with what I'll swear was a smile on her white face. For all that time not a single Palmyra dog had left her side.

And now as the *Gray's* gangway was hauled up, the busiest month of her short life was ending. She came to the side, her coat muddy and blood-stained, looking up at us, asking to be taken aboard. Someone heaved her on to the deck. But her escorts were not going to lose her as easily as this. In a body they clamoured around our side, barking frenziedly, howling dismally, and fighting among themselves. Several even managed to spring aboard, but firm hands quickly sent them flying back on to the pier.

But we hadn't finished with the dogs yet. As we moved astern two of them plunged in from the dock and were furiously swimming down the lagoon in pursuit of Butch. They followed us two hundred yards, encouraged by the barking and wailing of their colleagues ashore before they gave up in disgust.

Above the bedlam of the dogs we could now hear the islanders' farewell shouts, and presently they all joined in "Auld Lang Syne". Daley, who was aboard the *Baracuta*, called us up on the radio telephone to wish us a happy voyage, and I answered everybody with a prolonged blast on the siren. In all its history Palmyra lagoon had never seen anything like this.

As far as they could go down along the shore of the

lagoon, the islanders followed in their jeeps, until we streamed the tows and headed out through the passage into the Pacific swell. My last memory of Palmyra will always remain—fifty friendly waving folk, a chorus of frustrated, barking dogs, and, above it all, drifting sadly over the water, the strains of "Auld Lang Syne". By 4 o'clock Palmyra's palms were dropping over the horizon. Half an hour later they had gone.

Our first refuelling stop was Kwajalein in the Marshall Islands, 1,860 miles west of Palmyra. At nine knots I reckoned it would take about nine days. It did, and a splendid, trouble-free nine days they were too. This really was towing. No more 15, 30, 50, 70 painful crippled miles a day for us. The *Gray* had the bit properly in her teeth now. Every day she ticked off a proud two hundred miles or more. And the tow-lines? What a difference my new rig made. I felt no worry about them. I was very cheerful. The tows held position beautifully, not a strand of rope or wire parted, we almost began to forget we had them. I sent a signal to Colonel Gray, "TOWS DOING PERFECTLY EXPECT REACH MANILA FIRST WEEK DECEMBER." He radioed back, "BEST OF LUCK AND A QUICK PASSAGE."

Just after dusk on November 2 we were startled to see a brilliant object racing across the sky from west to east. It had a bright, white head and a streaming golden-red tail. It was not until it had disappeared in a spectacular spark shower that we realized we had seen a new comet. I got Sparks to flash a message to the United States Hydrographic Office reporting it. Perhaps we were the first to spot it. Perhaps it would be called *Gray's* comet. But we learnt later that it had been named after a man in Australia who had claimed to have seen it first.

As we approached the cluster of atolls that was Kwajalein, we became convinced that World War Three had broken out. The lagoon looked as if the entire United States Navy had moved in. For several miles, battleships, cruisers, destroyers and two-funnelled transports in grey war paint stretched in a forest of masts and funnels. I had not seen such a concentrated assortment of Naval striking power since the war. It was not until the pilot, a Navy Commander, came out, that we learnt the full story. The ships had recently been towed there from Bikini Island, over a hundred miles to the north. They had been the guinea pigs of the famous atom bomb explosion, were still radio-active and were lying at Kwajalein so that experts might keep them under close observation. As we steamed inside the lagoon we got a better look at them. Most astonishing to us was the apparent absence of the dreadful damage we had all come to associate with the A-bomb. With one exception every ship was still afloat. The exception was the former German pocket battleship, *Prinz Eugen*, and she had only recently gone aground in a typhoon. The Commander told us they would retain their lethal radio-activity so long, they would all sooner or later have to be towed out into the Pacific and sunk. It was only safe to be aboard dressed in special suits. After listening to him I felt far from happy as the *Gray* glided up to her anchorage, passing within a few yards of the deadly fleet. I didn't want to present the company with three radio-active ships, but the Commander laughed at my fears. "It's perfectly safe," he assured me, "they're only dangerous to board."

Nevertheless I was intensely relieved when we had refuelled and were safely at sea again. With stories of the Hiroshima victims' hair falling out fresh in my mind—the pilot had been a little bald—I tenderly felt my own at regular intervals for several days after that. But it remained as bushy as ever.

The day before we left I had more crew trouble. They wanted to spend a whole weekend ashore. Even Miranda wandered away for half a day without permission. Our nearness to the end of the voyage seemed to breed a new truculence. But there could be no question of leave at this stage. The Navy discouraged it and wanted us clear of the island as quickly as possible. In the end I had to threaten to call in the Navy police before they went back to work grumbling.

We sailed for Davao, on Mindanao in the Philippines on November 10. Manila was only another eight hundred miles up the Philippines coast. Impatient to catch up on some of my lost time I increased speed first to nine-and-a-half knots and later to ten. The *Gray* ploughed away westward, taking heavy rolling seas like a big liner. "This is more like it," she seemed to say. "This *is* what I was built for." And away astern the sweepers rode the swell like two loyal well-trained ducks. We had almost forgotten what a breakaway meant.

Between Nagatik and Nukuoro Islands in the Carolines we steamed, then down to within ninety miles of the Equator to avoid a reported typhoon, then north-west again toward the southern tip of Mindanao. Nothing could go wrong now, I thought, the voyage was all over bar the shouting. But fate had one final stab at us.

Sparks began to complain of acute pain from the tooth the Negro had broken in Panama five months before. A nasty-looking abscess had developed and within a few days his whole face had swollen like a Christmas pudding. He was in such terrible agony he could hardly speak, his eyes started to close, the pain began to spread down his body, he couldn't sleep, and went about the ship, a tormented figure, pathetically holding his head in his hands. We tried everything from hot and cold compresses to a bottle of whisky, but the abscess only got worse. I would have liked to pull the tooth out, but the amputation incident had left me thoroughly wary of further amateur surgery. In any case I had no dentists' tools. The fourth day of the swelling I honestly thought Sparks was dying. His face had reached an alarming shape and he seemed to

243

be fast losing interest in life. Then I remembered the penicillin. I began giving him shots in the arm every two hours. The effect was almost immediate. In forty-eight hours the swelling had subsided and Sparks was our normal cheerful wireless operator again.

We sighted the Philippines on November 28. Those 4,000-foot, hazy blue mountains did something to the *Gray*. In the space of an hour all the cares, grumblings, bitterness and weariness of the past five months vanished. In their place came a sudden new spirit, a spirit of friendliness, a last-minute will to work. The sight of the homeland many of them had several times never expected to see again transformed the Filipinos into a happy, smiling gang of men I had never seen before. As the coastline came nearer and began to show up out of the haze they lined the rail, excitedly pointing out familiar landmarks. Their laughter filled the ship, from the forecastle head drifted sounds of dance music from portable radios and gramophones, and everyone was either singing or whistling. How wonderful, to have had this atmosphere all the way. But for the ill-conceived tow-gear it might well have been. They were a rough-and-ready, and once a hopelessly inexperienced, bunch, these men, but despite the trouble they had given me I realized I had almost grown fond of them.

It was dawn next morning when we reached Davao. After pratique and Customs, when we were alongside the fuelling dock, I gave most of the crew shore leave. By 8 o'clock the ship was almost deserted, the crew fast getting drunk in Davao's saloons and bars. The company's agent took Sparks, Stephens and me ashore for a few drinks. For Stephens' sake I was glad he had our company. For into every bar we strolled, we were mysteriously followed by Ortiz, Lascano and Rocca. They had been drinking, and it was only too obvious what was in their minds. They were after Stephens. We felt quite uncom-

244

fortable in their presence. We stuck pretty close to Johnnie after that. It was all that saved him. Had we left him alone there is no doubt he wouldn't have ever come back to the ship.

Next morning we sailed for Iloilo, the port of Panay Island, about three hundred miles south of Manila. The Davao agent said the company would take delivery of the *Gray* and two sweepers there instead of Manila. On the voyage up I threw economy to the winds and opened up to twelve knots. We arrived there on December 3.

Of the voyage, there is not much more to tell. At the approaches to Iloilo harbour with its colourful church-sprinkled, Spanish-looking town, one of the company's local tugs came out and relieved us of the minesweepers. The last I saw of them, they were disappearing towards the workshops up the Iloilo river. Then we proceeded to the dock. I was mighty glad to get the *Gray* moored—for Cuesta's engines were beginning to play up again. They hesitated, stopped, restarted and by the time we came alongside the pier, had almost failed altogether. But this time they could drop out of the bottom into the harbour for all I cared. I should never need them again. We had arrived.

The crew lined the rail and cheered as the lines went ashore. One or two wives were waiting anxiously on the dock. Then Daley came aboard. He told me we were all to be flown to Manila next day and the crew paid off and sent back to their homes. The *Wallace R. Gray* was to be laid up for general overhaul. After this we had a visit from the Customs. They left with a small pile of arms that had eluded my mid-Pacific search.

I told Cuesta the ship was to be laid up and that he had best make his preparations for shutting-down the following morning, put bags of lime in the boilers and generally do whatever was necessary.

The Mate was ordered to have the men paint down the

funnel next morning and when it was completed I gave the order, "That will do the crew."

After that everyone furiously completed his packing. This time they were leaving for the last time. One by one they came, to shake hands and say good-bye before filing ashore with their suit-cases. They didn't look a bit like the same crew I had cursed, threatened and nursed for nearly seven months and fourteen thousand miles. Gone were the filthy beards, the greasy singlets and worn trousers, but it will not be by these that I shall remember most of them; it will be as a band of men who, starting out as fumbling incompetents, finished up as seamen whom I would not hesitate to ship again. Naturally there were a few I would like to single out for special mention, but after all each and every one had been through, I salute them all.

They went joyfully down the gangway clean-shaven, hair slicked down, neatly-pressed suits, spotless shirts and shining shoes. Some of them could easily have passed for prosperous business men. I stood in the wing of the bridge and watched them go and as they went they each gave the *Gray* a rousing cheer. They boarded a truck with their belongings and for some time I could hear their hubbub and laughter echoing through the streets of Iloilo.

With the exception of Johnnie Stephens all the officers had also gone. They had no need to say good-bye as I would be seeing them at the airport. So we both washed, packed and changed into clean clothing, took a final look around the decks that had been our home for so many months. Then I remembered something.

"Just a minute, Johnnie," I said, "we forgot to give a final ring-off."

"Heck, so we did. But it's not too late. I'll nip below, you go back on the bridge and we'll soon fix that," he replied.

"Ringing off," is one of the almost forgotten traditions

246

of the sea I have always been a little sentimental about, especially if I liked the vessel concerned, and I certainly liked the easy-handling *Gray*. So while Stephens in his best suit went scrambling back among the oil and pipes in the darkened engine-room I climbed the ladder to the bridge for the last time. Over went the telegraph lever, backward and forward, back came the reply and when the last ring had died away, Stephens' Southern accent came drawling up the voice pipe, "And let's thank the Almighty that's over, sir." By this time the agent was aboard and my last act was to hand him the various inventories, the ship's papers and finally the ship herself.

It was only when we reached the gangway on our way ashore, that I noticed Butch. Poor, miserable Butch. Forlorn, unwanted and forgotten, she had watched the crew leave. Nobody wanted her now, not even the man who brought her aboard.

She looked at us, her eyes beseeching us not to leave her. "What are we going to do with her?" I asked. "I'm afraid she's nobody's girl now." Johnnie thought hard for a moment. He looked at Butch and she seemed to sense his indecision. Her tail gave a faint, hopeful wag.

"I've been offered a job in the machine-shop here, sir." And then to Butch, "I guess I'll take you, you old good-for-nothing hound-dog. I'll be back to collect you next week." But not understanding, Butch slunk dejectedly away into the shadows of the fo'c'sle head. But the agent said he would take care of her in the meantime.

The company provided a meal ashore for us and then we boarded the two special planes for Manila. Slowly we climbed away over the gardens, the tiled roofs and towards the green hills. The waters of Iloilo Passage sparkled clear in the morning sunshine. And as the pilot circled to gain height, the whole panorama of the water-front spread itself below.

But it was not the view I pressed my nose hard against

the window to see, I was taking my last long look at a lonely grey tug four thousand feet below. Long after we were on our way, long after the other passengers had unfastened their safety belts and were sitting back, relaxing, smoking, reading, something kept me looking back.

And then a fluffy white cloud suddenly blotted out the harbour. When we emerged into the sunshine again Iloilo and the *Gray* were out of sight. Slowly I undid my safety belt. I sank back into the seat and lit a cigarette. My "holiday cruise" was over.

# Epilogue

I HAVE described the voyage of the *Wallace R. Gray* exactly as it happened. Although I haven't used most of their real names, every character actually lived, every incident took place. Not a single phase of what, in over thirty years at sea in sail and steam, was quite the most unpleasant voyage in all my experience, has been in the least coloured or exaggerated.

Perhaps some readers may be critical of my actions during this horrible voyage, but few can have had similar experiences, and unless they have, I hardly feel that they are qualified to judge. And, as for myself, I cannot say that I would do the same thing again, for in future I shall make very certain that I am not shanghaied on such a schooner-rigged expedition.

Some may even assert that I should not have sailed without the spare gear I had so often demanded. There is no argument against that. I did my best and have no excuses to offer.

Our tow ranks with the longest ever made. The total length of the voyage including that from Charleston to Panama, before I assumed command, was more than fourteen thousand miles. The only record I can find of comparable feats were the pre-war 13,000-mile tow in which several Dutch tugs hauled a floating dock from Newcastle, England to Wellington, New Zealand, and a tow of 12,995 miles from Tampa, Florida to a port in Malaya, made by two American Moran tugs towing a dredge. And in 1946, what is probably the longest tow ever attempted was made by the Dutch Government tugs *Beatrix* and *Margriet*. They took a floating crane from

Rotterdam to Curacao, off the coast of Venezuela, there transferred it to a floating dock which they towed across the Pacific to the Dutch East Indies—more than sixteen thousand miles in all. Ours was by a single tug.

What became of the crew of the *Wallace R. Gray* and the gallant tug herself? Where is she now?

When they reached Manila the crew were "paid off" and each given a bonus of $200. They then split up. Alonso left the Company and was appointed Master of a Philippine coastal vessel, and when I last saw him was "stand-by" Master of a 400-ton motor ship being made ready to be delivered to the Indonesian Government.

Miranda, one of the best navigating officers I have met, eventually secured a Panamanian Master's Licence and became Master of one of Philippine Cargo Handlers' vessels, but in October, 1953, died at Tacloban Leyte.

Harris (Sparks) has a shore job in Washington, D.C.

Ritter is now married and is manager of a recording studio.

Only recently I learned that Ferraro was killed in a motor accident in Honolulu.

As for the rest I do not know where they are, but I wish them all the best of luck. Perhaps I have made some of them appear rather incompetent and so at first many of them were, but it is to their credit that they all finished up very fine seamen.

Two years after I had left the Company, I was in Singapore on business as the General Manager of a shipping organization. Having a few hours to spare before catching a plane to Colombo, I took a stroll along the crowded waterfront. Out in the harbour among a jostling mass of sampans, tramp steamers and ocean liners, a large, smart-looking tug caught my eye. Something about her lines, her high bow, big funnel and radar platform seemed curiously familiar. Somehow I managed to borrow a pair of binoculars. But on the bow of this immaculate vessel was the name *Takapuna*. I turned to the man who had lent me the glasses and said, "You know, it's a strange thing but I could have sworn I knew that tug; seems I must be mistaken."

"You mean the old *Takapuna*?" he answered. "Smart-looking craft; one of the fastest round these waters. Belongs to a stevedoring company. They say she towed four minesweepers across from the States. Ran into a packet of trouble on the way, too. But she had another name then . . . let me see . . . yes, that was it—the *Wallace R. Gray*."